IMAGES
of America

JASPER AND HUNTINGBURG

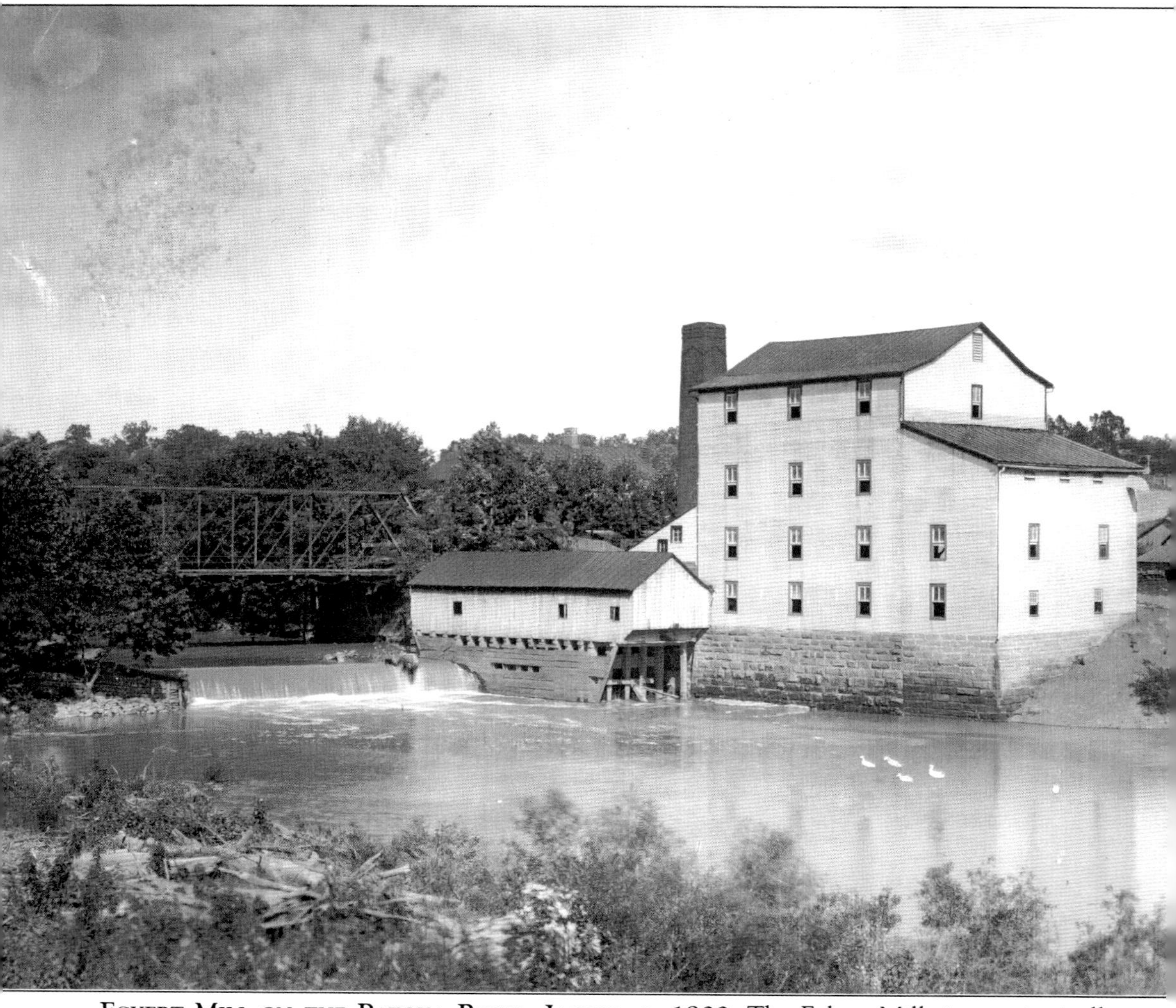

ECKERT MILL ON THE PATOKA RIVER, JASPER, C. 1900. The Eckert Mill rises majestically above the dam over the Patoka River in Jasper around the turn of the 20th century. This photograph was made directly from the original glass negative still in existence. The photograph was taken by Sprauer Studios of Jasper and used as the basis for a postcard. Note that there are no reflections of the ducks in the water, because the ducks are not real. Their images were painted onto the glass plate to make the scene more visually interesting.

IMAGES
of America

JASPER AND HUNTINGBURG

Ron Flick and Jane Ammeson

ARCADIA
PUBLISHING

ISBN 978-0-7385-3439-8

Published by Arcadia Publishing
Charleston, South Carolina

Printed in the United States of America

Library of Congress Catalog Card Number: 2005926082

For all general information contact Arcadia Publishing at:
Telephone 843-853-2070
Fax 843-853-0044
E-mail sales@arcadiapublishing.com
For customer service and orders:
Toll-Free 1-888-313-2665

Visit us on the Internet at www.arcadiapublishing.com

CONTENTS

ACKNOWLEDGMENTS

Dubois County is fortunate to have so many people dedicated to preserving its history and willing to work so hard at doing just that. A book like this would not be possible without the help of all those who are willing to give their time and energy to share the stories and the photographs of their towns.

There are so many people to thank, including my co-author, Ron Flick, who not only shared knowledge, but went to his safety deposit box to take out precious photographs of the Eckert Mill, his home, and his family, so that we could scan them; Phyllis and Ralph Johanneman, who welcomed me into their home and even took me on a tour; John Fierst, a walking encyclopedia of historical data, who spent hours going through photographs of Jasper with me to the point where he was late for a family gathering; and to Delbert Himsel Jr., who helped open many doors for us and also shared the photographs of Ireland that he has painstakingly collected. I also owe a big thank you to the Sisters at Monastery Immaculate Conception, including Sister Christine Kempf and Sister Mary Dominic Frederick, as well as Karen Katafiasz, Director of Communications for the Monastery; and thanks also to Loma Hartke, who gives so much time and effort in his volunteer work at the Museum of Huntingburg. Another thank you to Dave Buehler of Jasper, who let me take photographs off his wall to scan for this book.

But there are many others to be acknowledged, including: Nancy Eckerle of the Jasper Chamber of Commerce; Tom Ellsworth of Huntingburg; Don Flick of Indianapolis; the Hanselman family, owners of the Schnitzelbank Restaurant; Kathy Lett, Director of the Huntingburg Public Library, and the other staff members there; Bernard and Sharon Messmer; July Olinger; Christine Prior of the Huntingburg Chamber of Commerce; Kristen Seitz of Dubois County Tourism; and Ruth Uebelhor, owner of the Harvest Moon Bed & Breakfast in Ferdinand. Printed sources that provided valuable information included the Jasper Centennial publication, *This Our Town* (1966), Arthur Nordhoff's *Pictures from the Past* (1966), Sr. M. Frederica Dudine's *The Castle on the Hill* (1967), *Jasper Area History* (1989), Hugo Songer's *History of Huntingburg* (1987), and R. L. Menke's *Hoosier Vignettes* (1991), as well as the indexed volumes of *Jasper Courier* and *Jasper Herald* newspaper articles, compiled by Lillian Doane and John Fierst, at the Jasper Public Library.

The people of Dubois County should be proud that their traditions and past are in such caring hands.

Jane Ammeson

INTRODUCTION

The past fades away quickly. What was once known and very familiar to all soon disappears, often to be lost forever. But it is through old photographs and memories that we can retain the past, which is the case with Jasper and Huntingburg in Dubois County in southern Indiana. Here, there is so much history—from the Germans who immigrated with their woodworking skills and willingness to work long hours to make their towns prosperous, to the four Sisters of St. Benedict who traveled thousands of miles from their home in Germany to what was then an unknown and almost wild area of a new country. There were other settlers too, of Irish, Scottish, and French descent. There was even a Croatian priest, Father Kundek, the young pastor of a poor, small congregation of German Catholic immigrants in Jasper. While riding through an uninhabited patch of land between the Patoka and Ohio Rivers, he decided that there needed to be churches strung along the way for the faithful. Thus, he established many Catholic churches in southern Indiana, including one in a small town called Ferdinand, which was nearby. Father Kundek was the driving force behind the waves of German Catholic immigrants who swept into the county and the surrounding area. And while his vision shaped much of Dubois County, another settler, Colonel Jacob Geiger also proved instrumental. Geiger was a man of vision, but his reason for moving here was more prosaic. A devoted hunter, he had heard from his father, a Revolutionary War hero, that the hunting was good in the rolling hills and woods of an area which he named Huntingburg. Geiger, who came from Kentucky, had been a slave owner. But he freed his slaves when he moved to Indiana and those slaves formed the Freedom Settlement just south of Huntingburg.

Today, more than a century later, Dubois County remains a charming and prosperous area. Many of the buildings in towns tucked into the hilly, sylvan landscape dotted with lakes and rivers are on the National Register of Historic Places. There is a growing effort to preserve and restore this unique and colorful past, rather than allowing it to be destroyed. Huntingburg's downtown is so quintessential 19th-century Victorian that Hollywood has even taken notice. The late 19th-century Southern Railway depot in Jasper has recently been rebuilt, and there are ambitious plans to recreate the old Eckert Mill that once stood on the Patoka River. Soon, empty warehouses will be converted into offices and retail shops, an invitation for all to enjoy the river and the way of life that makes Dubois County so wonderful.

One

RIVERS AND RAILROADS

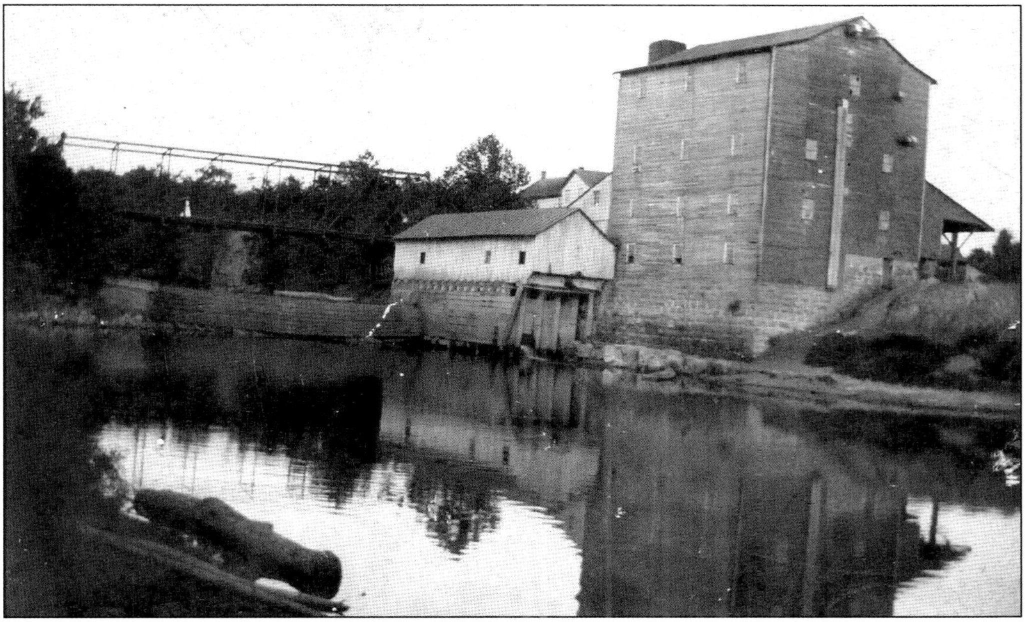

ECKERT MILL ON THE PATOKA RIVER, JASPER, C. 1885. The history of the mill in Jasper dates back to 1817 or so, when Colonel Andrew Evans, a veteran of the War of 1812, came to Dubois County from Kentucky with a handful of slaves. They constructed a wooden dam and grist mill, with waterwheel, on the Patoka River at an ancient Indian ford and buffalo crossing. In 1820, the Joseph Enlow family purchased the land and acquired the mill. Joseph's wife, Eleanor, was the woman who gave the fledgling community the name Jasper, after choosing it from the Bible's Book of Revelation. Subsequent owners of the mill were Mathew Foster, John Johnson, and J. A. and W. C. Graham. In 1847, Francis Xavier Eckert, and his cousin, Alois Eckert, immigrants from Pfaffenweiler, Baden, purchased the mill and surrounding property soon after their arrival. The Eckerts operated the business until the late 1850s, at which time the mill was closed due to its deteriorating condition. In 1865, after giving careful consideration to relocating the mill elsewhere, Francis Eckert decided to construct a steam-powered mill with chimney on the same site, adjacent to the original mill. The first mill was finally disposed of in 1870, when some boys from town shoved the decrepit structure into the river. The following year, Francis's three sons—Andrew, Jacob, and Conrad—assumed ownership, and thus began a period of rapid expansion and explosive growth. Flatboats of flour were sent down river as far south as New Orleans, and with the opening of the railroad in 1879, train shipments reached the east coast. Water power was reintroduced in 1880 with the rebuilding of the wooden dam and the construction of a new forebay, which housed a horizontal turbine wheel. In 1883, the mill was closed for four months to allow for the installation of a new system of roller machinery, which produced a finer flour than was possible with the older grindstone process. A small addition was added to the west side of the mill after the turn of the 20th century, and a stone dam was built after the flood of 1913. However, only 20 years later, in 1933, the mill fell victim to progress and milling operations ceased. The building served as a feed mill and storage warehouse until a devastating flood in the early months of 1964 weakened its foundations beyond repair. The mill was demolished a few months later, nearly 100 years after its construction. (Photograph courtesy of John Fierst.)

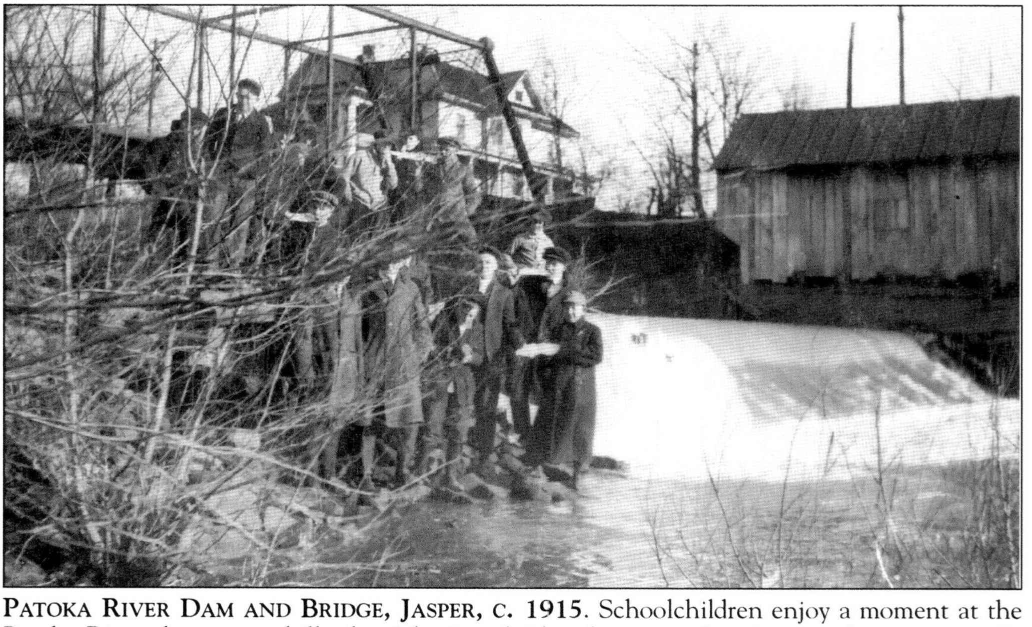

PATOKA RIVER DAM AND BRIDGE, JASPER, C. 1915. Schoolchildren enjoy a moment at the Patoka River dam on a chilly day. The iron bridge shown in the photograph was originally erected in 1879 and replaced an earlier wooden covered bridge. In the background is the newly-constructed Louis Eckstein residence, which was built on the same site as the home of his wife Josephine's parents, Andrew and Caroline Eckert. (Photograph courtesy of John Fierst.)

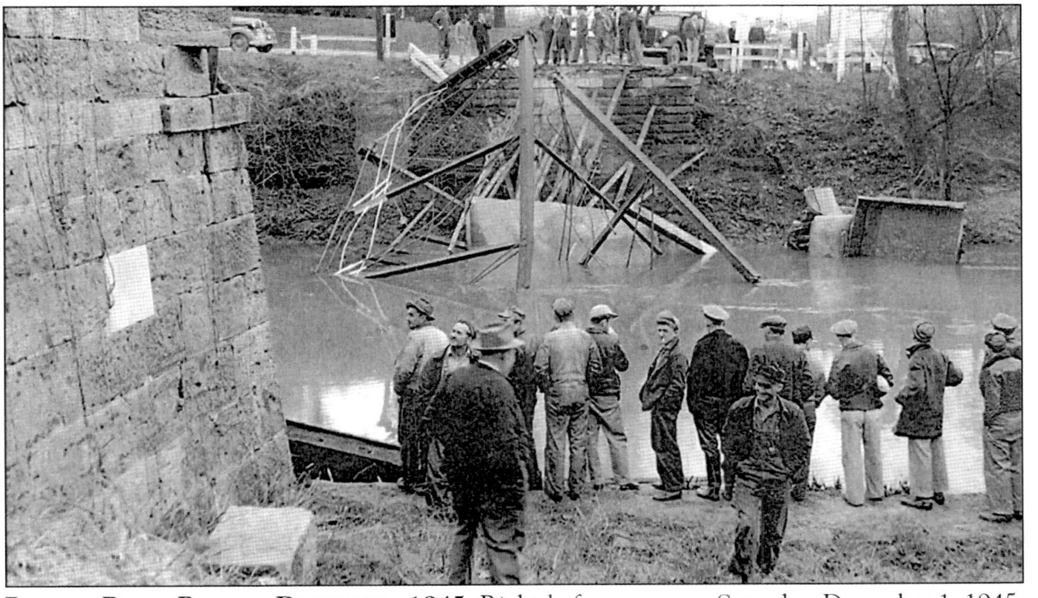

PATOKA RIVER BRIDGE, DECEMBER, 1945. Right before noon on Saturday, December 1, 1945, local resident Clarence Sermersheim, a state highway worker, was driving west on the road overlooking the Patoka River when the brakes on his truck failed. He swerved to miss a lumber truck driving on Highway 162 and careened into the bridge over the Patoka, knocking the iron structure off its stone foundation and into the river. Luckily no one was hurt. Residents south of the river were forced to drive eight miles to get to town until a temporary bridge was erected the following month. A year later, the present concrete bridge was constructed. (Photograph courtesy of John Fierst.)

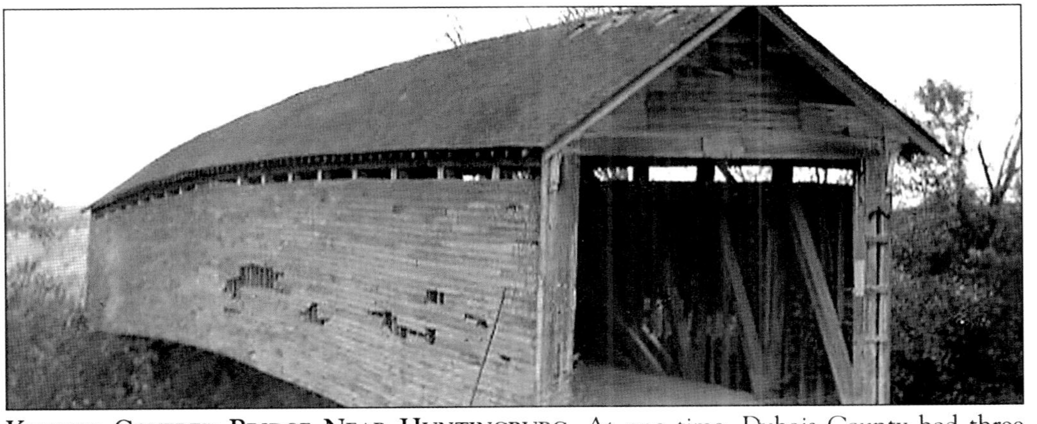

KESSNER COVERED BRIDGE NEAR HUNTINGBURG. At one time, Dubois County had three covered bridges. A covered bridge was built over the Patoka in Jasper prior to the Civil War and replaced in 1879. A bridge over Postelthwaite creek was completed in 1870 and stood for only a few decades. The third was the Kessner covered bridge, shown in this photograph. The bridge, built in 1877, crossed the Patoka River northwest of Huntingburg near the small town of Duff. This single-span, burr-arch truss structure had a length of 156 feet, or 160 feet, including the 2-foot overhang at each end, with a portal clearance 14 feet wide by 12 feet high. The Kessner bridge was the last remaining covered bridge in the county. It was destroyed by fire in 1965. (Photograph courtesy of the Museum of Huntingburg.)

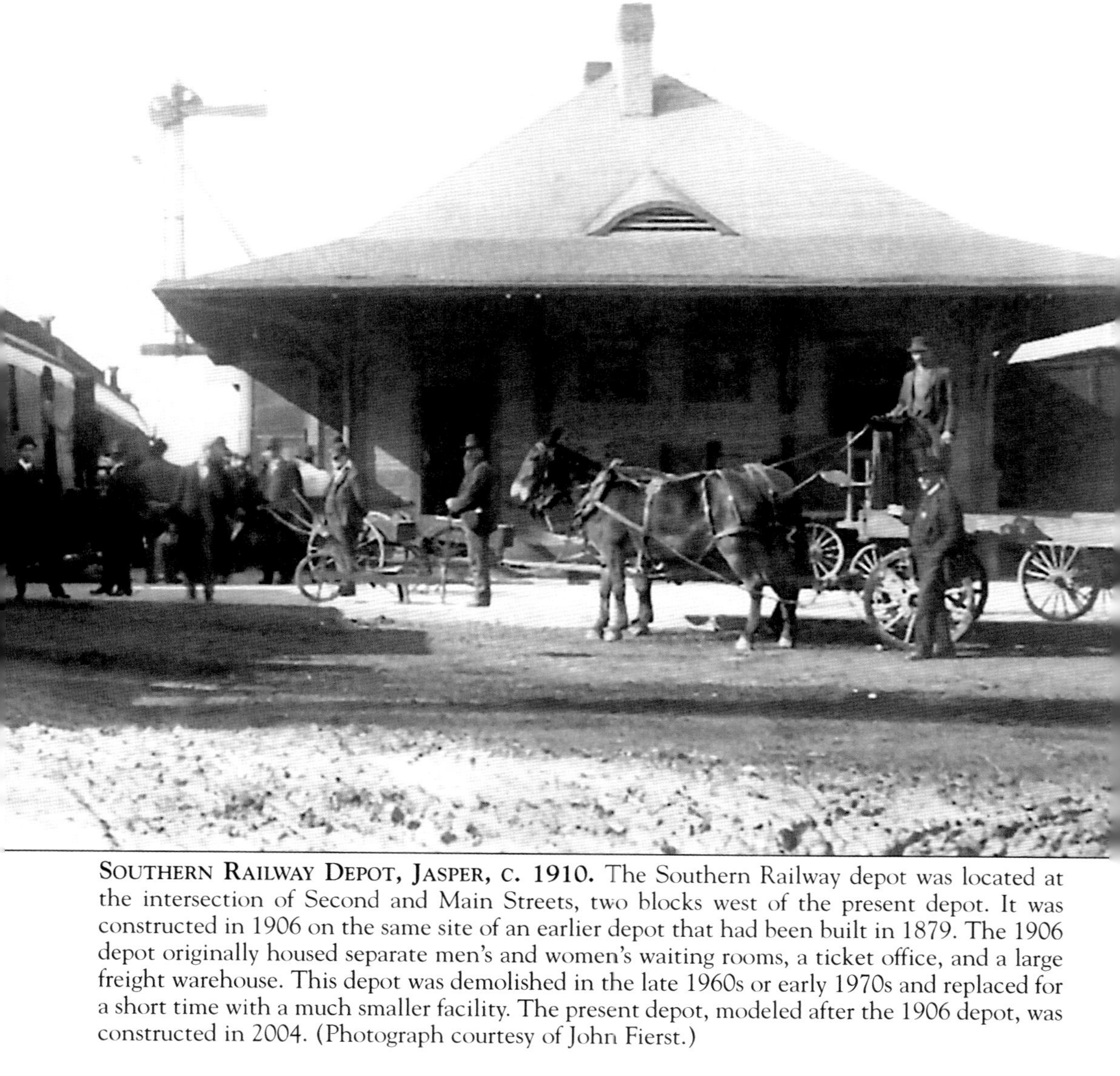

SOUTHERN RAILWAY DEPOT, JASPER, C. 1910. The Southern Railway depot was located at the intersection of Second and Main Streets, two blocks west of the present depot. It was constructed in 1906 on the same site of an earlier depot that had been built in 1879. The 1906 depot originally housed separate men's and women's waiting rooms, a ticket office, and a large freight warehouse. This depot was demolished in the late 1960s or early 1970s and replaced for a short time with a much smaller facility. The present depot, modeled after the 1906 depot, was constructed in 2004. (Photograph courtesy of John Fierst.)

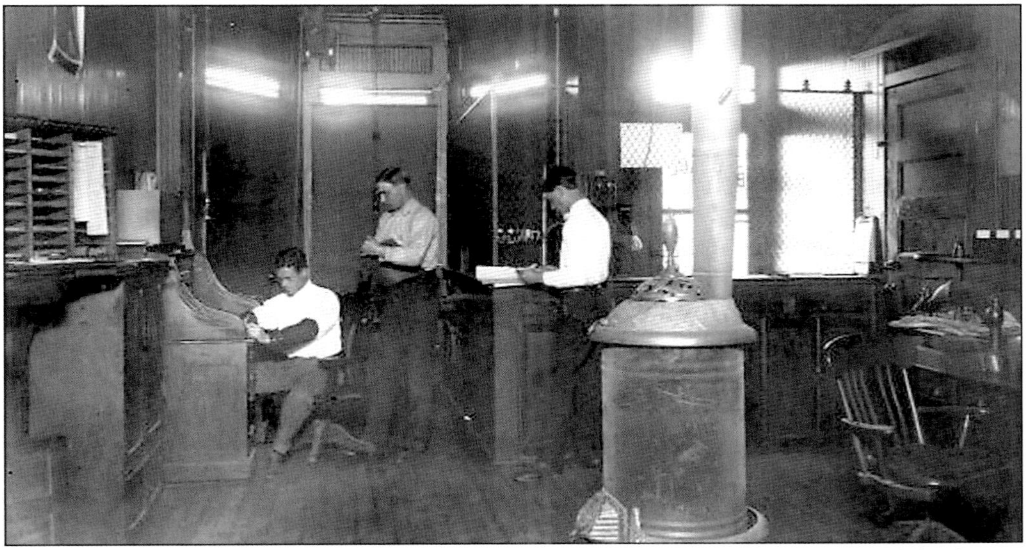

SOUTHERN RAILWAY DEPOT TICKET OFFICE, JASPER, C. 1910. This photograph of the depot's ticket office was taken looking to the south. (Photograph courtesy of the Dudine Family.)

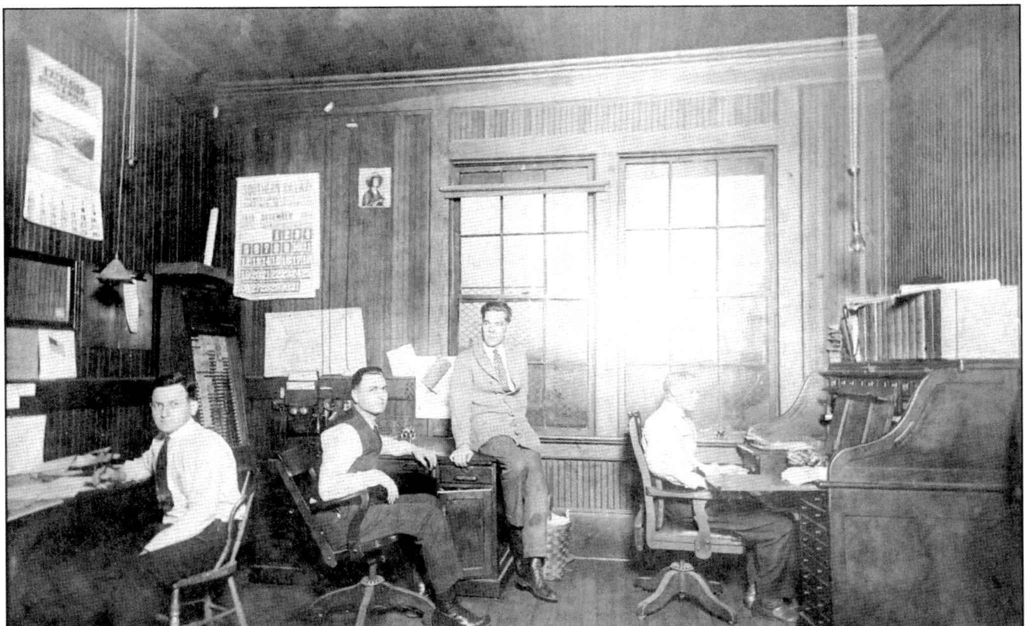

SOUTHERN RAILWAY DEPOT TICKET OFFICE, JASPER, 1915. This photograph of the depot's ticket office was taken on December 17, 1915, looking to the north. The gentlemen shown in the photograph are Henry Kress, Romus Chambers, Ted Dudine, and Lloyd Claycomb. A dozen years before, Henry, Romus, and Lloyd were all schoolmates at Jasper High School, at a time when only 18 total students were enrolled in all 4 grades. (Photograph courtesy of C. Mae [Kress] Ploetner.)

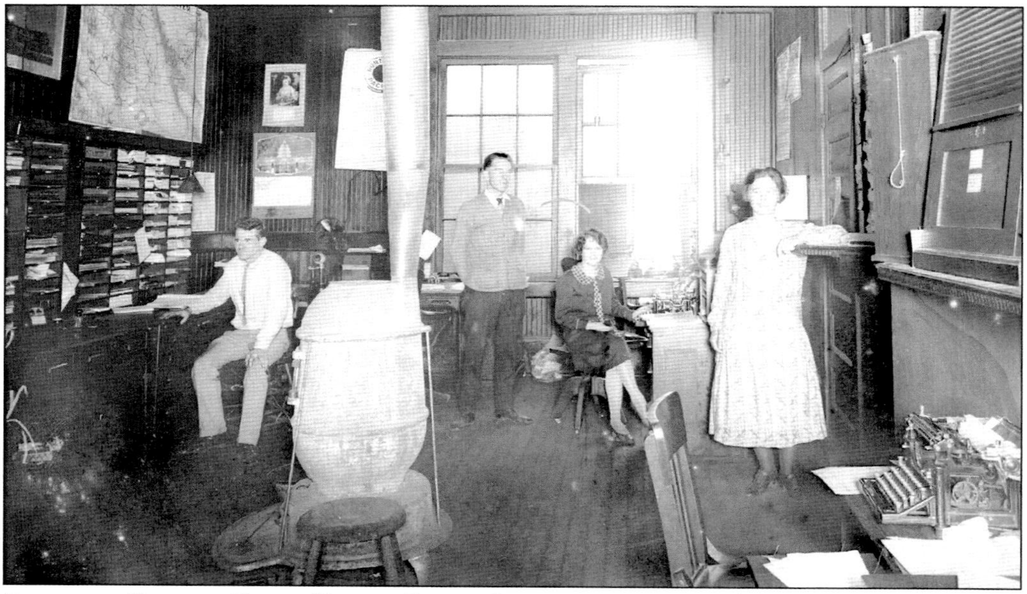

SOUTHERN RAILWAY DEPOT TICKET OFFICE, JASPER, 1930. Pictured inside the 1906 depot are, from left to right: Julius Buettner, Theodore Dudine, Helen Buettner, and Sarah Hartke. Julius Buettner worked for the Southern from January 1, 1918, until March 5, 1965. By the time he retired, he had top seniority as a clerk for the railroad's Danville, Kentucky, and St. Louis Division. (Photograph courtesy of John Fierst.)

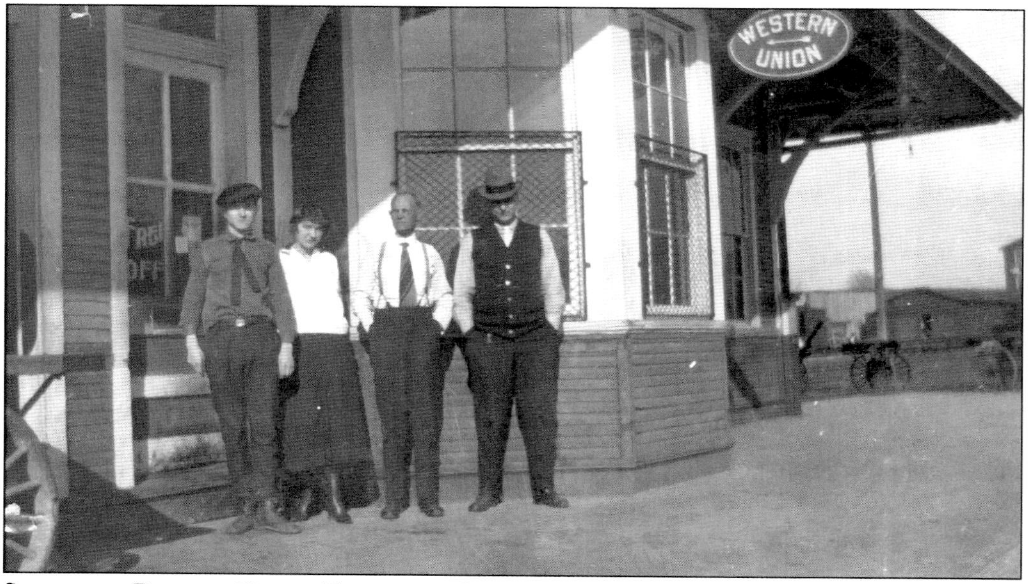

SOUTHERN RAILWAY DEPOT EMPLOYEES, JASPER, C. 1920. Pictured here are Julius Buettner, Mrs. Ted Dudine, Victor Claycomb—who was the railroad agent—and Romus Chambers. According to the book, *Jasper Area History* (1989), Victor Claycomb, known as Mr. Southern Railway, was named agent for the station in 1894 and worked there until 1935. (Photograph courtesy of John Fierst.)

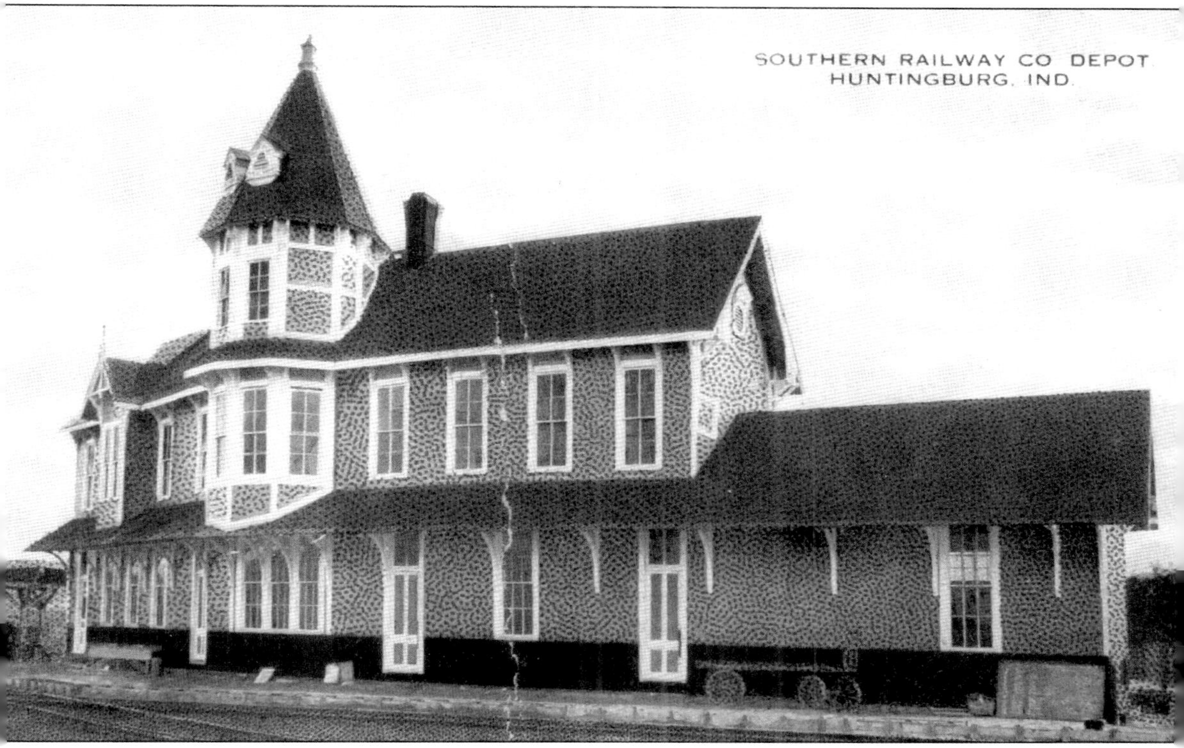

SOUTHERN RAILWAY DEPOT, HUNTINGBURG. According to Judge Hugo C. Songer in his book, *The History of Huntingburg*, the depot, built by local contractor Henry Winkenhoefer, was completed in December 1882. Having railway service opened the town up to news from outside (Songer says the train delivered newspapers the same day they were printed—allowing people quick access to world events) and also allowed residents to travel to destinations such as Louisville and St. Louis more quickly and easily than stagecoaches or horses could move along dirt roads that were often impassable in wet weather. Songer writes, "Special excursion trains were run to every conceivable event and purpose. Lacking an auditorium, the Huntingburg Cornet Band sponsored an excursion to Marengo Cave in 1885, round trip $1.00, and held a grand concert in the cave. Several hundred attended. Another special train was run to Milltown, which 1,000 excursionists attended from Princeton (another Indiana town), Huntingburg, and points along the route. The train, gaily decorated with bunting and flags, was composed of one baggage car and ten coaches." (Photograph courtesy of the Huntingburg Public Library.)

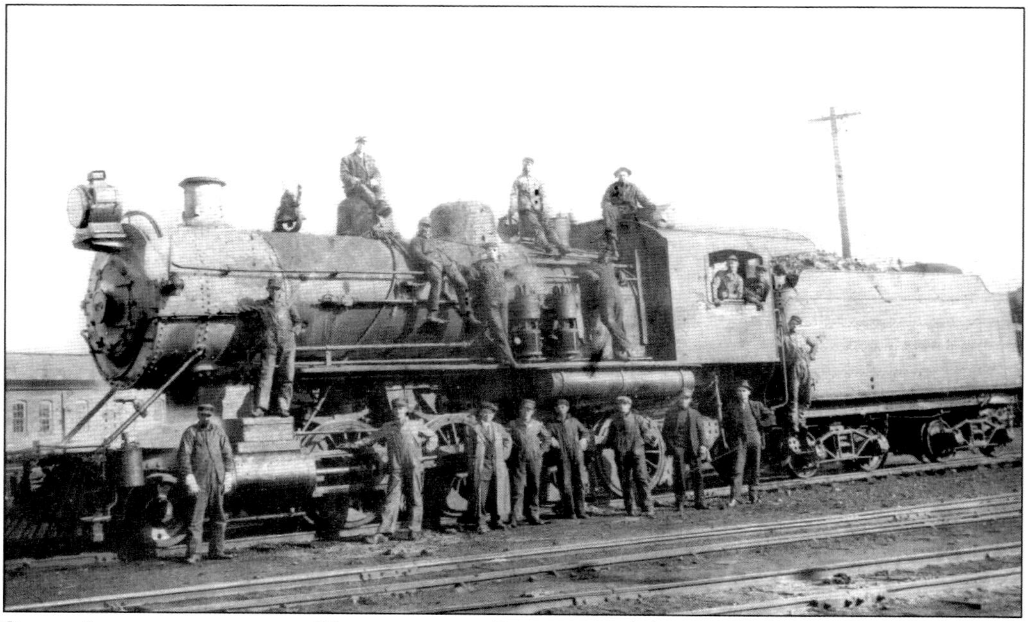

Steam Locomotive in the Huntingburg Railyards. (Photograph courtesy of the Museum of Huntingburg.)

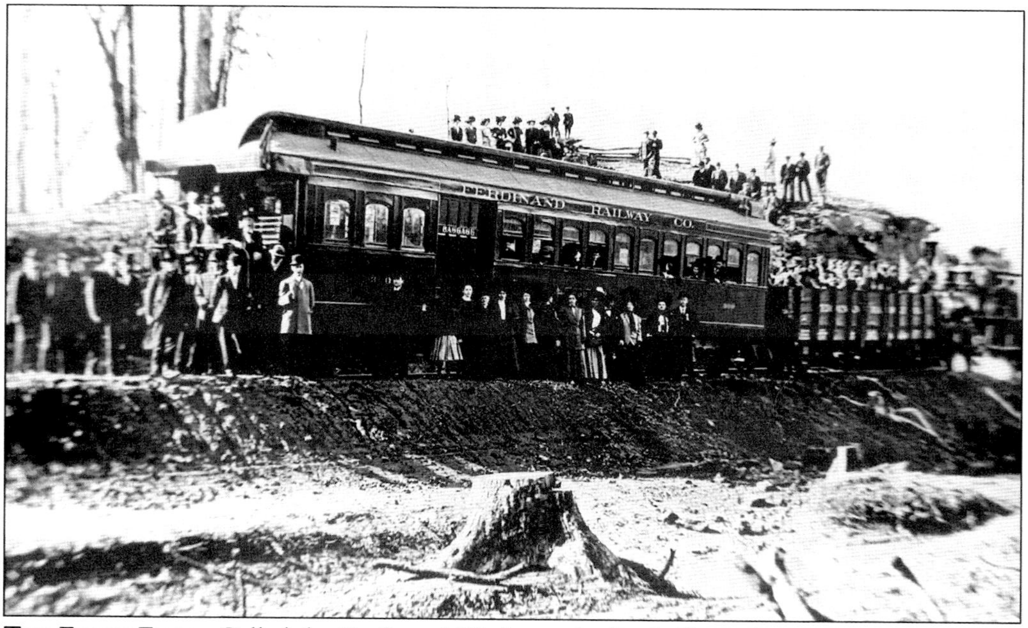

The Ferdy Flyer. Called the Ferdinand Blinky or the Ferdy Flyer, this train carried students from Ferdinand to attend school in nearby Huntingburg. (Photograph courtesy of the Huntingburg Public Library.)

Two

GOVERNMENT

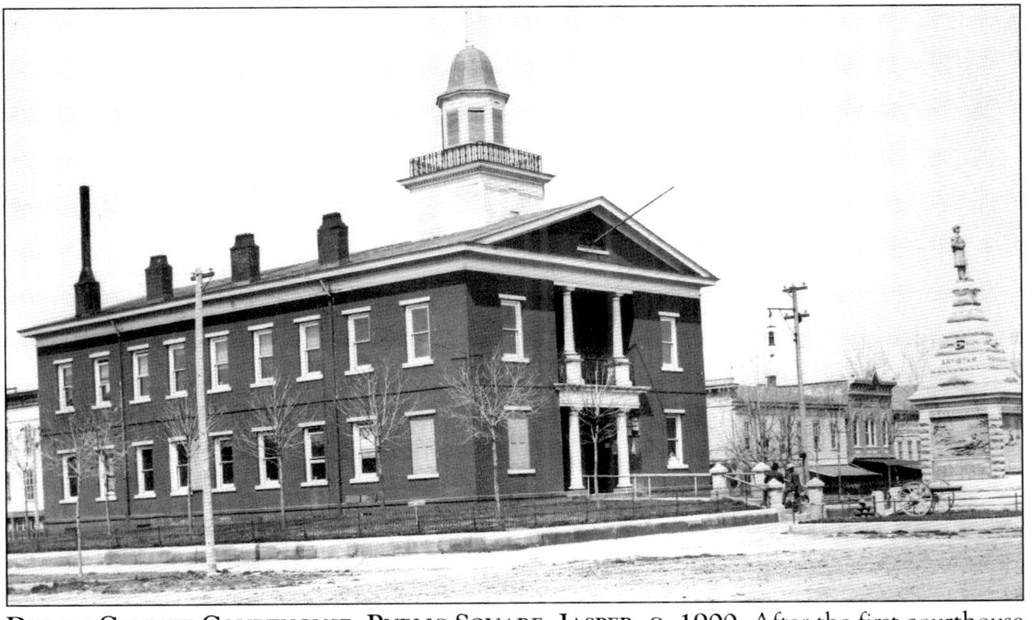

DUBOIS COUNTY COURTHOUSE, PUBLIC SQUARE, JASPER, C. 1900. After the first courthouse burned down in 1839, court was held in the home of James Condict at the southwest corner of Fifth and Jackson. Alexander McGroves was given the contract to build the new courthouse, but after the foundation was finished, he quit, putting the project on hold. Then, Father Joseph Kundek, the area's first resident Catholic priest, undertook the responsibility of getting the courthouse finished. He signed on as general contractor on December 3, 1844. According to the book *Jasper Area History*, "the lime used in the building was burned from rocks obtained at the foot of Reider's Hill. Michael Marendt was paid $28 for two lower stone columns in the front of the courthouse, including the stone caps; for the two upper columns, which were in two parts he was paid $30. He dressed the columns in a quarry near Jasper. The brick courthouse was completed in 1847 and cost $6,773. An addition, which doubled the size, was added in 1875 by [local brickmason and contractor] E. A. Hochgesang. By the early 1900s, the courthouse was deemed too small and was torn down in 1909, to allow for the construction of a newer and larger facility." (Photograph courtesy of John Fierst.)

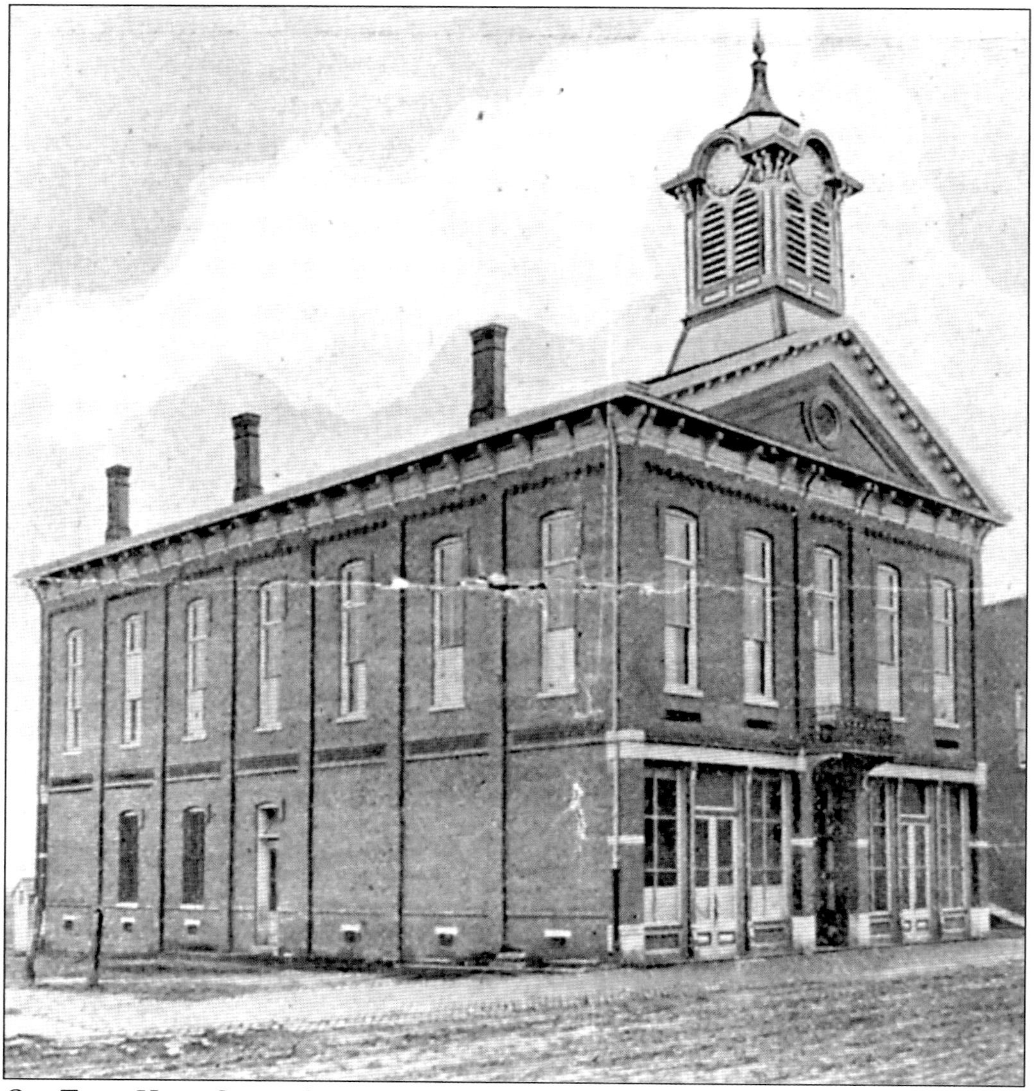

OLD TOWN HALL, GEIGER STREET, HUNTINGBURG, C. 1890. The building, now immaculately restored, houses the Chamber of Commerce. According to Judge Hugo C. Songer, in his book *The History of Huntingburg*, the city hall was designed by Henry Mursinna, an Italian architect who worked for an Evansville firm. The hall, completed on June 10, 1886, cost $13,600. Songer goes on to note that part of the new building was used as an opera house and was rented to traveling theatre companies for $7.50 a night and to local companies for the lesser fee of $5.00. The town's fire company, founded a year after the hall was built, was located on the first floor of the building for a period of time. (Photograph courtesy of the Huntingburg Public Library.)

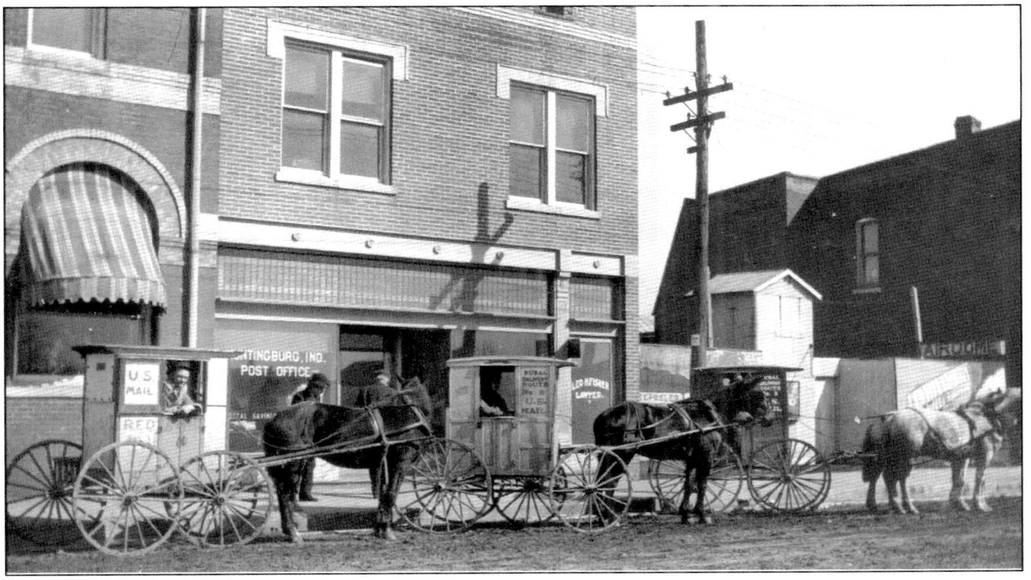

Huntingburg Post Office, 304 Fourth Street, Huntingburg. The post office is an example of late Victorian-Commercial architecture and was built c. 1900. The building housed the post office until 1927. That year, Armin Brace bought the building and remodeled it to use as Brace's Bakery. Over the years, it was also known as Ruch's Bakery and in the 1940s, Cossie M. Day relocated his business, The Electric Shoe Hospital, in the building. A decade later, the building was sold to Kermit Ruttkar to become Ruttkar's Flower Shop. It was later a candle and gift shop. The two mail carriers in the wagons are Ira Katterhenry and Jim Miller. (Photograph courtesy of the Huntingburg Public Library.)

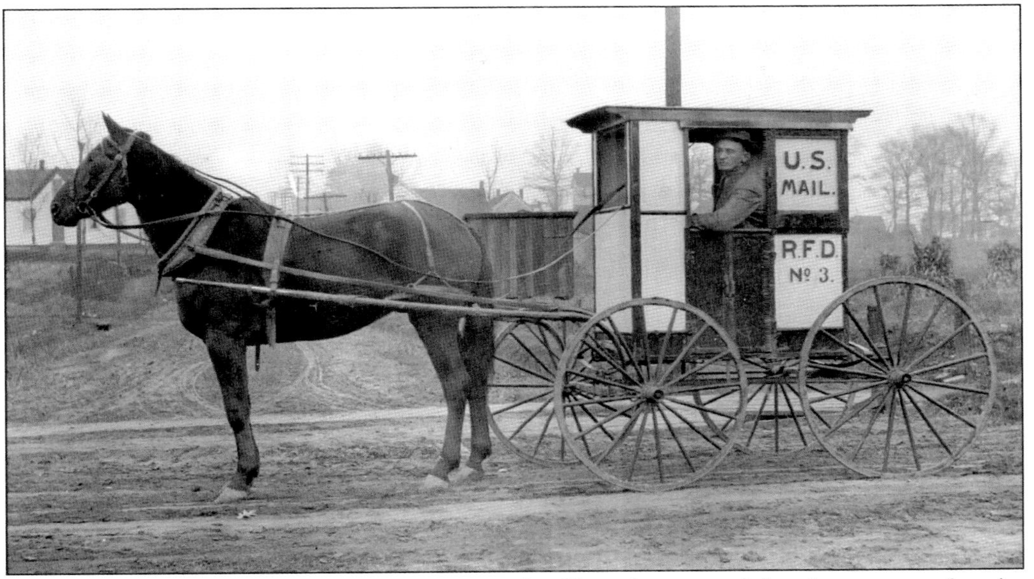

Mail Delivery in Huntingburg, 1914. Ira Katterhenry and his horse pose for the photographer while delivering the mail on Route No. 3 in Huntingburg. (Photograph courtesy of the Huntingburg Public Library.)

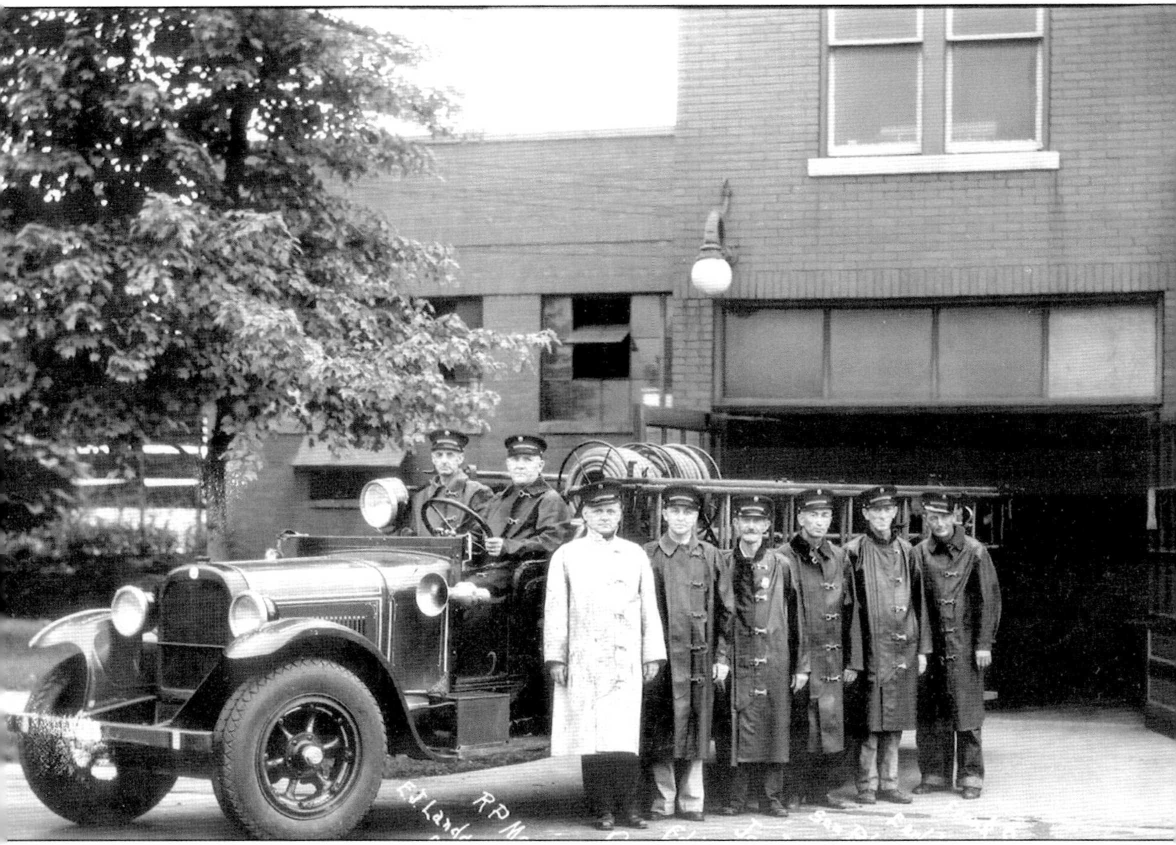

HUNTINGBURG FIRE DEPARTMENT, 1934. Fire Chief C. M. Day (in light-colored coat) poses with his department. Seated are E. J. Landgrebe and R. P. Metz. Flanking the chief, from left to right, are firefighters Ed Utz, Joe Dittmer, Blemker, Earl Young, and Frank Smith. (Photograph courtesy of the Museum of Huntingburg.)

Three

Downtown

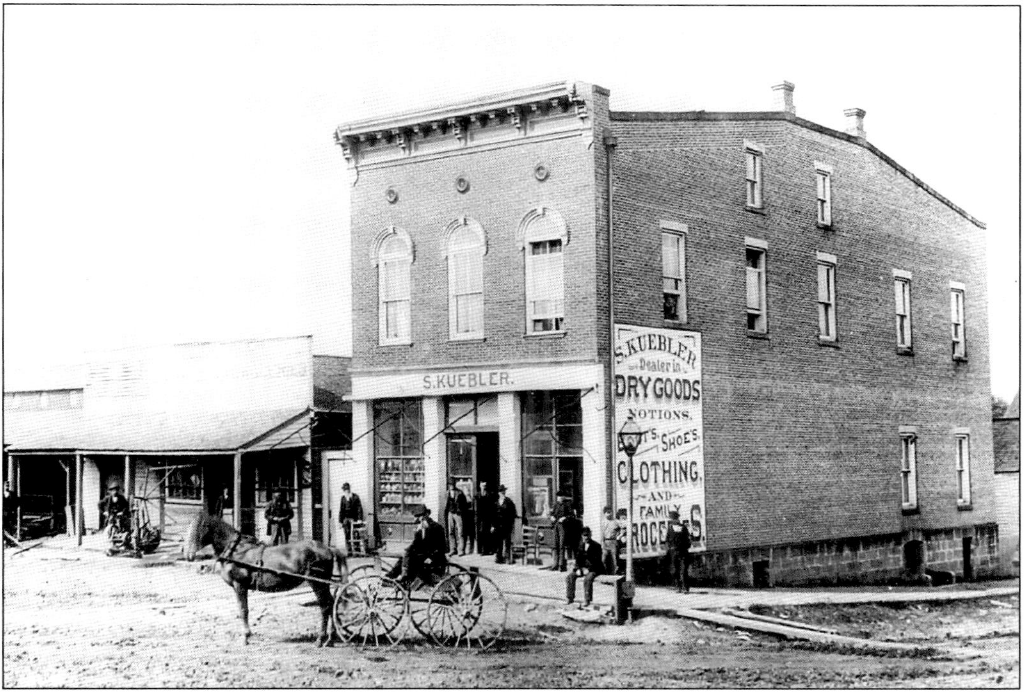

Kuebler Building, Public Square, Jasper, c. 1885. Standing west of the courthouse is one of the two oldest buildings still in use on the Public Square. Built in 1880 by Sebastian Kuebler, the building was constructed to house his general store. Prior to this time, Kuebler, a native of Grissheim, Baden, had been a blacksmith and manufacturer of farm implements and wagons. Kuebler then began to deal in tobacco and other commodities, which led to a successful retail trade in dry goods, clothing, and groceries, as the sign confirms. In 1895, the frame buildings shown in the photograph were removed and the large, two-story brick Kuebler Block was erected. (Photograph courtesy of John Fierst.)

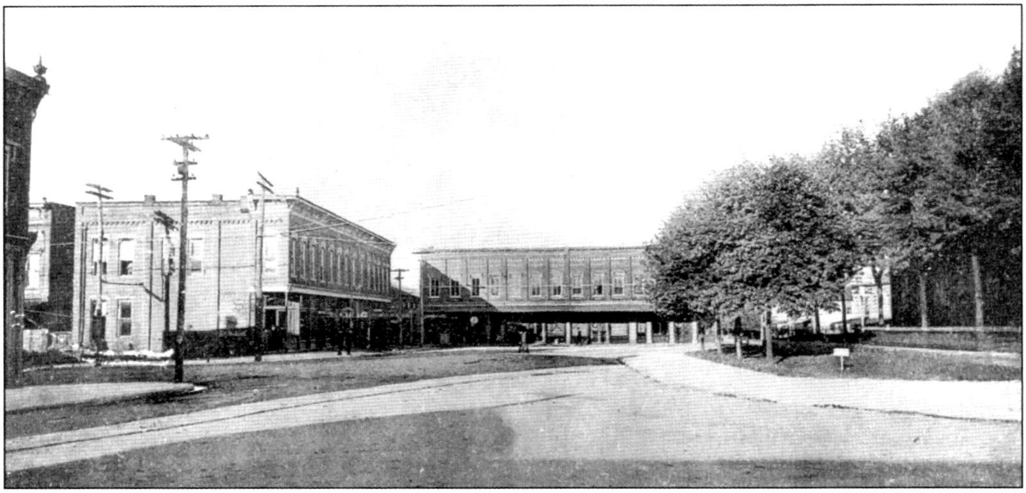

SOUTHWEST SIDE OF PUBLIC SQUARE, JASPER, C. 1906. This photograph, taken from a postcard dated May, 1907, shows the southwest side of the square in the early 1900s. The long, two-story building on the left, south of the courthouse, is the Spayd Building, also known as the Spayd Block. It was constructed in three phases. The east half was built in 1894 by Leo Spayd to house his shoe store. The central portion, 18 feet in width, was built in 1895 as the first location of the Farmers and Merchants Bank. The westernmost 32 feet of the building were constructed in 1900 as lease space. Adjacent to the Spayd Block is the Kuebler Block, facing east toward the courthouse. This 75 feet wide, two-story brick building was erected in 1895 by Sebastian Kuebler. At the north end of the Kuebler Block, obscured by the trees around the courthouse, is the original brick Kuebler Building. (Photograph courtesy of Ron Flick.)

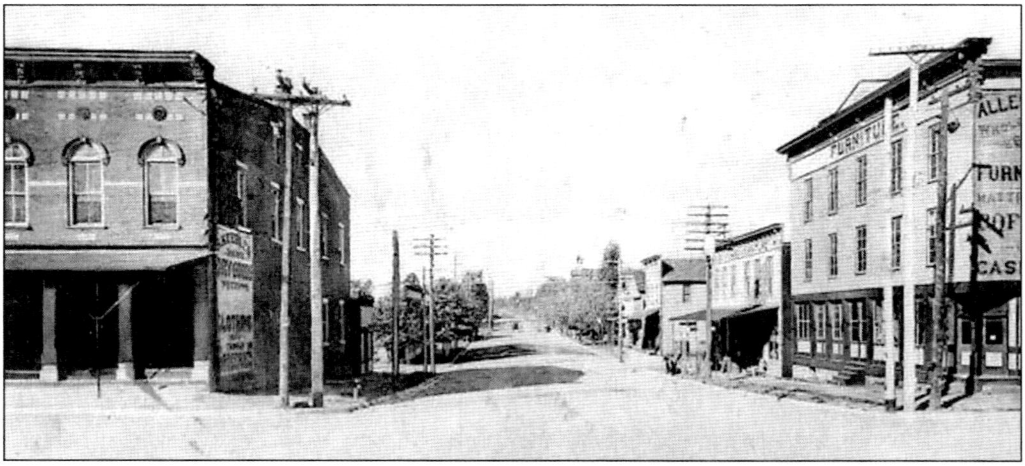

WEST SIDE OF PUBLIC SQUARE, JASPER, C. 1900. This view is from the courthouse, looking west on Sixth Street. On the left is the Kuebler Building, constructed in 1880. On the right, in the foreground, is Alles Brothers Furniture Store, which was torn down in 1907. Behind Alles Brothers is the wood-framed Lorey Brothers Furniture Store, which was originally built by John Lorey in 1891 and expanded in 1898. Beyond Newton Street, on the northwest corner of Sixth and Newton Streets, is a two-story frame building which housed Prechtel's Saloon prior to 1901, and Karl Weigel's harness shop after that year. The tower of the public school rises further to the west. Across the street, on the southwest corner of the Sixth and Newton intersection, barely visible in the trees, is the upper floor of the Union Hotel. (Photograph courtesy of Don Flick.)

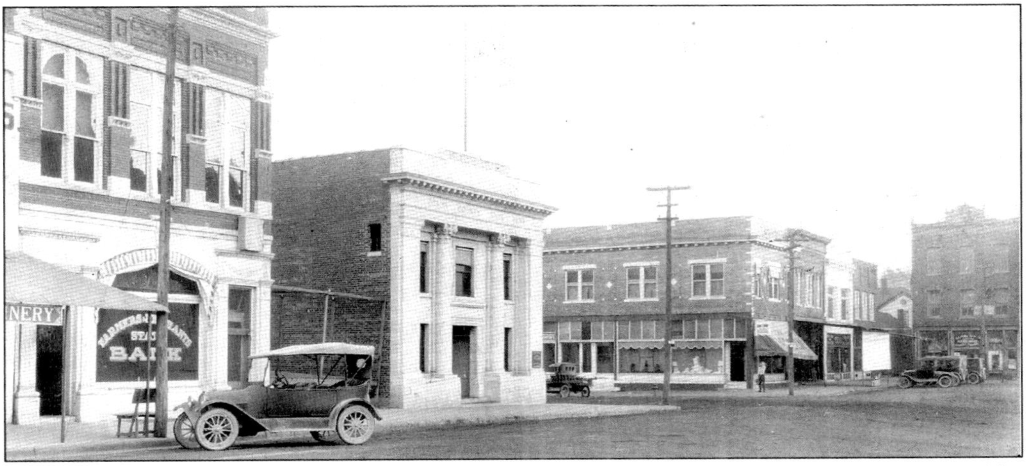

EAST SIDE OF PUBLIC SQUARE, JASPER, C. 1925. In this view of the east side of the Jasper Public Square, at the far left can be seen a small portion of the Sprauer Building, dating from 1880. Next is the Farmers and Merchants Bank Building, constructed in 1905. Beyond the empty lot is the Dubois County State Bank Building, finished in 1916. Across Main Street is the 1912 Urich Building, which has housed the Siebert family clothing store since 1924. The next three buildings are the 1908 Melchior Building, the 1915 Ideal Building, and the 1912 Haberly Building. In the southeast corner is a restaurant and bar building that has housed numerous businesses. Turning the corner, standing at three stories, is the Joseph Friedman Building, erected in 1886, which has been the home of Sturm's Hardware since 1895. (Photograph courtesy of John Fierst.)

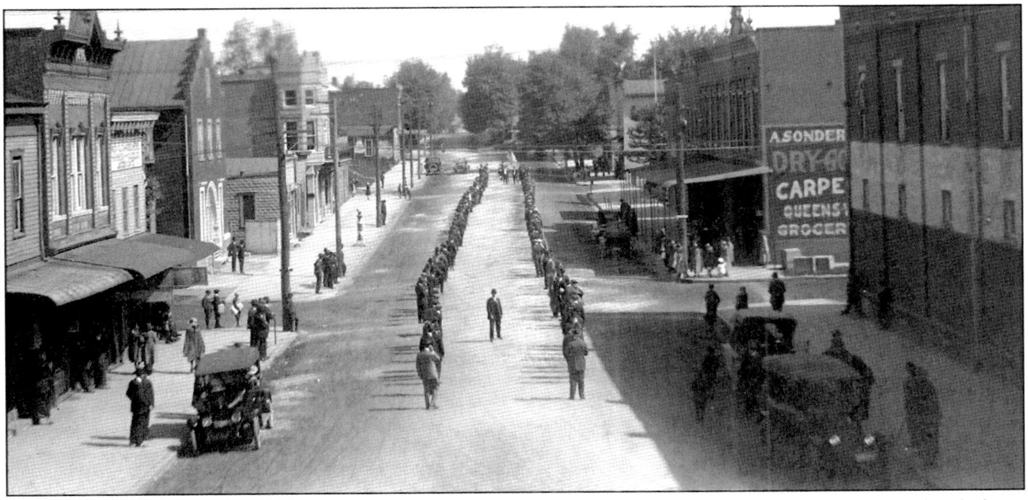

NORTH MAIN STREET, JASPER, C. 1920. Looking north from the courthouse, on the left, is a portion of Kunkel's Hall, built in 1884 and torn down in 1923. Next are the brick Troxler Building, built in 1896 and the wood–framed Troxler Building, which preceded its brick neighbor by a decade or two. Across Seventh Street is the Gramelspacher-Gutzweiler House built in 1849, in its original location. The next major structure to the north is the turreted William Wilson Building, built in 1910, which served as the main offices for the German-American Bank. On the right side of the photograph is the sidewall of the Sermersheim Building, built in 1896. Beyond the street is the 1893 Sonderman Building, which housed Sonderman's Dry Goods Store. Next come the two Wagner Company buildings: the showroom, built in 1893, and the blacksmith shop, constructed in 1888. (Photograph courtesy of Ron Flick.)

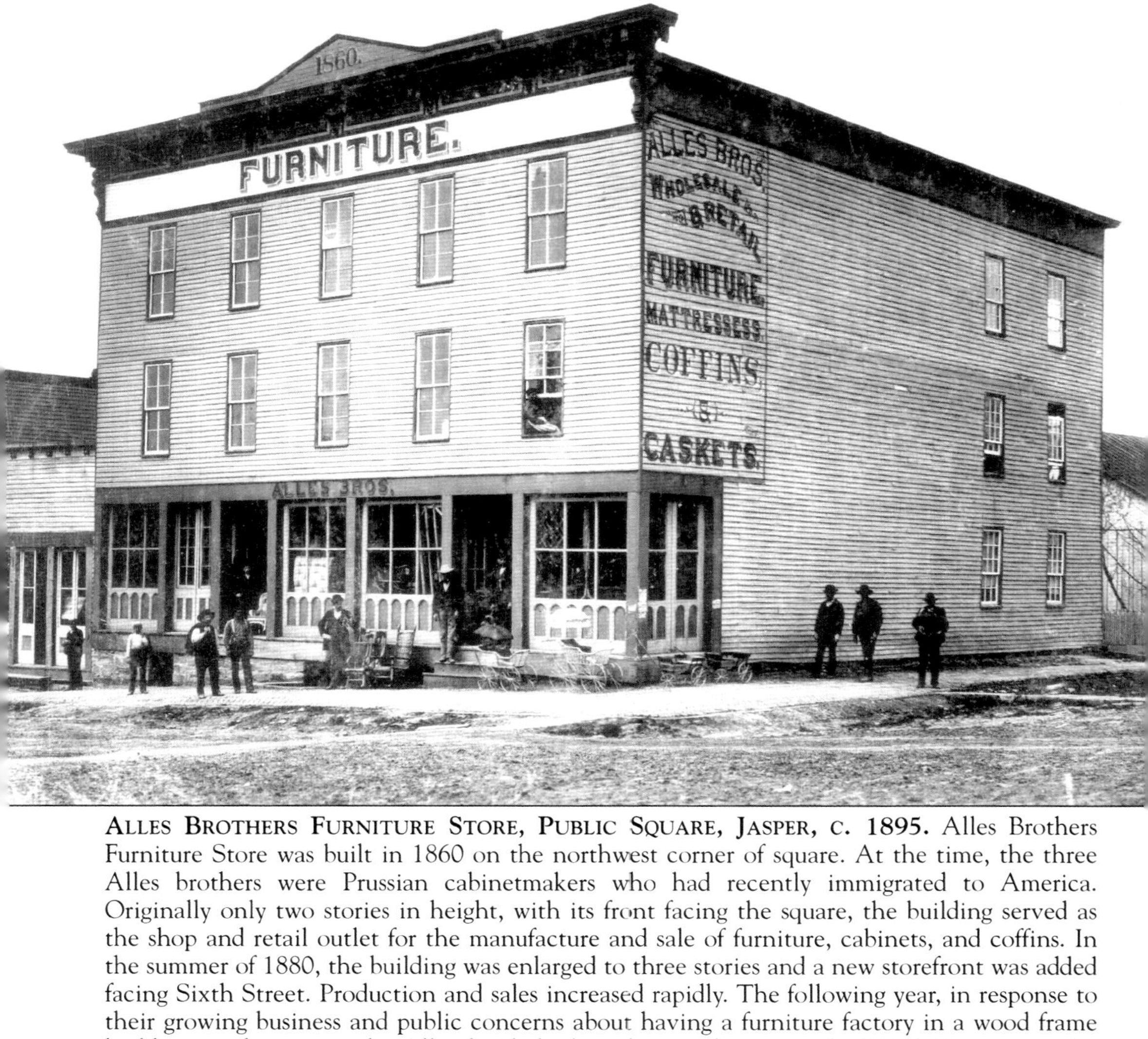

Alles Brothers Furniture Store, Public Square, Jasper, c. 1895. Alles Brothers Furniture Store was built in 1860 on the northwest corner of square. At the time, the three Alles brothers were Prussian cabinetmakers who had recently immigrated to America. Originally only two stories in height, with its front facing the square, the building served as the shop and retail outlet for the manufacture and sale of furniture, cabinets, and coffins. In the summer of 1880, the building was enlarged to three stories and a new storefront was added facing Sixth Street. Production and sales increased rapidly. The following year, in response to their growing business and public concerns about having a furniture factory in a wood frame building on the square, the Alles family built a plant at the east end of Sixth Street near the Patoka River. This new facility became the Jasper Furniture Company in 1886, and later the Jasper Desk Company. The Alles brothers eventually sold their interest in the company to the Kuebler, Gramelspacher, and Joseph families. The original building on the square was then obtained by John Lorey, who razed the aging edifice and erected a two-story brick building on the site in 1910. (Photograph courtesy of John Fierst.)

L. H. STURM HARDWARE STORE, PUBLIC SQUARE, JASPER, C. 1900. In 1886, Joseph Friedman erected a three-story brick hardware store on the southeast side of the square. Nine years later, he sold the building and business to his niece's husband, Louis Sturm, and his partner, John Lorey. The two men remained partners until 1909, after which the business became known as L. H. Sturm Hardware. More than 100 years after the Sturm family purchased it, members of the family still own and operate the business in Jasper. The building to the right is the Joseph and Martin Friedman Building, built in 1900 to house Haberly's Confectionary. (Photograph courtesy of Bernard and Sharon [Sturm] Messmer.)

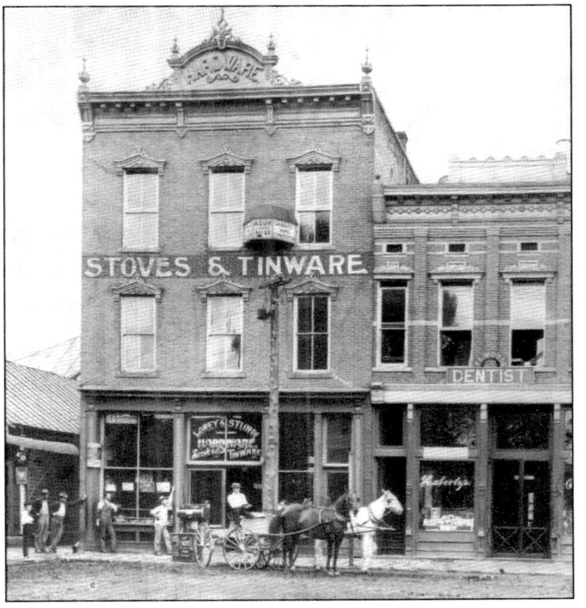

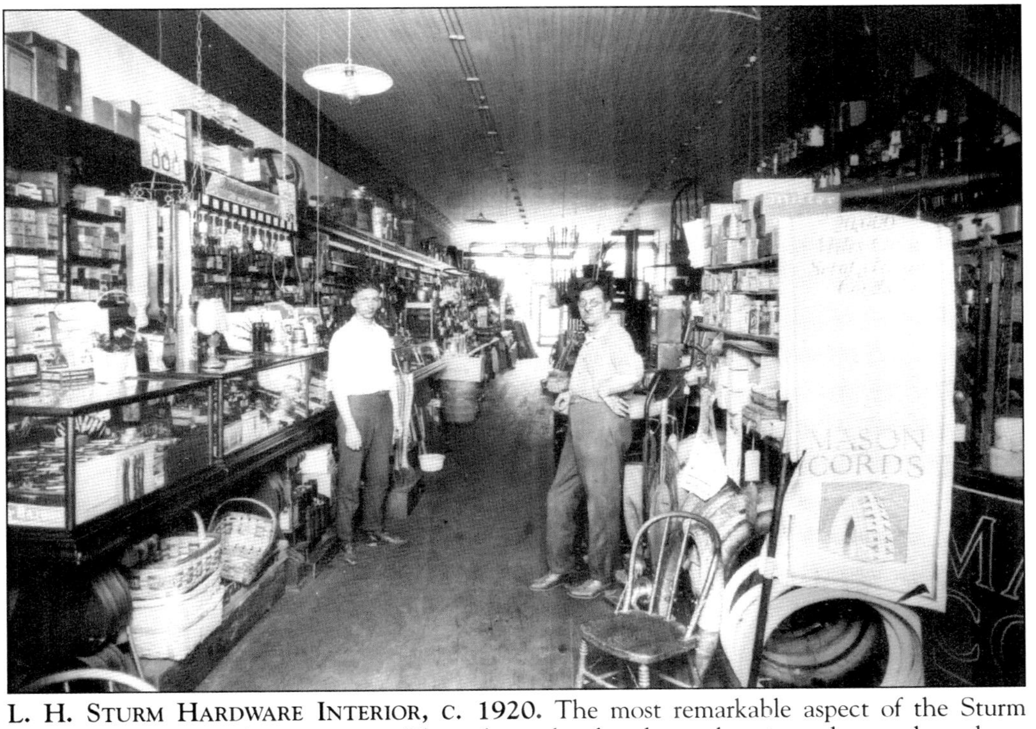

L. H. STURM HARDWARE INTERIOR, C. 1920. The most remarkable aspect of the Sturm building is its state of preservation. Throughout the decades, only minor changes have been made to the building, both inside and out. The store contains original cabinetry and shelving along with displays of vintage merchandise and period advertising throughout. A potbelly stove, rolling ladder, spiral staircase, and hand-operated elevator all add historical charm. Sturm Hardware is on the National Register of Historic Places. Featured in the photograph are Louie Sturm and his son, Hugo. (Photograph courtesy of Bernard and Sharon [Sturm] Messmer.)

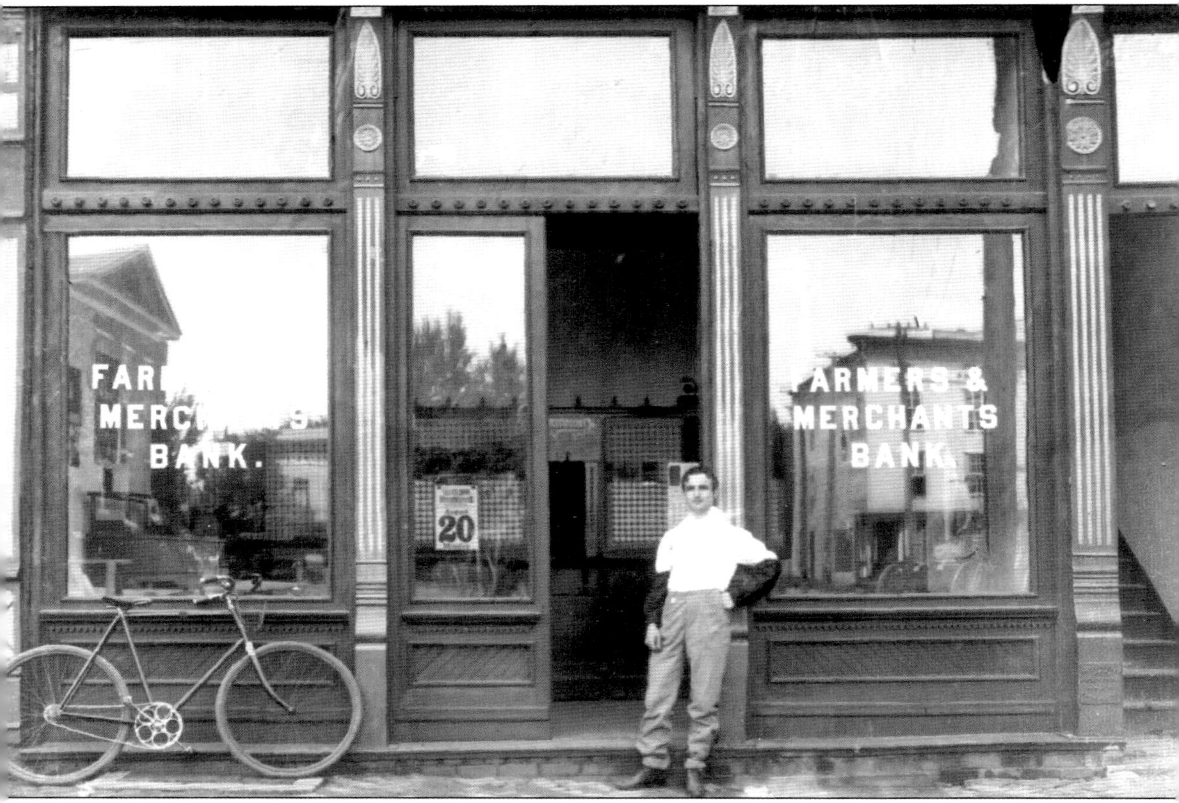

Farmers and Merchants Bank, Public Square, Jasper, c. 1900-1905. The F & M Bank is shown in its original location on the southwest side of the Square, occupying the central portion of the Spayd Building. The bank had moved into the building in 1895 after its incorporation. The portion of the building to the right of the bank, shown only partially in the photo, was not constructed until 1900. In 1905, the bank had a new building constructed on the east side of the Square. Reflected in the windows are the mirrored images of the original brick courthouse, which was torn down in 1909, the Alles Brothers furniture store, razed in 1907, and Kunkel's Hall. (Photograph courtesy of the Jasper Chamber of Commerce.)

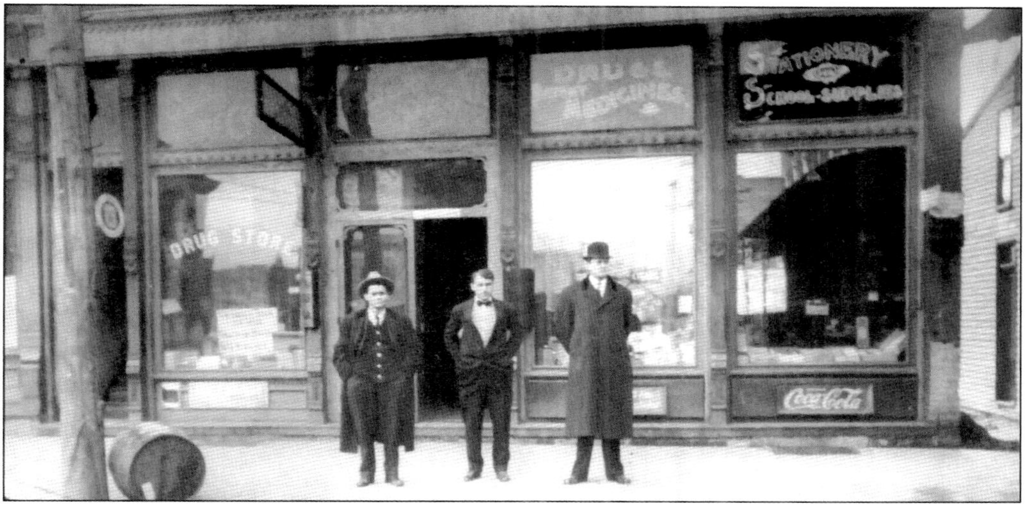

FLICK & PFAU DRUG STORE, PUBLIC SQUARE, JASPER, C. 1910. The Flick & Pfau Drug Store was located in the western-most portion of the Spayd Block on the southwest side of the square. The owner, A. W. "Gus" Flick, is shown standing in the center of the photo, with George Kremp, the local soft drink distributor, on the left. The gentleman on the right has not been identified. The store had its beginnings in 1894, when Dr. B. B. Brannock opened the Model Drug Store on the east side of Jackson Street, between Fourth and Fifth Streets. Later that year, Dr. Brannock moved the store to the new Spayd Building on the square. In 1904, the business was sold to Millard Holly of St. Louis. Two years later, the drugstore was purchased by 24-year-old Gus Flick and his father-in-law, Henry Pfau. In 1916, the store was sold to Victor Salb, who renamed it the Crescent Pharmacy. Six years later, Gus repurchased his old business, renaming it Flick's Drug Store. In 1957, ownership of the business passed on to Gus's children, Robert "Chub" Flick and Connie (Flick) Battle, and their second cousin, Denny Bell. In 1981, the drug store was sold to Rick Stradtner, who still operates it today. (Photograph courtesy of Ron Flick.)

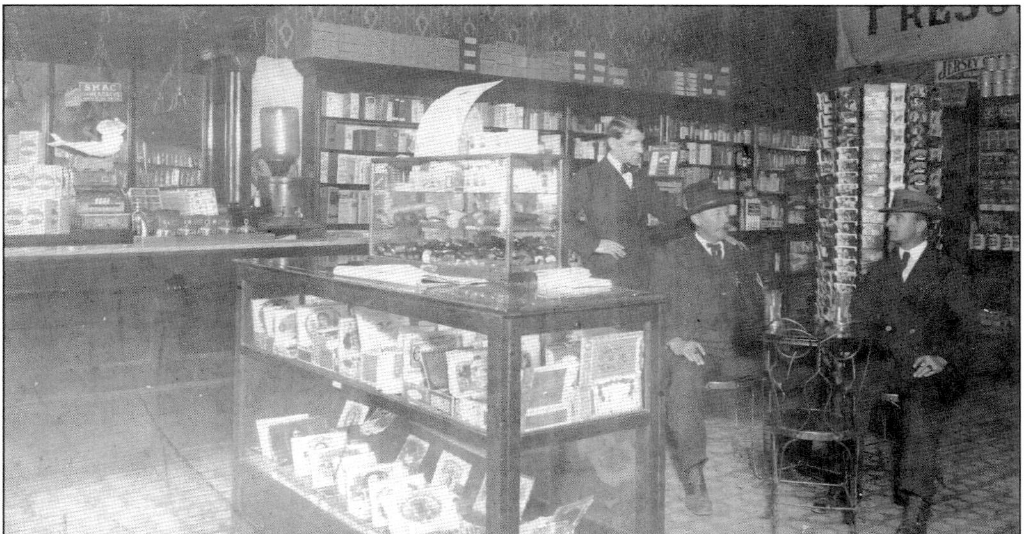

A. W. "GUS" FLICK, JASPER, C. 1910. Pharmacist A. W. "Gus" Flick chats with two well-attired patrons. (Photograph courtesy of Ron Flick.)

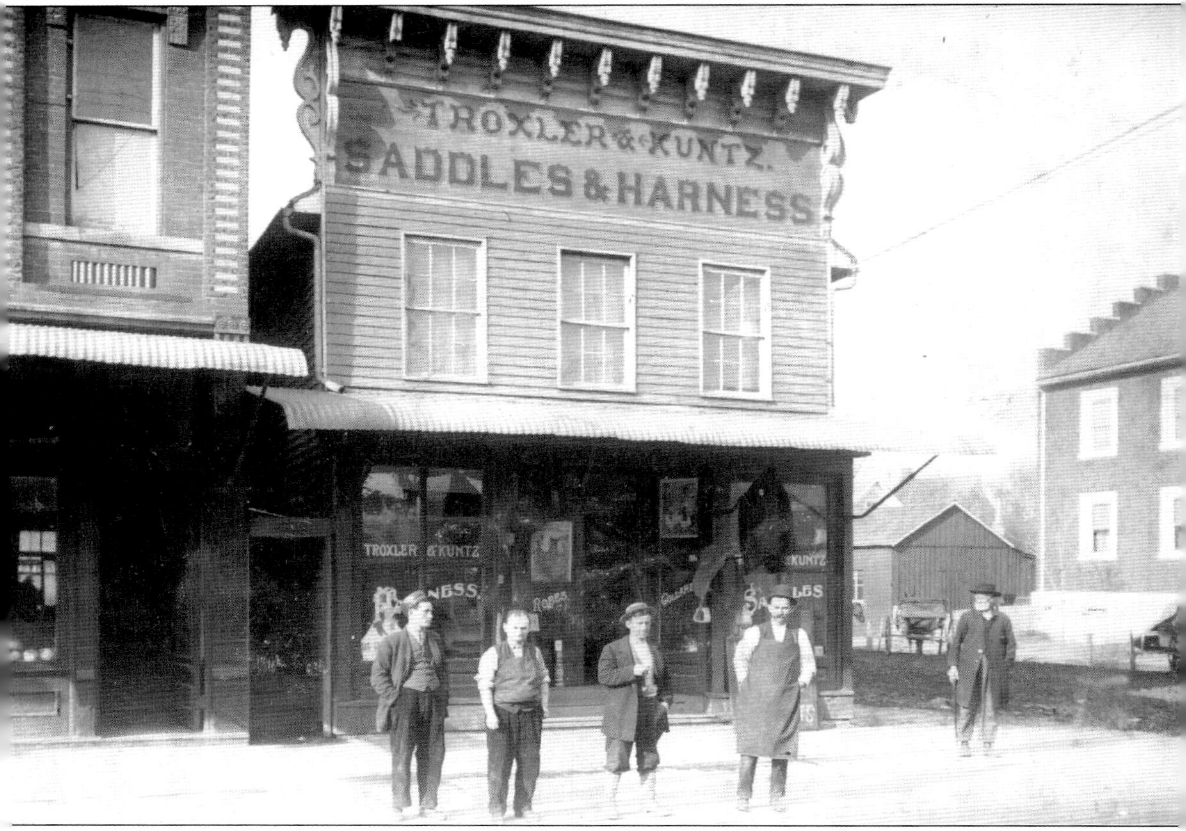

TROXLER AND KUNTZ SADDLE AND HARNESS SHOP, JASPER, 1911. This photograph, dated December 23, 1911, shows the owners and employees of the Troxler and Kuntz Saddle and Harness Shop, located on the southwest corner of Seventh and Main Streets in Jasper. The frame building was built by John Troxler, most probably in the 1870s or 1880s, as his shop and residence, although newspaper accounts mention Troxler's saddle shop as early as 1860. As his business concerns increased, Troxler had the two-story brick building constructed, in 1896, shown adjacent to the frame building. The business was eventually taken over by his son, Charles Troxler, who along with his partner, Jacob Kuntz, formed the partnership of Troxler & Kuntz. By 1920, Kuntz bought out Charles Troxler's interest and moved the shop to the Spayd Block on the Square. The Gramelspacher-Gutzweiler House is on the right. (Photograph courtesy of John Fierst.)

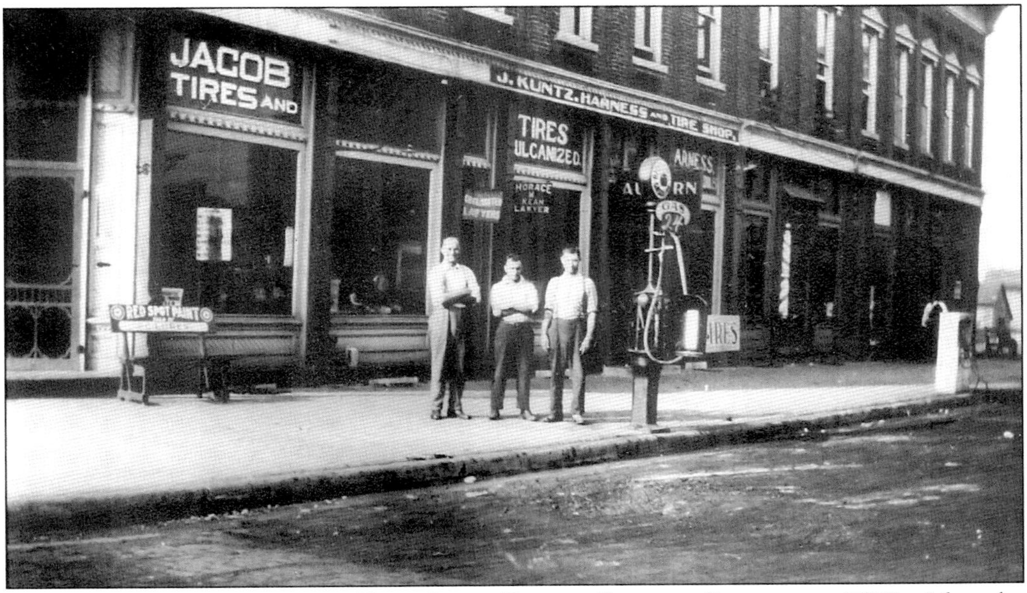

JACOB KUNTZ HARNESS AND TIRE SHOP, PUBLIC SQUARE, JASPER, C. 1925. After the dissolution of Troxler & Kuntz, Jacob Kuntz relocated his business to the Spayd Block on the southwest side of the square. With the transition from horse to automobile, the former "saddle and harness" shop became a "harness and tire" shop. Eventually, Kuntz became a Chevrolet automobile dealer. New cars were allowed to be parked on the courthouse square for viewing and sale. In 1931, after more than 45 years in a business that experienced tremendous change, Jacob Kuntz closed his shop and retired to his home, where he conducted a shoe repair shop until his death, four years later. (Photograph courtesy of John Fierst.)

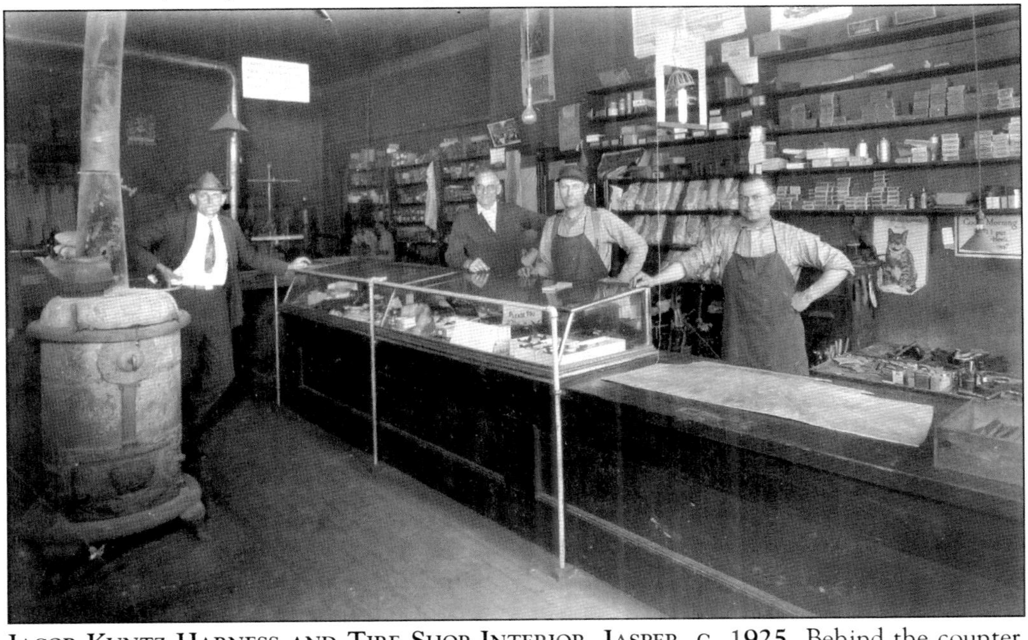

JACOB KUNTZ HARNESS AND TIRE SHOP INTERIOR, JASPER, C. 1925. Behind the counter, from left to right, are Jacob Kuntz, and two gentlemen named Schutz and Troxler.

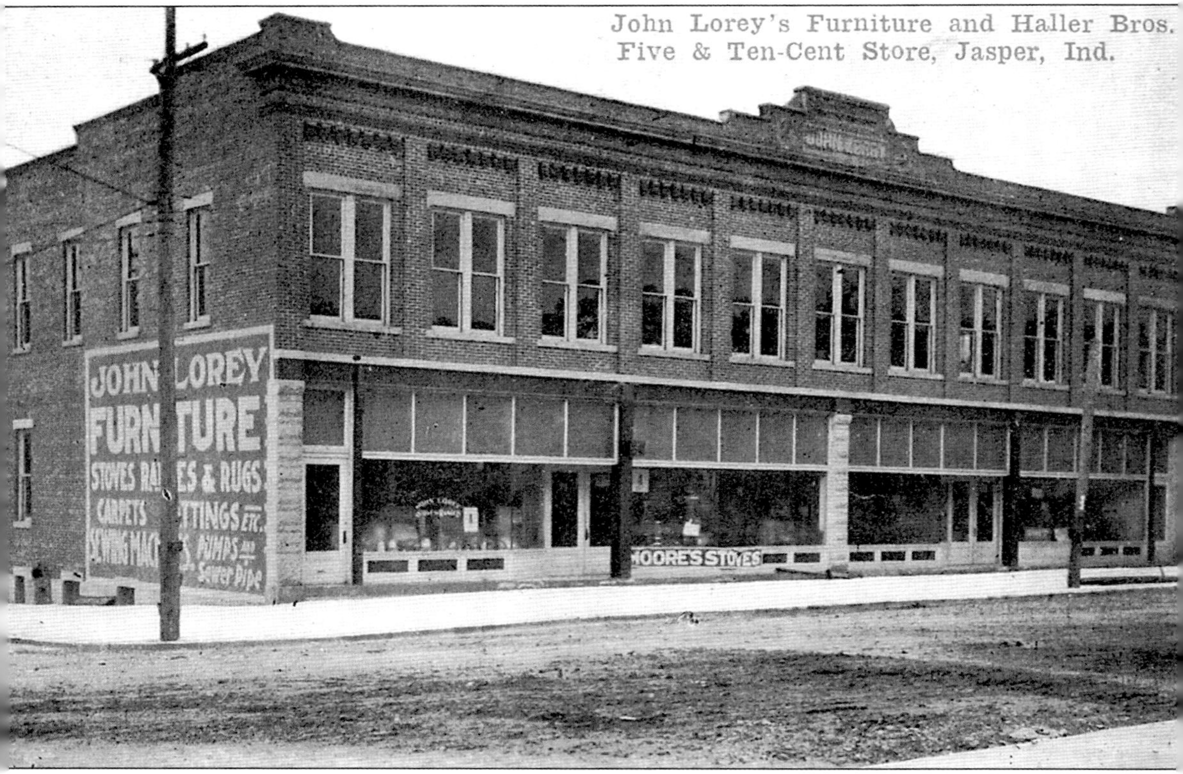

John Lorey Building, Public Square, Jasper, c. 1910. John Lorey learned the tinsmith trade as a young man and built a wood-frame building on the northeast corner of Sixth and Newton in 1891 to sell stoves and tinware. The next year, he formed a partnership with Louis Sturm and helped operate Lorey and Sturm Hardware on the square. The wood-frame Lorey Building doubled in size in 1898, and evolved into the Lorey Brothers Furniture Store. John was assisted in the business by his younger brother, Jacob. In 1909, John Lorey dissolved his partnership with Sturm and began the construction of a two-story brick building where the Alles Brothers Building once stood. The structure would house an expanded John Lorey Furniture Store and Haller's 5 & 10 Cent Store. The following year, younger brother Jacob Lorey decided to break off and build his own furniture store east of the square, at Sixth and Mill Streets. In 1914, John Lorey passed his furniture business on to his two sons, Ray and Silas. Lorey then devoted his time to family, church, and politics, becoming Jasper's second mayor in 1934. In 1924, the Quaker Maid Grocery Store moved into the first floor, while the furniture showroom moved upstairs to the second floor. In 1935, Haller's 5 & 10 was replaced by a Ben Franklin Store, run by Ott Lorey, a nephew of John Lorey. The Ben Franklin store remained a popular "dime store" on the Square for decades. It eventually grew to encompass the entire first floor of the building. In 1978, Ben Franklin relocated to the Northwood Park shopping center on Jasper's north side and its emphasis was shifted to artificial flowers, craft supplies, and framing. Today, the building on the square is occupied by Sternberg Furniture and other tenants. (Photograph courtesy of Ron Flick.)

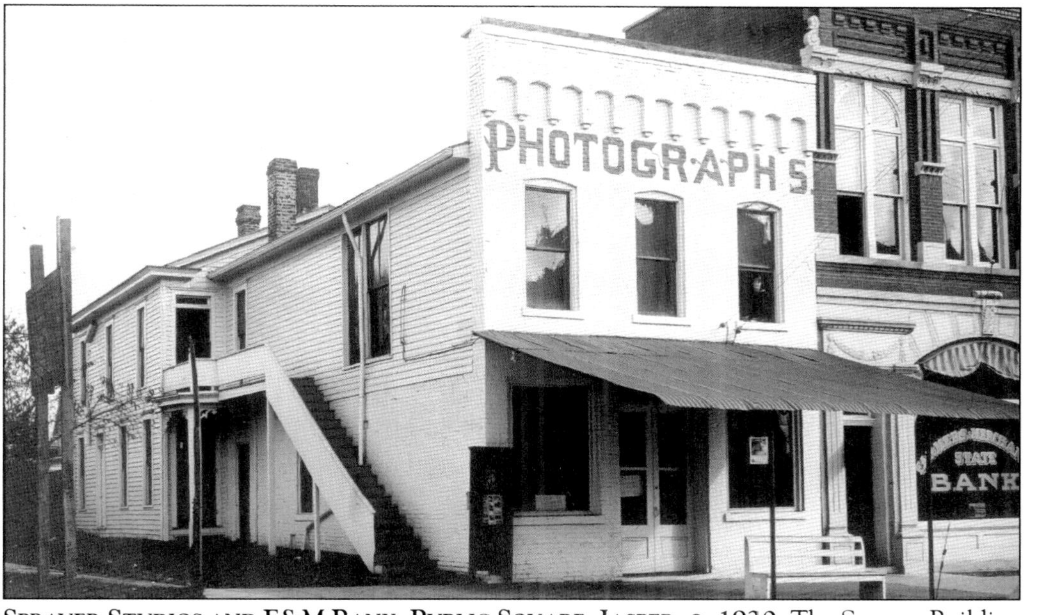

SPRAUER STUDIOS AND F&M BANK, PUBLIC SQUARE, JASPER, C. 1930. The Sprauer Building was constructed in 1880 as a two-story wood frame building. Originally, the Sprauers ran a grocery store on the first floor with their residence in the rear. Over the years, the main level retail space has housed numerous other businesses, including a saloon, a jewelry store, a tailor shop and, more recently, a book store. Located upstairs was the Sprauer photography studio, founded by Alois Sprauer. The studio endured for decades, eventually passing on to Sprauer's son, Albert. Sometime around 1940, the open stair on the north wall was enclosed and the building's exterior was remodeled. (Photograph courtesy of Lena Sprauer.)

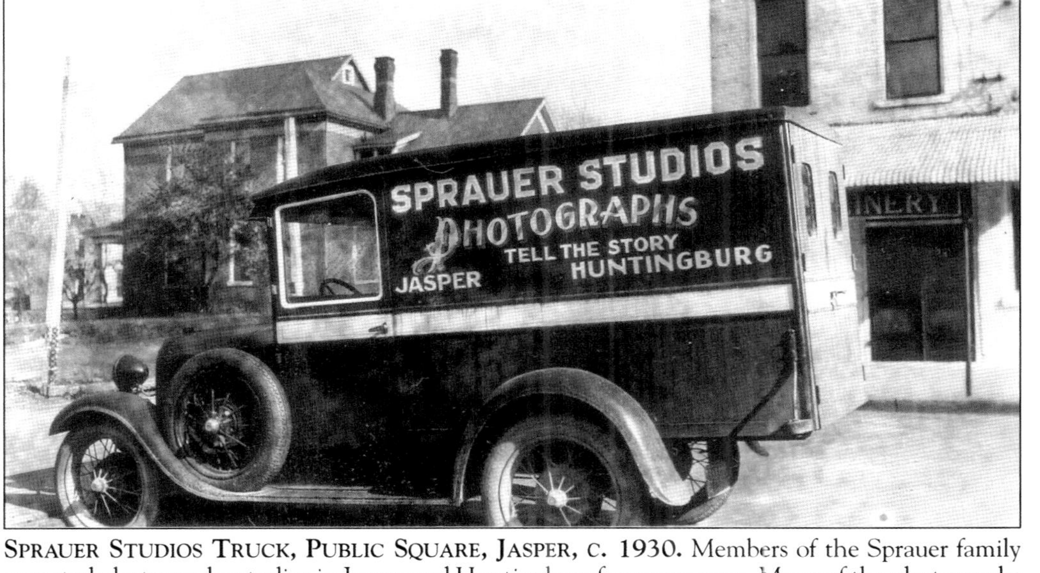

SPRAUER STUDIOS TRUCK, PUBLIC SQUARE, JASPER, C. 1930. Members of the Sprauer family operated photography studios in Jasper and Huntingburg for many years. Many of the photographs reproduced in this book were taken by the Sprauers. (Photograph courtesy of Lena Sprauer.)

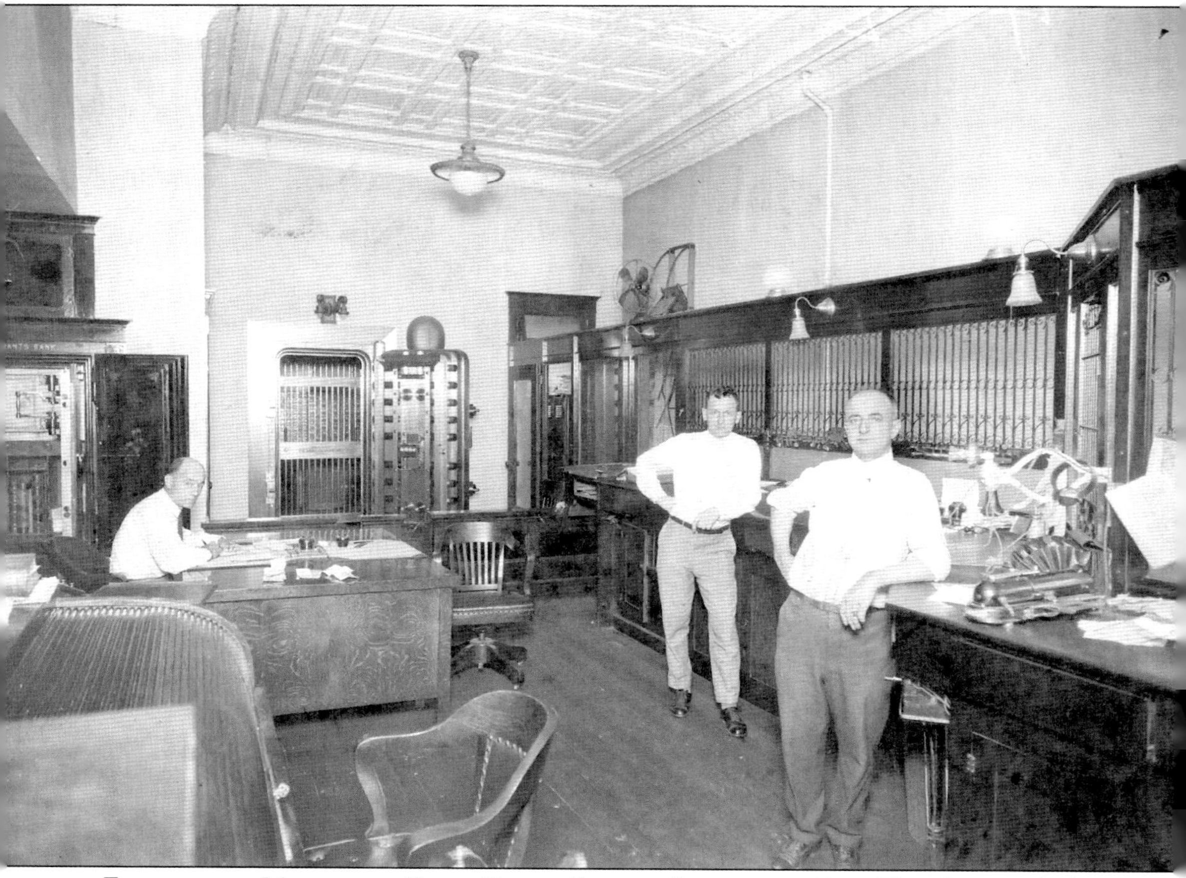

FARMERS AND MERCHANTS BANK, PUBLIC SQUARE, JASPER , C. 1920S. This photograph shows the interior of the Farmers and Merchants Bank on the northeast side of the square in downtown Jasper. The gentlemen working in the bank at the time were Gustave Gramelspacher, Henry Kress, and John Judy. During the years following World War I and into the Great Depression, the bank struggled to stay in business. In 1931, like many other banks around the county, the F&M went into voluntary liquidation. Fortunately, all depositors received 100 percent of their deposits before the bank closed its doors in 1934. (Photograph courtesy of C. Mae [Kress] Ploetner.)

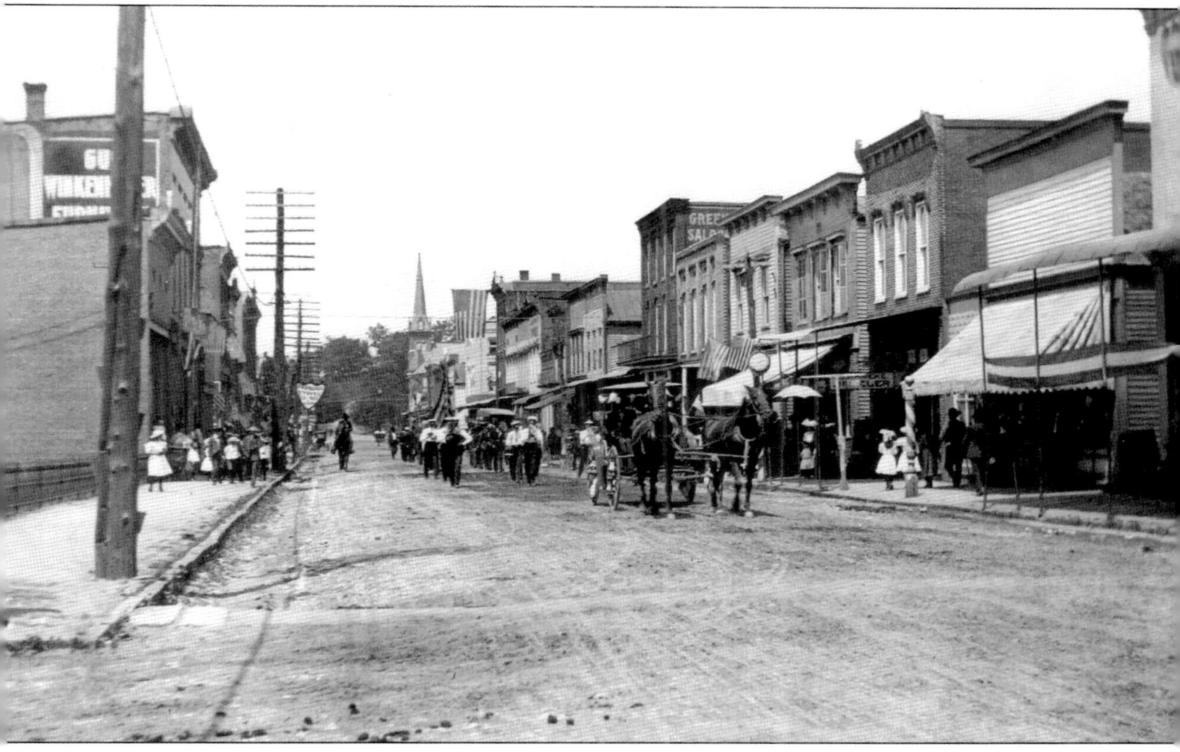

FOURTH STREET LOOKING WEST, HUNTINGBURG, 1911. The city's historic Fourth Street has been meticulously maintained and preserved, conveying the feeling of the turn of the 20th century when many of the stores first opened. Many of the storefronts shown are still standing. Note the steeple of the Salem Church rising in the distance. (Photograph courtesy of the Huntingburg Public Library.)

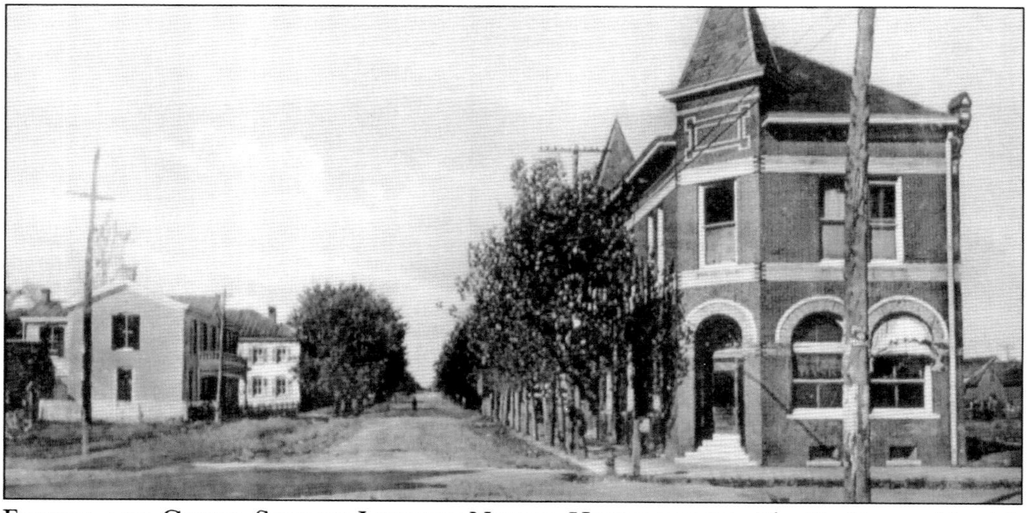

Fourth and Geiger Streets Looking North, Huntingburg. The St. George Hotel is on the left, and the imposing Huntingburg Bank building is on the right. (Photograph courtesy of the Museum of Huntingburg.)

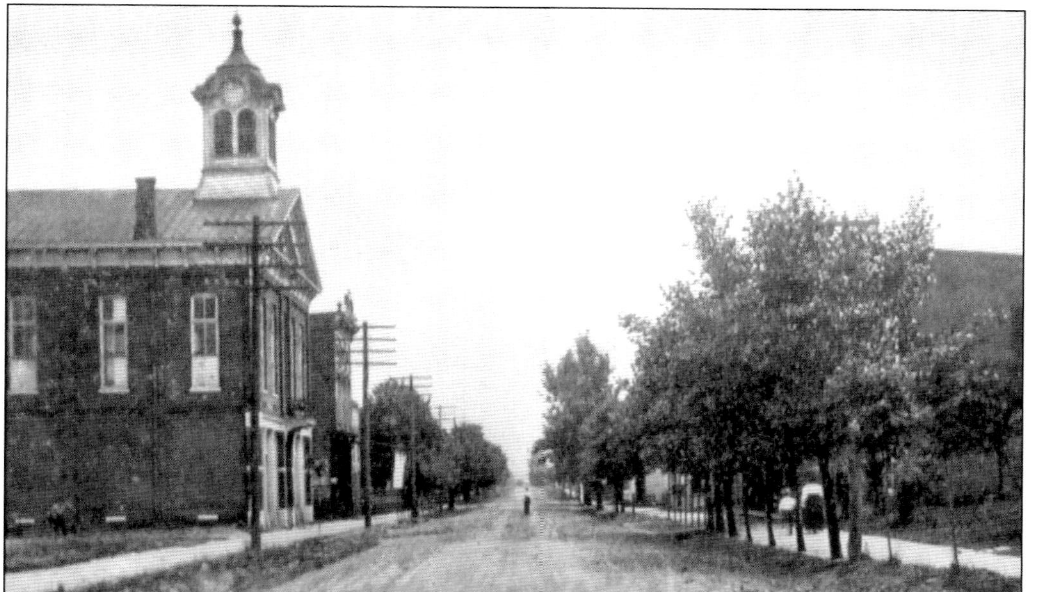

Fourth and Geiger Streets Looking South, Huntingburg. The old town hall stands on the left. (Photograph courtesy of the Museum of Huntingburg.)

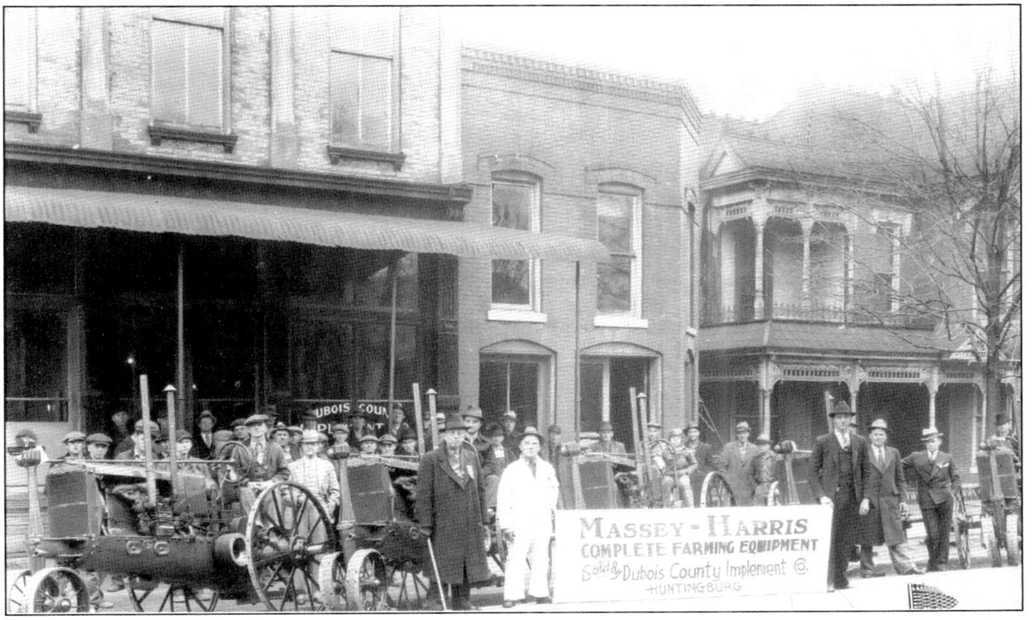

GERHARD HACKMAN SR. Hackman, a salesman, is seated on the tractor. These buildings stood on Geiger Street, south of the old town hall. The Dufendach Residence, on the right, is still standing. (Photograph courtesy of Gerhard Jr. and Shirley Hackman and the Museum of Huntingburg.)

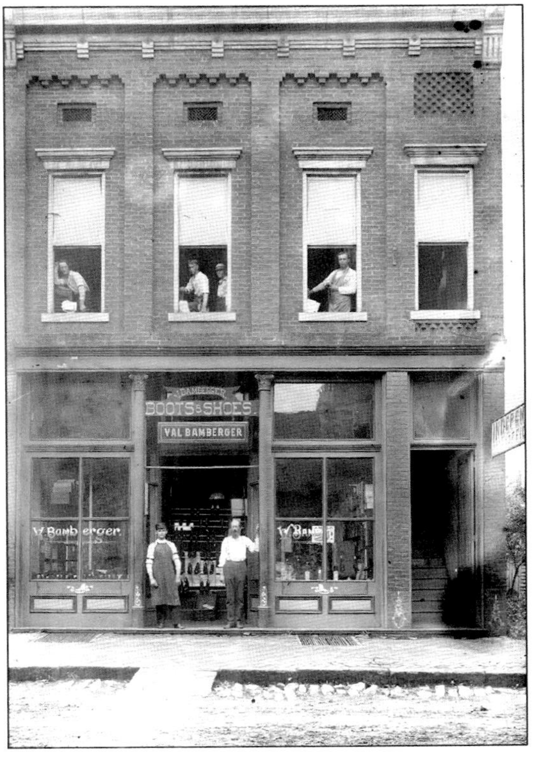

BAMBERGER BUILDING, HUNTINGBURG. Standing in front of the shop are Valentine and his son Leo, one of five children born to Valentine and his wife, Wilhelmina Hildebrand. According to the *History of Pike and Dubois Counties, Indiana* (Chicago: Goodspeed Bros. & Co., Publishers, 1885), Valentine, a manufacturer and dealer in boots and shoes, was born in Dubois County on January 22, 1850. He was the son of Peter and Catherine (Frick) Bamberger, natives of Germany. Peter Bamberger came to the United States about 1850 and located on a farm in Dubois County, where he lived until 1881, when he retired from business. Located upstairs was the Independent. From left to right are Dave, Al, Charlie, and Ed Dufendach. (Photograph courtesy of the Huntingburg Public Library.)

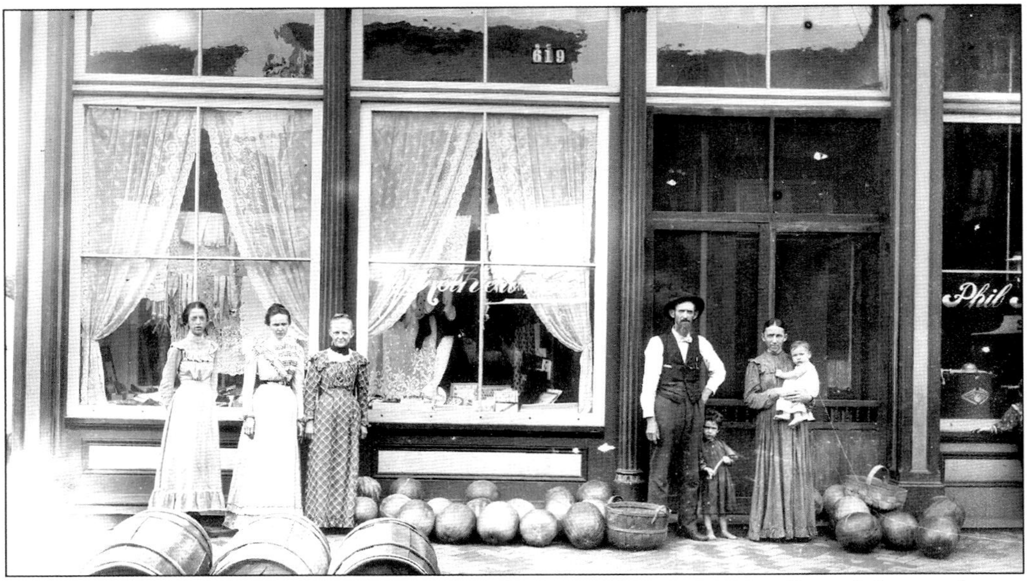

JOHN ROTHERT GENERAL STORE, FOURTH STREET, HUNTINGBURG. From left to right are Florence and Carrie Rothert, Nora Poetker Katterhenry, and Mr. and Mrs. John Rothert and their two young children. (Photograph courtesy of the Huntingburg Public Library.)

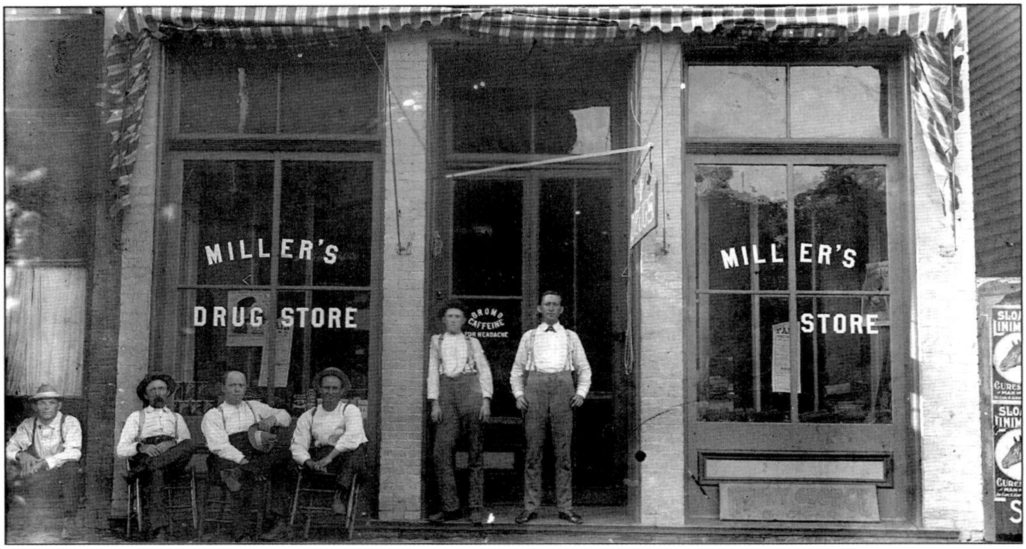

HARRY MILLER'S DRUG STORE, 319 FOURTH STREET, HUNTINGBURG. According to the Huntingburg Chamber of Commerce, after the "devastating fire of 1889, prominent Huntingburg businessmen F. H. Poetker and J. B. Miller decided to erect a 'fine' building to encourage revitalization." In the 1920s, it became Lukemeyer's Grocery Store, and an advertisement from 1928 stated that the store sold "staple and fancy groceries." Lukemeyer was also the mayor of the city during Prohibition. According to the Chamber, "Mayor Lukemeyer would confiscate illegal alcoholic beverages and store them in the rear of the grocery store. It was noted that sometimes customers would leave Lukemeyer's through the back door." A. H. (Harry) Miller Jr. is shown standing on the right, while Dr. Kilian, a dentist, is seated third from left, and Al Beeler is seated nearest the door. (Photograph courtesy of the Huntingburg Public Library.)

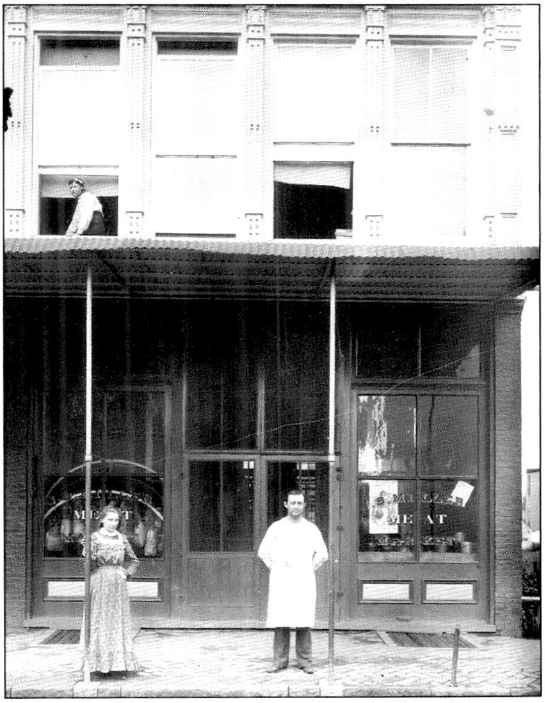

MILLER MEAT STORE, HUNTINGBURG. Standing in front of the Miller Meat Store are Ella Miller, daughter of John "Butch" Miller, and Louis Wellman, a meat cutter. The store was built shortly after a fire decimated parts of Huntingburg in 1889. (Photograph courtesy of the Huntingburg Public Library.)

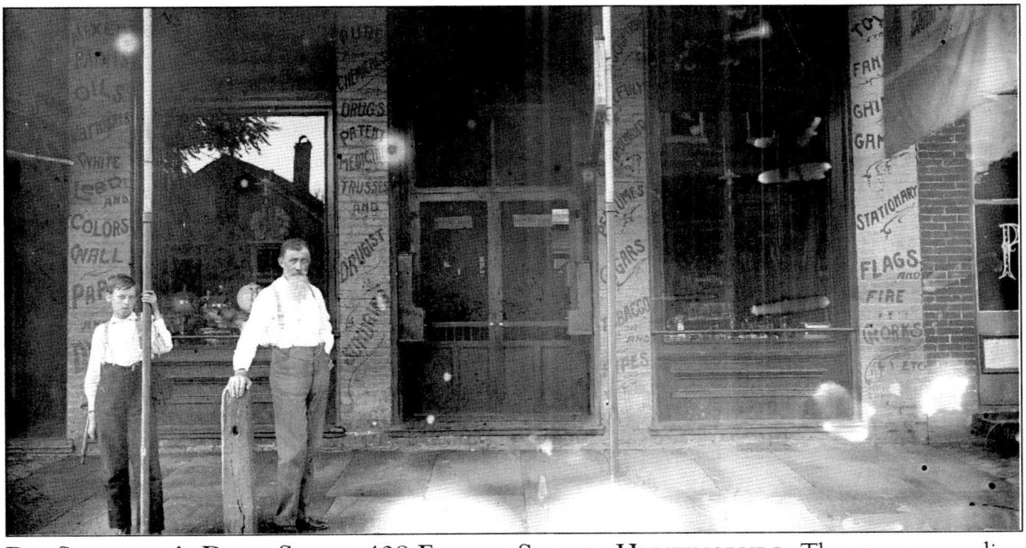

DR. SCHWARTZ'S DRUG STORE, 408 FOURTH STREET, HUNTINGBURG. The store, according to information provided by the Huntingburg Chamber of Commerce, was built around 1885 and is representative of the Italianate architectural style. In 1900, Dr. C. W. Schwartz bought the building from Fred Katterhenry in order to open his drug store. Around 1940, he sold it to Mr. Willard Utt who changed the name to Utt's Drug Store. In 1953, Utt sold the store to John Kesling, who renamed it the Kesling Rexall Drug Store. The photograph shows Dr. Schwartz standing in front of the store next to an unidentified boy. The doctor also served two terms as mayor of Huntingburg. He and his wife had five children. (Photograph courtesy of the Huntingburg Public Library.)

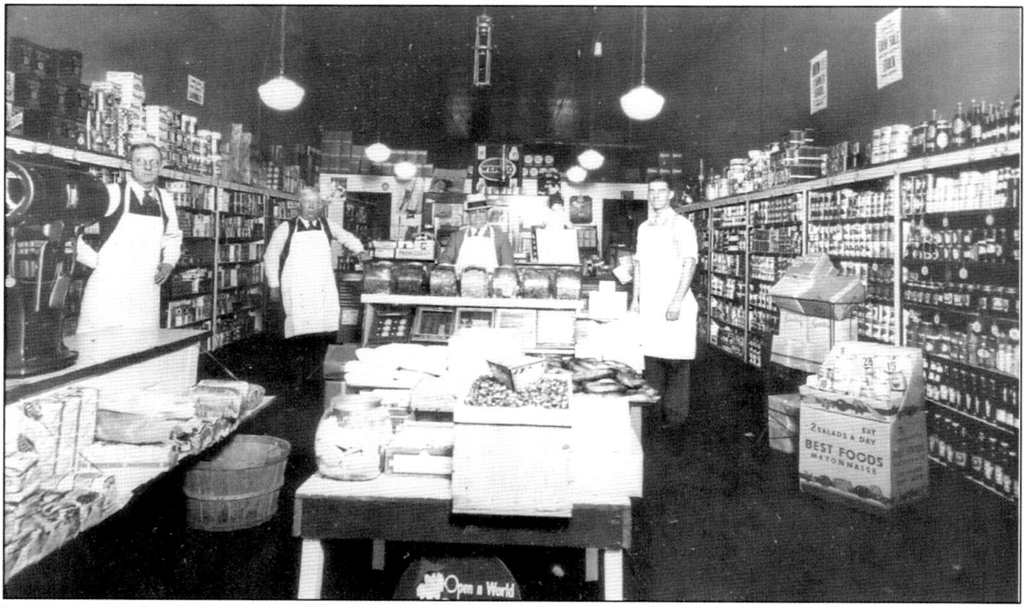

LUKEMEYER STORE INTERIOR, 319 FOURTH STREET, HUNTINGBURG. The Lukemeyer Grocery Store was located in the Poetker-Miller Building during the 1920s. From left to right are Edwin Lukemeyer, John Geiss, Eldo Wood, and Kenny Crider. (Photograph courtesy of the Huntingburg Public Library.)

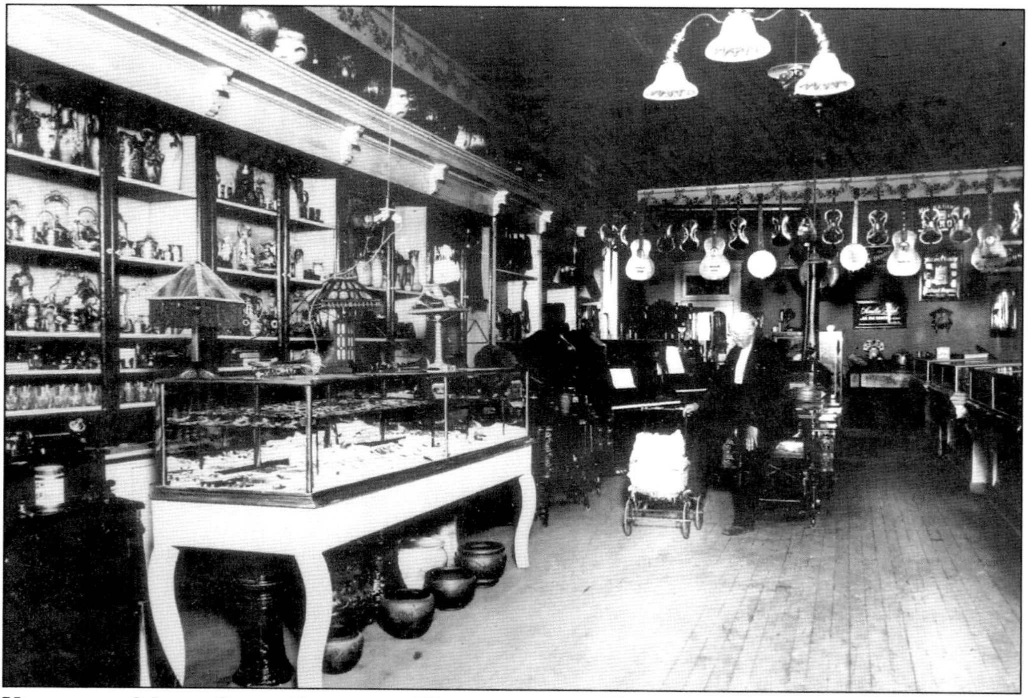

KONRUMPF MUSIC STORE INTERIOR, HUNTINGBURG. The music store was located on Geiger Street north of the Huntingburg Bank. Christian Konrumpf was organist and choir director at the Salem Church for 53 years. (Photograph courtesy of the Huntingburg Public Library.)

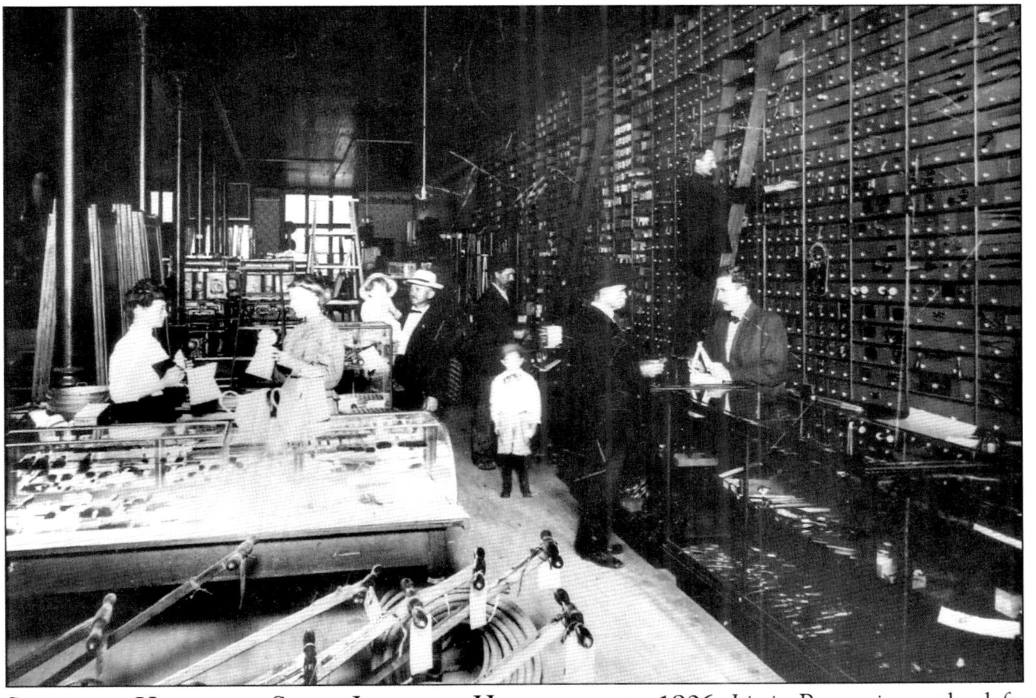

STRATMAN HARDWARE STORE INTERIOR, HUNTINGBURG, 1906. Lizzie Berger is on the left, Bill Mundy on the ladder, and Adam Kordes on the right. The store was located on Fifth Street between Van Buren and Washington. (Photograph courtesy of the Huntingburg Public Library.)

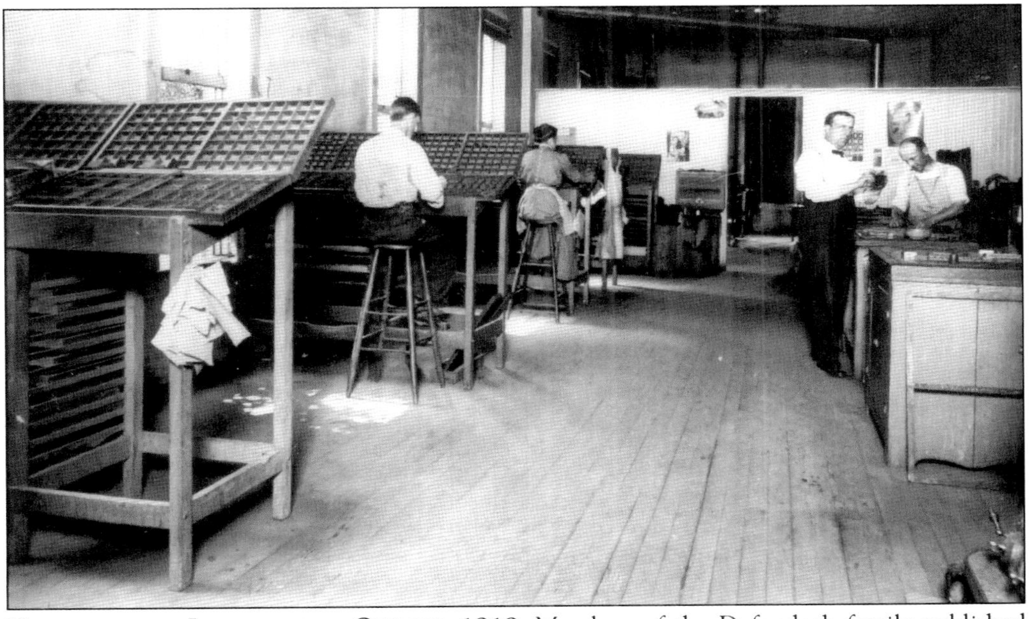

HUNTINGBURG *INDEPENDENT* OFFICES, 1919. Members of the Dufendach family published the *Independent*, a Huntingburg newspaper which began in 1886. Shown in the photograph, from left to right, are Charles, Sadie, Ed, and Dave Dufendach. (Photograph courtesy of the Huntingburg Public Library.)

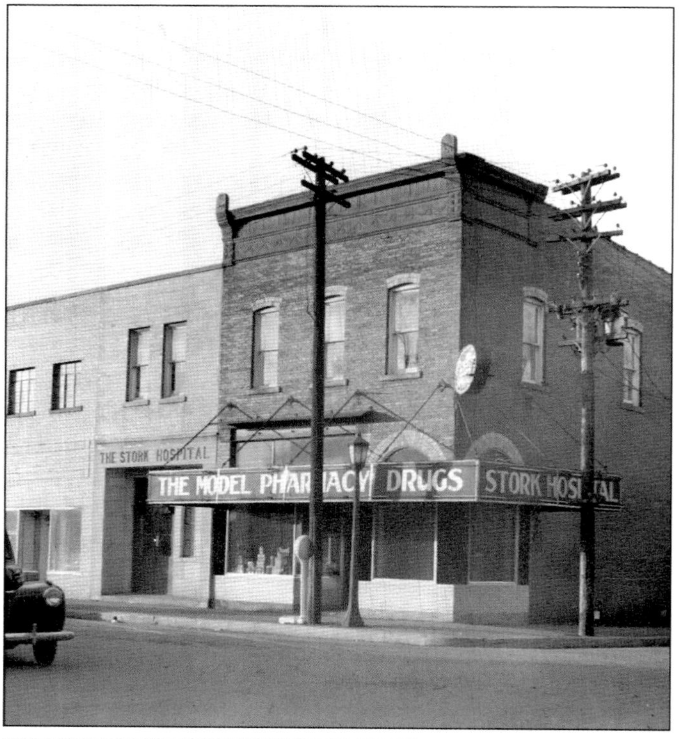

MODEL PHARMACY AND STORK HOSPITAL, HUNTINGBURG. Notice the Romanesque-style side-by-side doors. Huntingburg is famous for its wonderfully preserved downtown, which is on the National Historic Register. This building is located at Fourth and Van Buren Streets. (Photograph courtesy of the Huntingburg Public Library.)

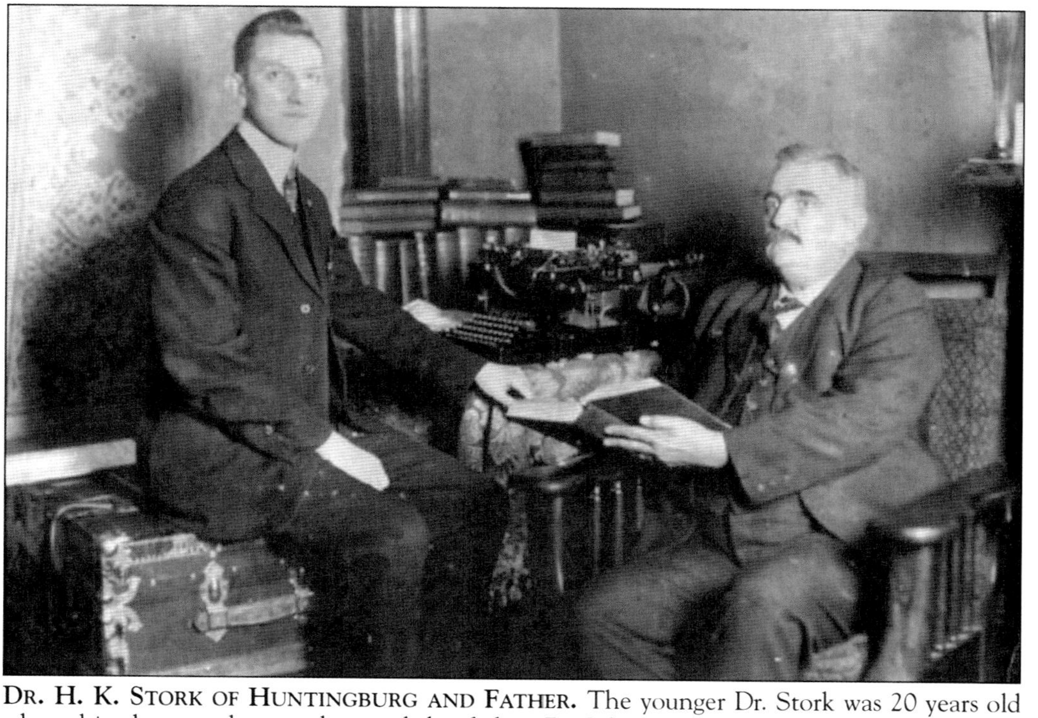

DR. H. K. STORK OF HUNTINGBURG AND FATHER. The younger Dr. Stork was 20 years old when this photograph was taken with his father, Dr. John H. Stork. (Photograph courtesy of the Museum of Huntingburg.)

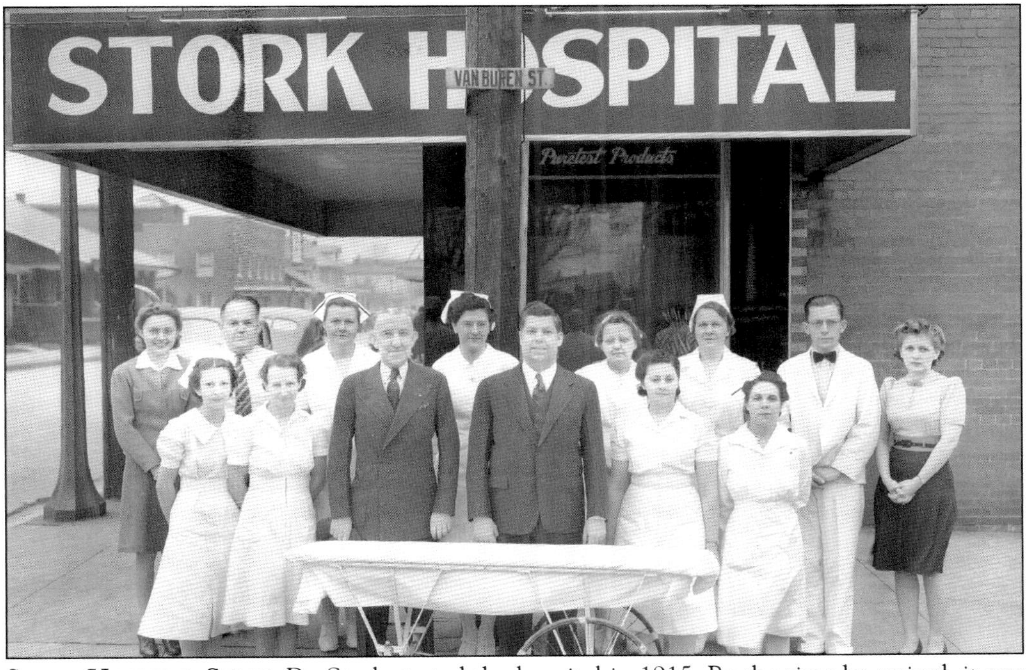

STORK HOSPITAL STAFF. Dr. Stork started the hospital in 1915. By the time he retired, it was reported by the *Evansville Press*, in an article written on May 31, 1951, the hospital had 27 beds, 9 bassinettes, 12 registered nurses, and 3 doctors on staff. The 8,200 square-foot hospital also housed a pharmacy. (Photograph and information courtesy of the Museum of Huntingburg.)

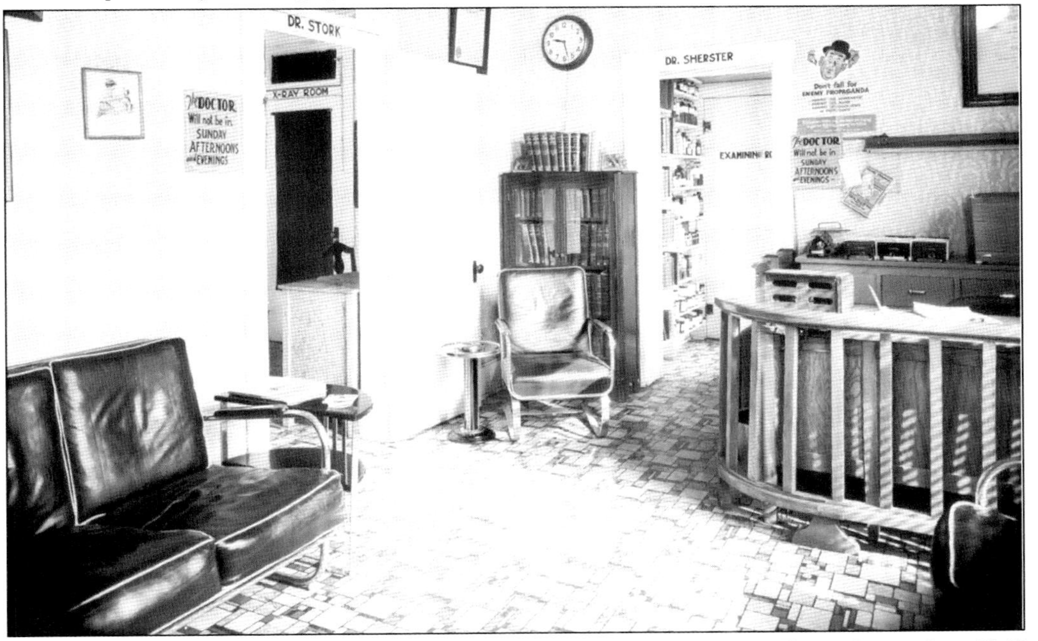

STORK HOSPITAL WAITING ROOM, HUNTINGBURG, MARCH 1935. From September 1940 to April 1951, the hospital admitted 9,995 patients—doctors performed 5,752 operations and delivered 4,614 babies. (Photograph and information courtesy of the Museum of Huntingburg.)

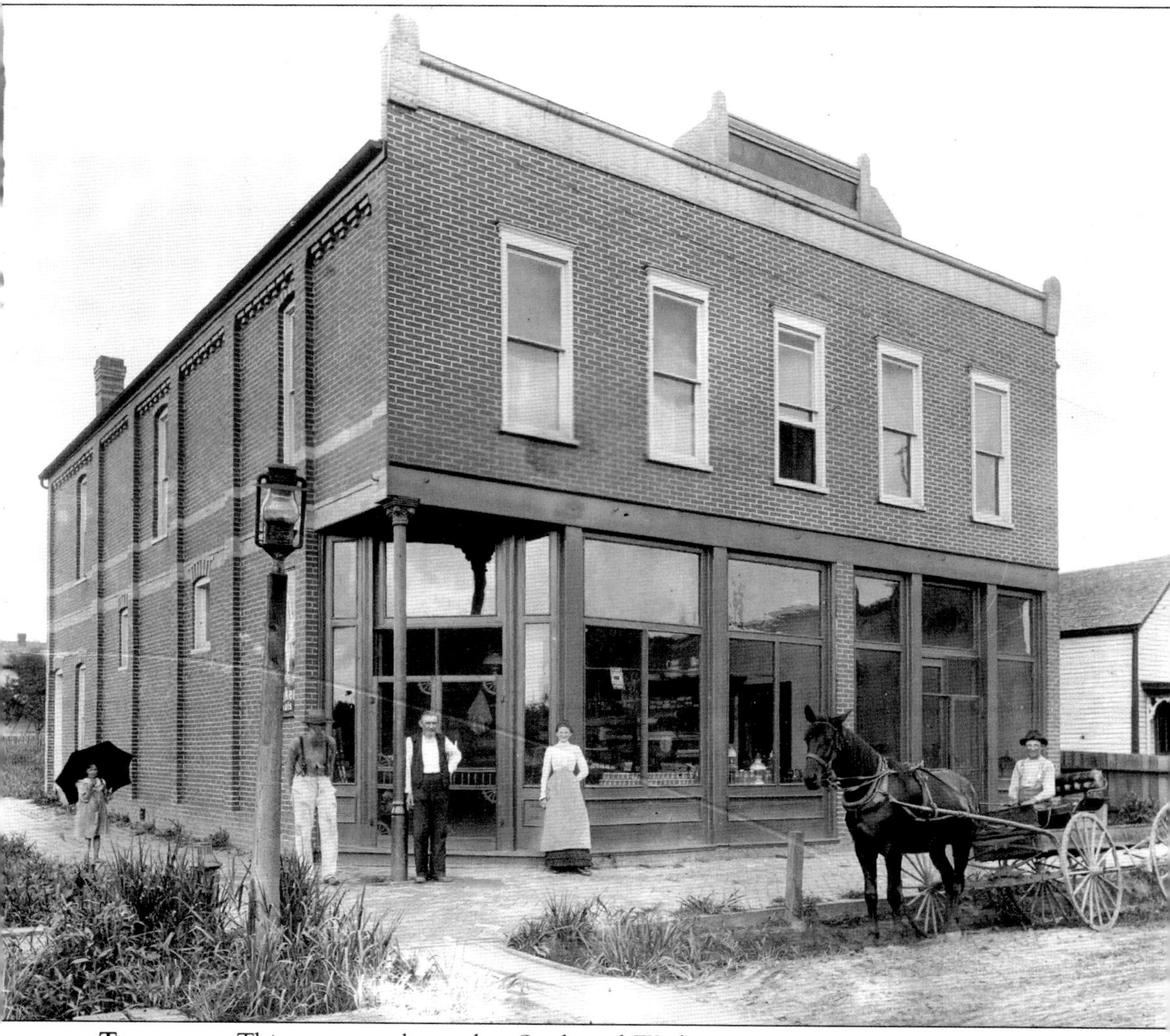

TODRANKS. This store was located at Sixth and Washington Streets and was later called the Hillemeyer Store. (Photograph courtesy of the Huntingburg Public Library.)

Four

BUSINESS AND INDUSTRY

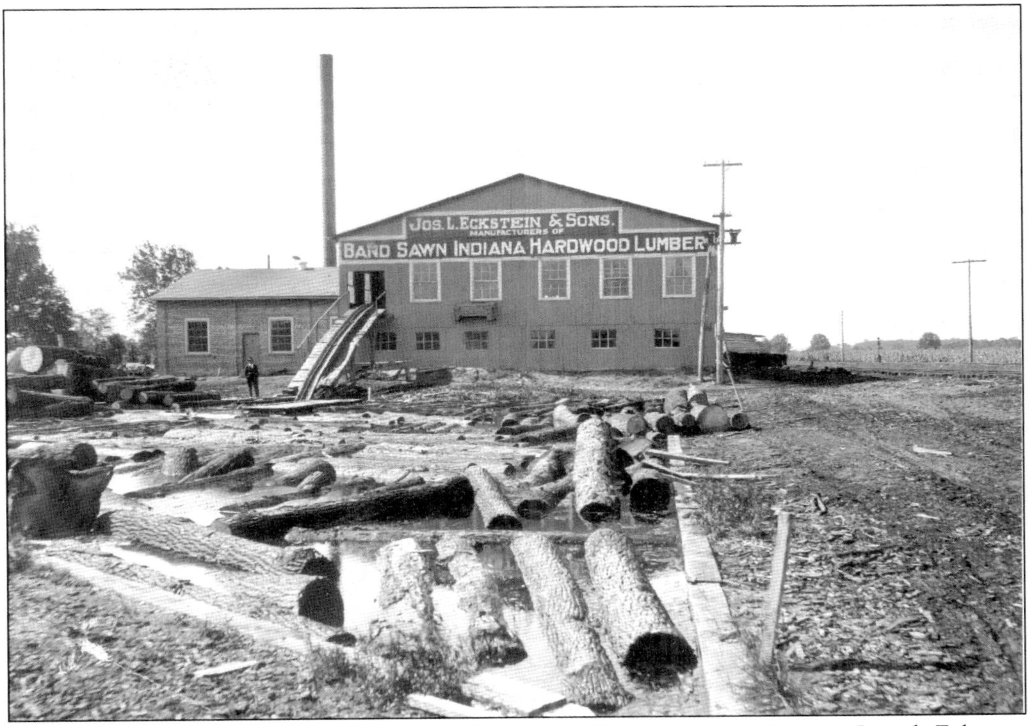

JOSEPH L. ECKSTEIN LUMBER COMPANY, FIRST AND CLAY STREETS, JASPER. Joseph Eckstein was born in Ripley County, Indiana, and came to Dubois County as a youngster. In 1889, in partnership with Ben Dupps and William Schuler, he purchased a steam thresher and sawmill, threshing farmers' wheat during growing season and sawing lumber throughout the year. The partnership dissolved in 1889, with Eckstein taking over the sawmill portion of the business and moving it to the northeast side of Jasper. As the business grew and the years passed, Joseph's sons, Clem and Louis, joined the company. Eventually, it became necessary to expand the facilities. In 1919, the Ecksteins decided to relocate the mill to property adjacent to the railroad track, west of Clay Street, near the river. The Eckstein Lumber Company remained in operation at this location for many decades. (Photograph courtesy of John Fierst.)

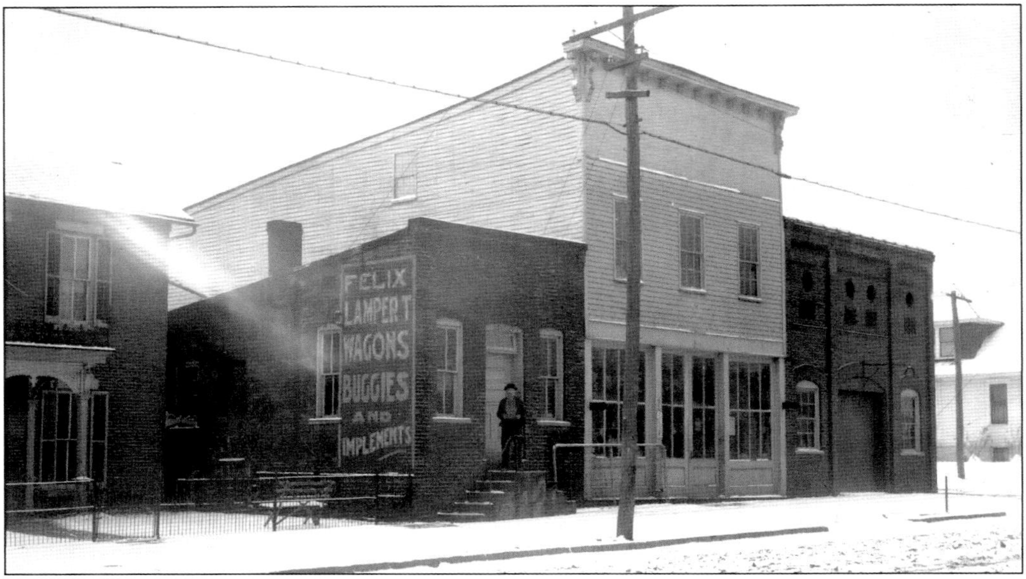

FELIX LAMPERT IMPLEMENT STORE, JASPER, JANUARY 1907. The Felix Lampert Implement Store was located on the south side of the 200 block of West Sixth Street. Felix Lampert stands in front of his shop. Born in Wagshurst, Baden, he learned the blacksmith trade at the age of 19 from Sebastian Kuebler, who also owned a blacksmith business in Jasper. In 1861, Lampert opened his own blacksmith shop on the lot in the photograph. The small brick building on the left of the three buildings was later used as a taxi stand. After that, all of the buildings were used as a farm implement store. In 1944, the buildings were sold to Joseph Gutzweiler, and the brick building on the right became a meat-packing locker, while the middle frame building was torn down. The house at the far left was the Lampert home, razed in 1964. (Photograph courtesy of John Fierst.)

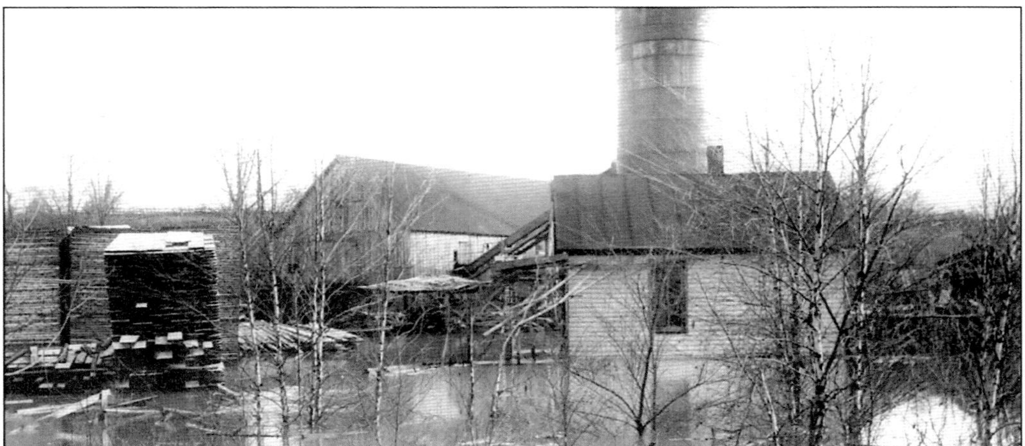

MOSSMAN-BAYLESS LUMBER COMPANY, JASPER, JANUARY 1907. This photograph was taken by local photographer Will Sprauer on January 6, 1907, and was featured in the *Jasper Herald* five days later. It was one of six photographs that were published to show the effects of a winter flood that had struck the area. The photograph's caption read, "The Mossman band mill, above the raised road leading to the Patoka bridge at Eckert's mill." The mill had been constructed in 1900. Years later, the buildings were destroyed by fire, after which the operations were moved to Tennessee. (Photograph courtesy of Lena Sprauer.)

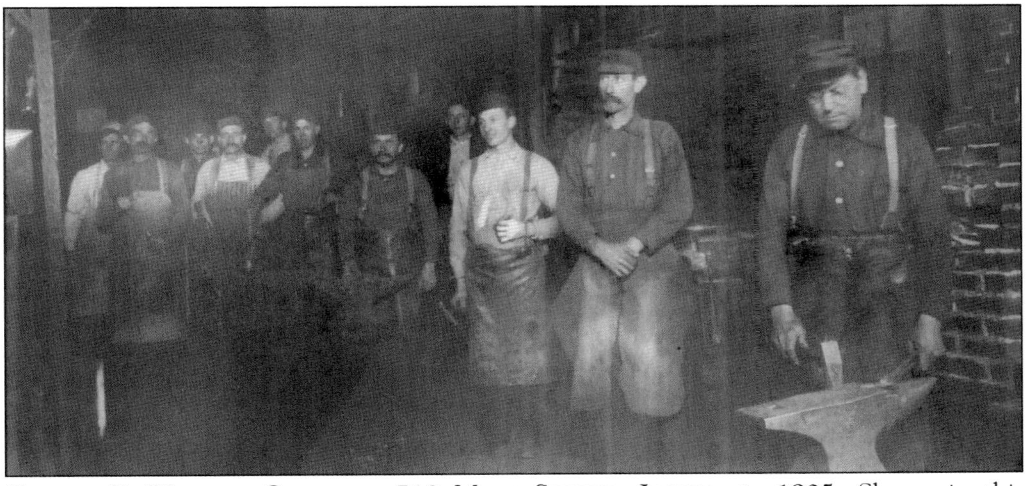

GEORGE P. WAGNER COMPANY, 710 MAIN STREET, JASPER, C. 1905. Shown in this photograph are the employees of the George P. Wagner Company, including master blacksmith William Flick, at the anvil. The company had its beginnings in 1886, when Wagner purchased the blacksmith shop of his employer, William Gasser. After a devastating fire destroyed his shop in 1888, Wagner built a two-story brick building with blacksmith shop in its place. In 1893, Wagner had a second building constructed to the south. By this time, the Wagner Company had become one of the leading manufacturers of wagons and carriages in the area. In addition to his successful business enterprises, George Wagner was a prominent community leader. When Jasper became an incorporated city in 1915, the community elected Wagner as its first mayor. (Photograph courtesy of Ron Flick.)

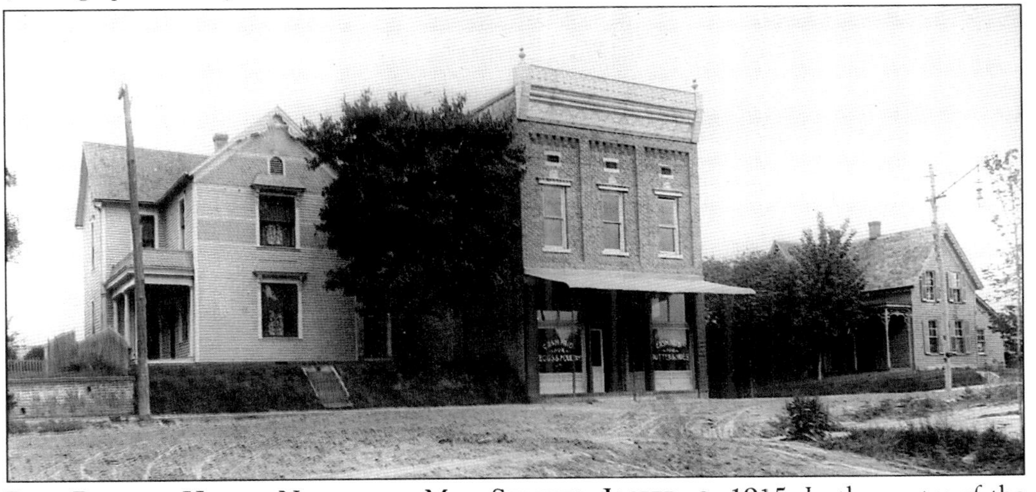

PFAU POULTRY HOUSE, NINTH AND MILL STREETS, JASPER, C. 1915. In the center of the photograph is the Pfau Poultry House, a business founded by Henry Pfau in 1891. The two-story, brick building was erected in 1900 and replaced an earlier frame structure. The firm purchased poultry and egg products from local farmers and sold them to local townsfolk. The one-and-a-half-story home on the right, built in 1885, was the residence of Henry and his wife, Mary (Biggeleben) and their eight children. The two-story house on the left, constructed in 1895, served originally as the home of Henry's widowed mother-in-law, and later was the first home for Henry's daughter Helen, her husband, August Flick, and their children. (Photograph courtesy of Ron Flick.)

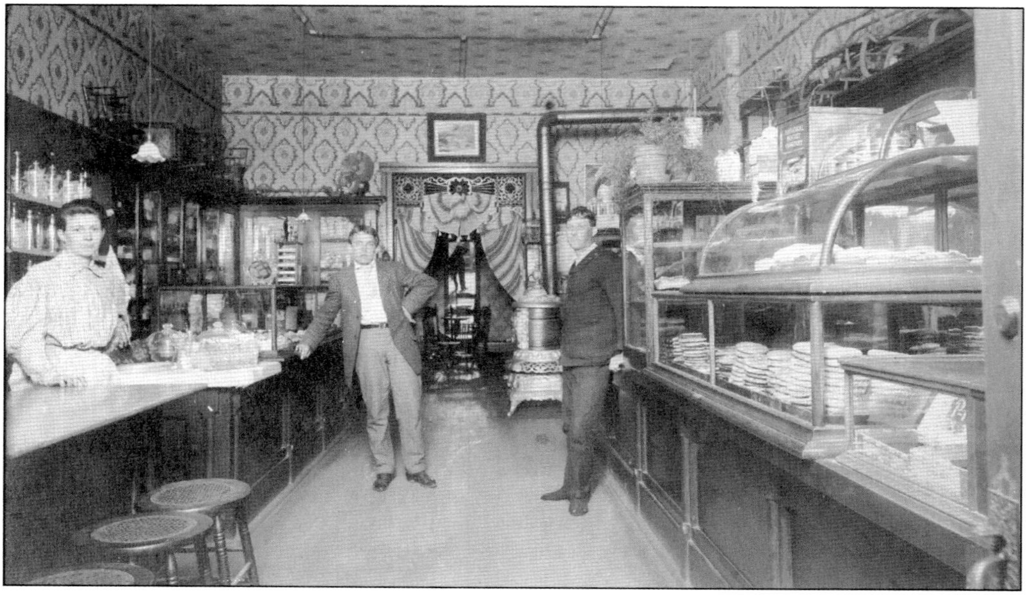

JASPER CITY BAKER INTERIOR, C. 1905. In 1894, prominent Jasper businessman, John Gramelspracher, contracted with local brick mason, Anthony Hochgesang, to construct a two-story brick bakery building on Jackson Street for his daughter and son-in-law, Anna and Henry Moutoux. During its earliest years, the bakery was the first business in Jasper to install a telephone and the first to sell Coca Cola. Moutoux's baker, Henry Mertens, purchased the business in 1897, sold it back to Moutoux in 1899, repurchased it in 1903, and sold it again in 1905, to Frank Seibert and his wife, who are shown in the above photograph with cousin Frank Basedow. (Photograph courtesy of the Jasper City Bakery.)

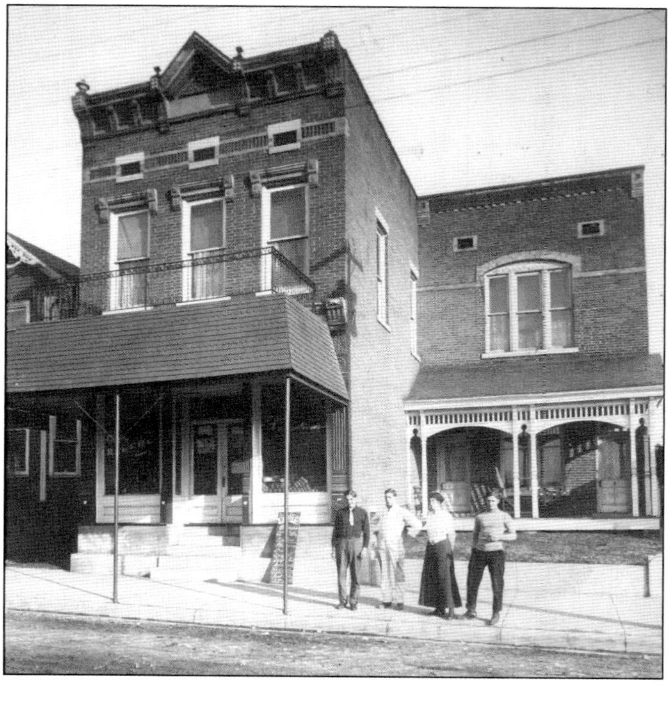

JASPER CITY BAKERY, JASPER, 1913. In 1908, Martin Gosman, who had previously operated a saloon on the square, purchased the bakery from Frank Seibert and his partners. Three years later, Gosman traded the business to the Joseph Haller family for the Indiana Hotel, which sat across the street. The Hallers, some of whom are pictured here, operated the bakery until 1984, when it was acquired by Gene and Marlene Hochgesang. The Hochgesangs owned the business until 2005, when it was sold to Keith Mandel and Alan Winkler.

OK GROCERY AND MEAT MARKET, JACKSON STREET, JASPER. The OK Grocery was a longtime Jasper tradition, occupying a small building on the east side of Jackson Street, two doors north of the Jasper City Bakery. The building, only 16 feet wide, was built in 1905 as the office of Dr. B. B. Brannock, whose home was next door to the south. (Photograph courtesy of John Fierst.)

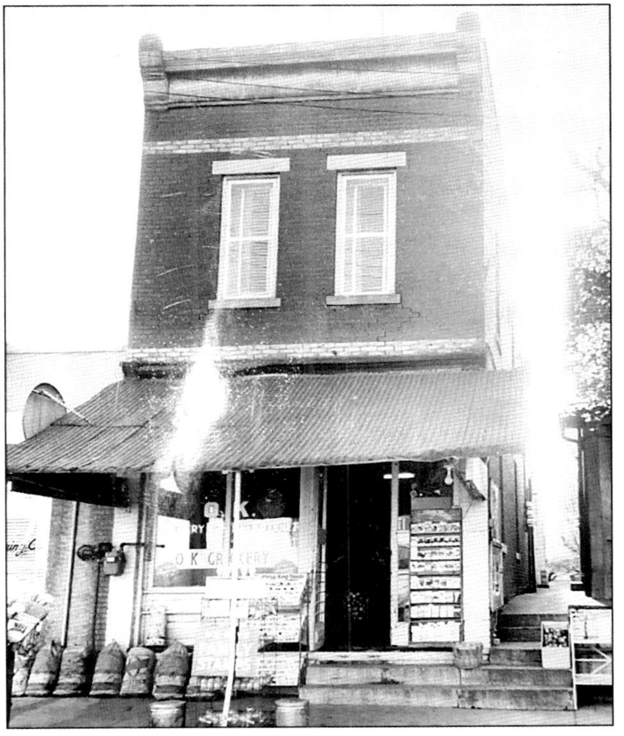

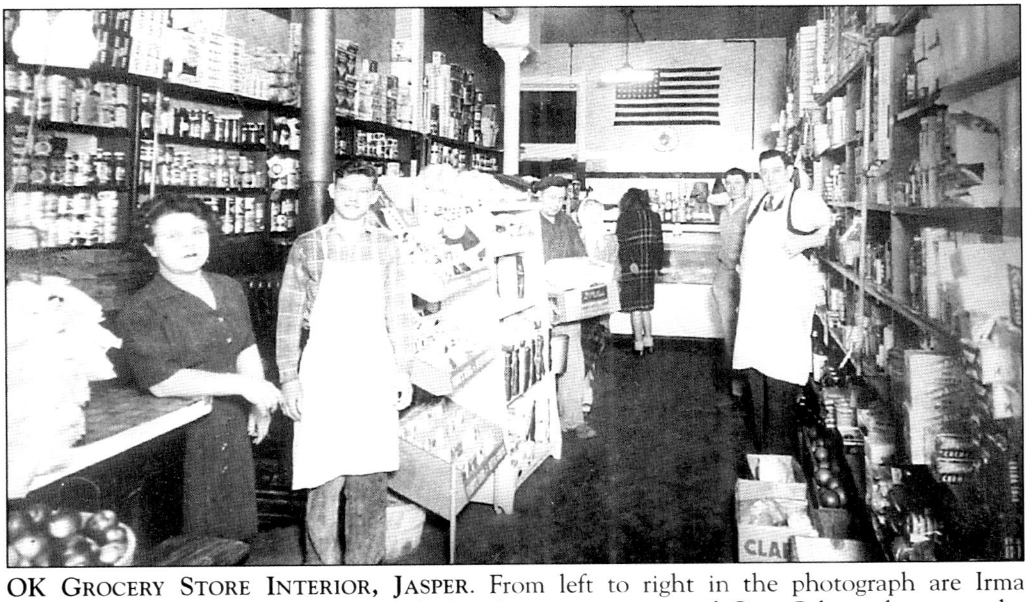

OK GROCERY STORE INTERIOR, JASPER. From left to right in the photograph are Irma Schwinghammer; Don Taber; Bill Schultz, the meat cutter; and Otto Schwinghammer, the proprietor. For many years, the store offered home delivery of groceries to their customers. The grocery store closed in the late 1980s. Later, Duvall's Fish Hut opened in the building and sold quite a few tasty fish sandwiches, especially during Lent, to the many Catholics in Jasper. The building was torn down in the mid 1990s, when the Fish Hut was moved to the square. (Photograph courtesy of John Fierst.)

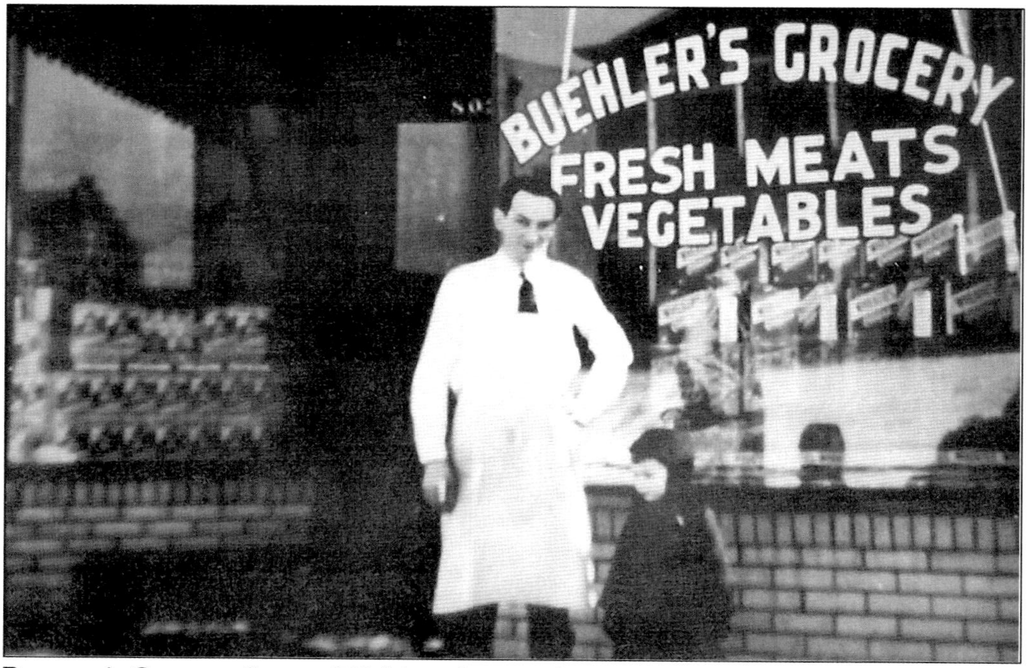

BUEHLER'S GROCERY STORE, 802 MAIN STREET, JASPER, C. 1943. Pictured is Gabe Buehler with his son, Dave, in front of the family grocery store. The store was founded in 1940 and was initially located in a tiny, wood-frame building on the west side of Main Street, between Seventh and Eighth Streets. The following year, the business moved across the street to the Krodel Building at the northeast corner of Eighth and Main. In 1957, the store was relocated to a spacious new building in the Northwood Park shopping area on the north side of Jasper. Today, Buehler Foods has more than 60 stores throughout southern Indiana, Illinois, Kentucky, North Carolina, and Virginia. (Photograph courtesy of Buehler Foods.)

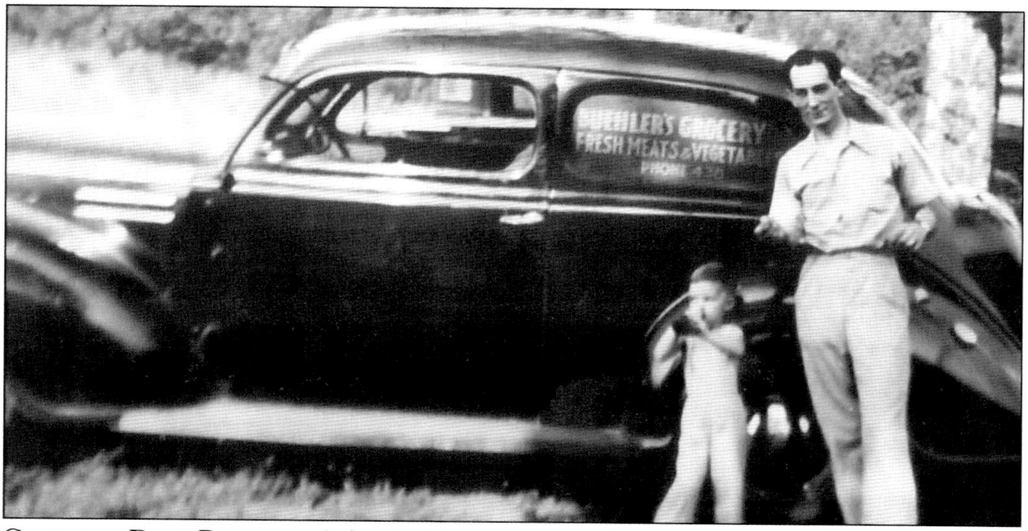

GABE AND DAVE BUEHLER. Gabe Buehler stands proudly in front of the family car, on which is advertised the family business, Buehler's Grocery. Meanwhile, his young son, Dave, enjoys some liquid refreshment. (Photograph courtesy of Buehler Foods.)

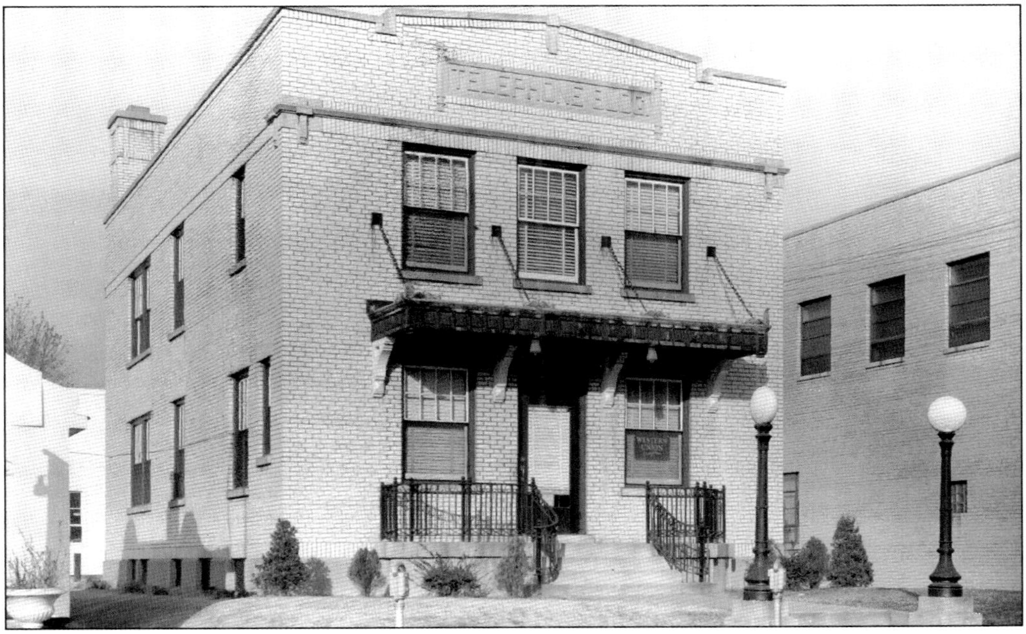

INDIANA TELEPHONE CORPORATION BUILDING, JASPER, C. 1950S. In the early 1900s, Jasper was served by two separate telephone companies, the Dubois County Telephone Company and the Cumberland Telephone Company, both of whom sought subscribers from families and businesses in town. In 1914, Cumberland sold its equipment and rights to its competitor. The Southern Indiana Telegraph and Telephone Company then purchased the Dubois County Telephone Company in 1926, and commenced to construct a new exchange and office building on the west side of Newton Street, between Fifth and Sixth Streets. Unfortunately, the telephone company could not escape the financial woes of the Great Depression. It went bankrupt and was reorganized in 1935 as the Indiana Telephone Corporation, with main offices in Seymour, Indiana. During the 1960s, a large, windowless addition was constructed beside the old building. (Photograph and information courtesy of Guido Seaton.)

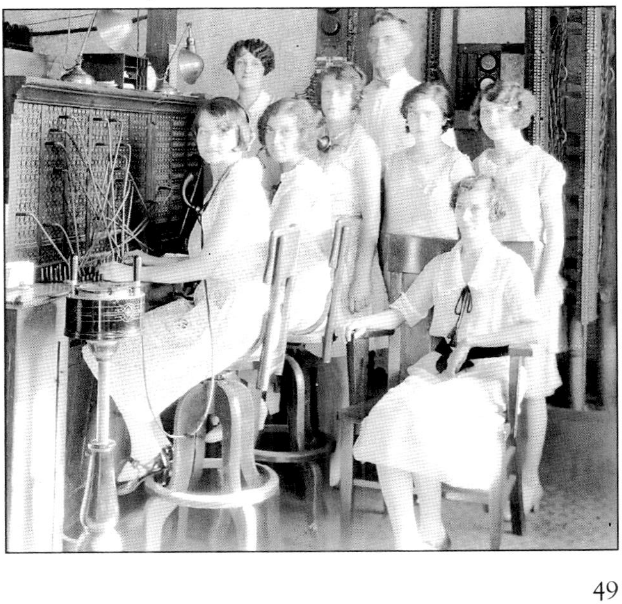

TELEPHONE OPERATORS, JASPER, SEPTEMBER 1928. Seven of the eight employees of the telephone company in Jasper are identified in this photograph taken in 1928. The two women at the switchboard are Louannah Bence, a day operator, and Josepha Marks, a night operator. The woman seated in the chair is Clara M. Buechlein, the chief operator and cashier. Three of the girls standing are Lorena Schuetter, Louisa Giesler, and Connie Melchior. The gentleman in the back is the office manager, John J. Himsel. (Photograph and information courtesy of Guido Seaton.)

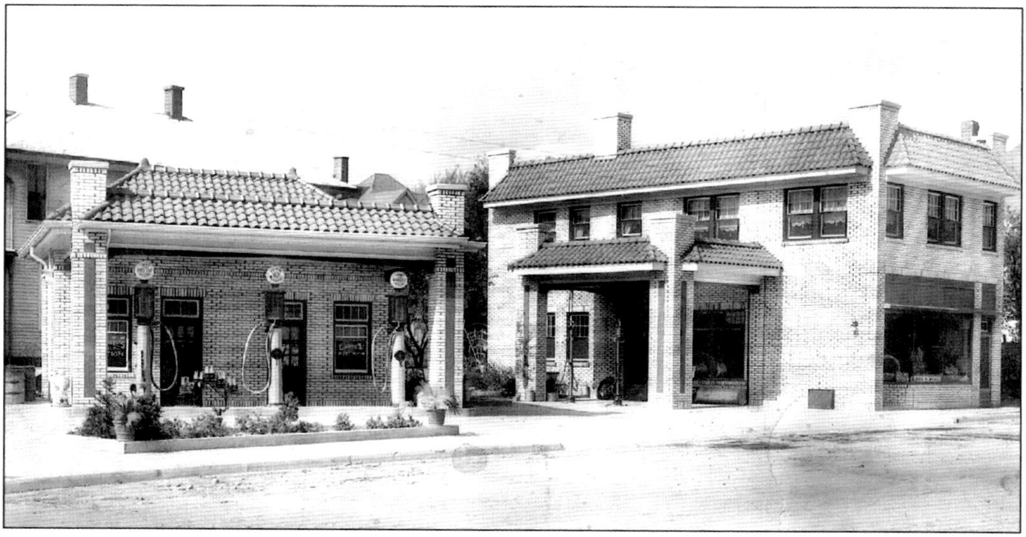

KARL WEIGEL SERVICE STATION, JASPER, 1926. In 1901, Karl Weigel purchased a former saloon building from Conrad Prechtel at the northwest corner of Sixth and Newton Streets and opened a harness shop. In 1926, Weigel removed the frame building and constructed a service station of buff-colored brick and green roof tile. A matching building to the north served as the new harness shop and as the family residence, which was located upstairs. The station eventually was acquired by the Brescher family. Later, the buildings were remodeled and converted to retail and office space. In the late 1990s, the Bronx Bagel, a trendy eatery, was opened in the building. (Photograph courtesy of the Bronx Bagel.)

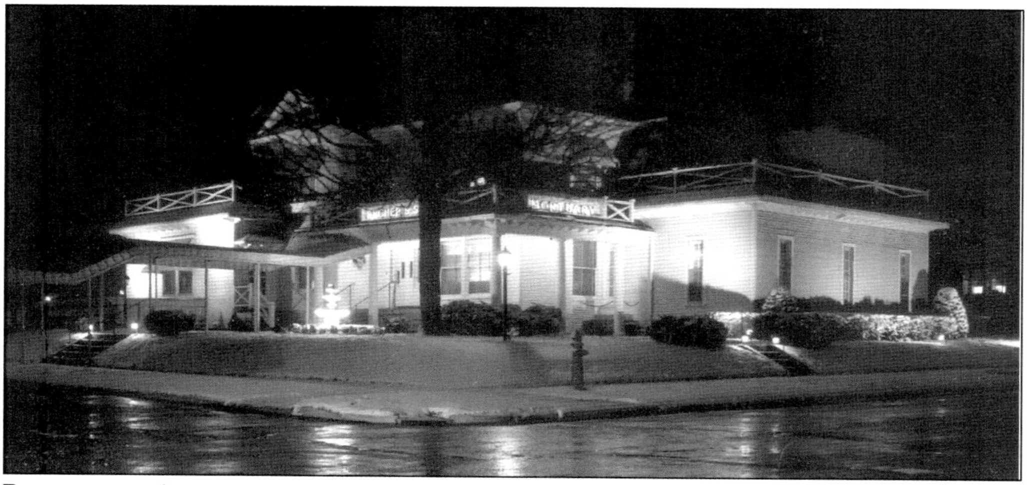

BECHER AND SON FUNERAL HOME, JASPER, C. 1960S. The Becher-Kluesner Funeral Home, formerly Becher and Son, had its beginnings in 1938, when St. Meinrad native Ralph "Tommy" Becher purchased the former Schwenk Funeral Home at 213 West Sixth Street. In 1945, he relocated the business to the Hennessy-Eckerle Funeral Home, the former William Traylor residence, on East Seventh Street at Mill Street. Joseph Hennessy, a Hammond native, had operated at the location since 1932. As the years passed, Tommy was assisted in the business by his father, Robert, and his brother, Gervase. In 1973, Arnold Kluesner, a Celestine native who had joined the business in 1967, became a partner. Today, Tommy's son John has assumed his father's position as partner in the business. (Photograph courtesy of Laurie Becher.)

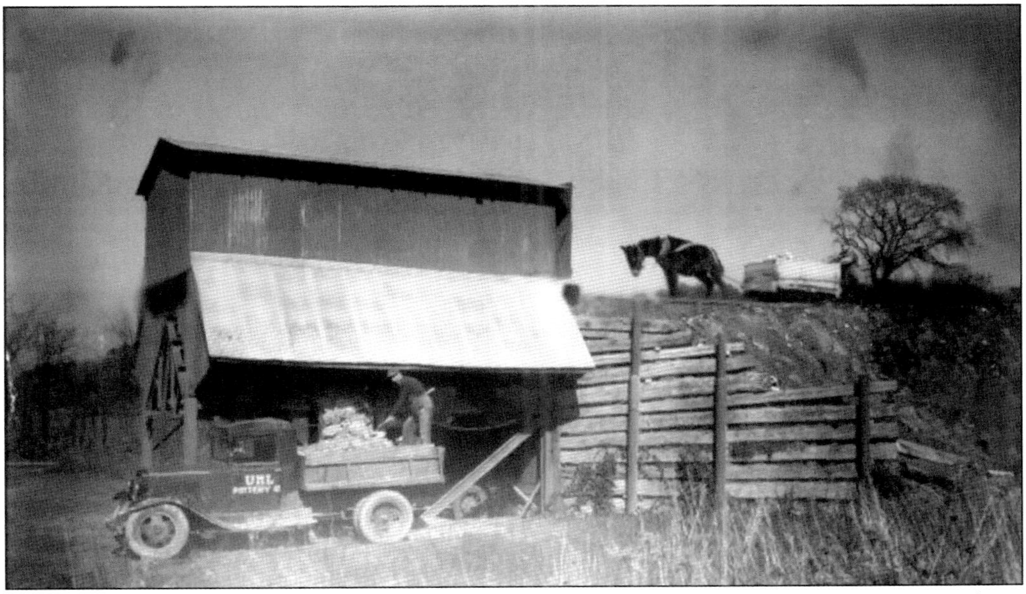

UHL POTTERY, HUNTINGBURG. In "The History of the Uhl Pottery," posted on the Huntingburg Library website, Mrs. Hannah Uhl Switzer writes: "In 1929, clay was the third most valuable mineral resource of Indiana. Only coal and ore exceeded it. In 1931, there were 101 plants in Indiana engaged in solely the manufacture of clay products." (Photograph courtesy of the Museum of Huntingburg.)

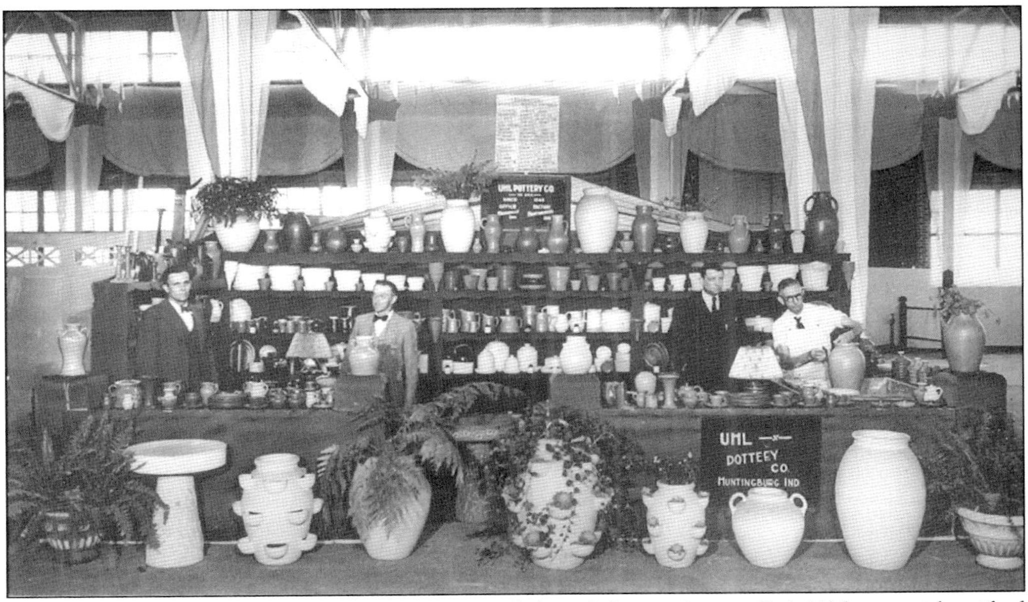

UHL POTTERY DISPLAY BOOTH, 1934. Pictured, from left to right, are Bob Uhl; an unidentified salesman; Louis Uhl; and Bernie Jeffries, who is turning the pottery wheel. (Photograph courtesy of the Museum of Huntingburg.)

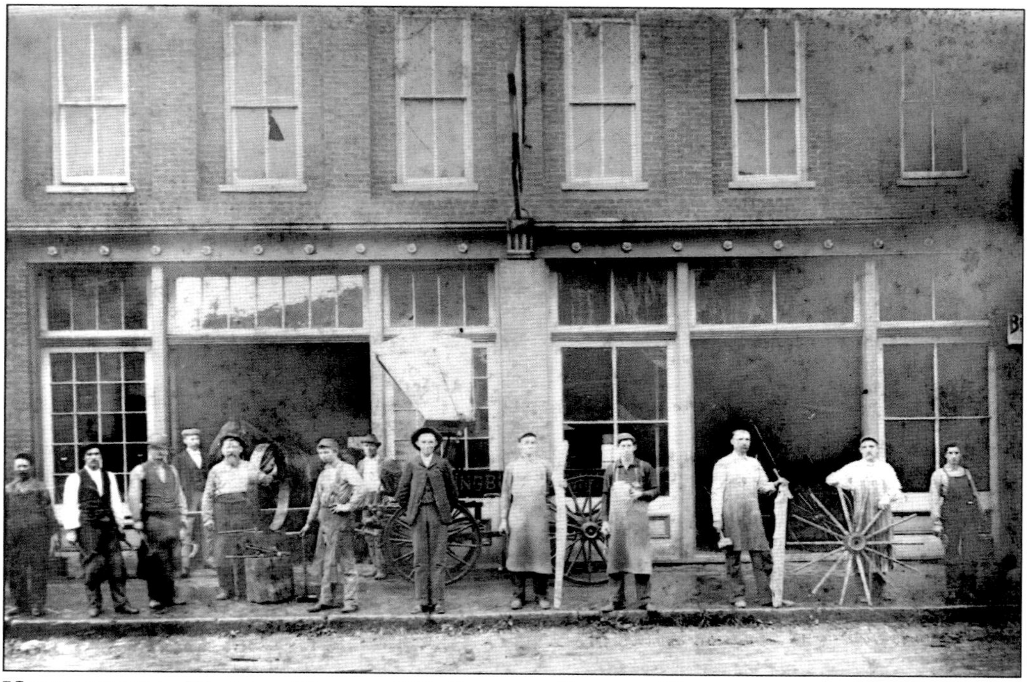

HUNTINGBURG WAGON WORKS, 321 FOURTH STREET, HUNTINGBURG. Also known as William Roettger's Wagon Shop, the building was sold in 1902 to Henry Dufendach, who opened a hardware store there. In the 1930s, Dufendach sold his hardware business to Reutepohler Hardware Company. Reutepohler enlarged the store and also sold furniture, rugs, and household supplies. In this photograph, William Roettger is dressed in a suit. (Information provided by the Huntingburg Chamber of Commerce. Photograph courtesy of the Huntingburg Public Library.)

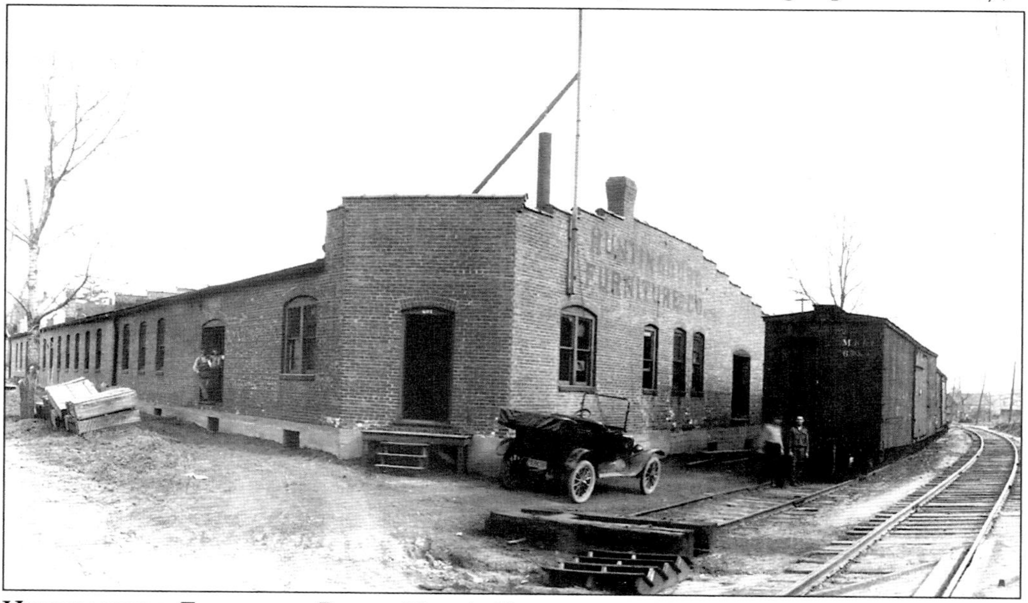

HUNTINGBURG FURNITURE PLANT NO. 1, EIGHTH AND VAN BUREN. Plant No. 1 of the Huntingburg Furniture Company was constructed in 1911. The building is now owned by DMI.

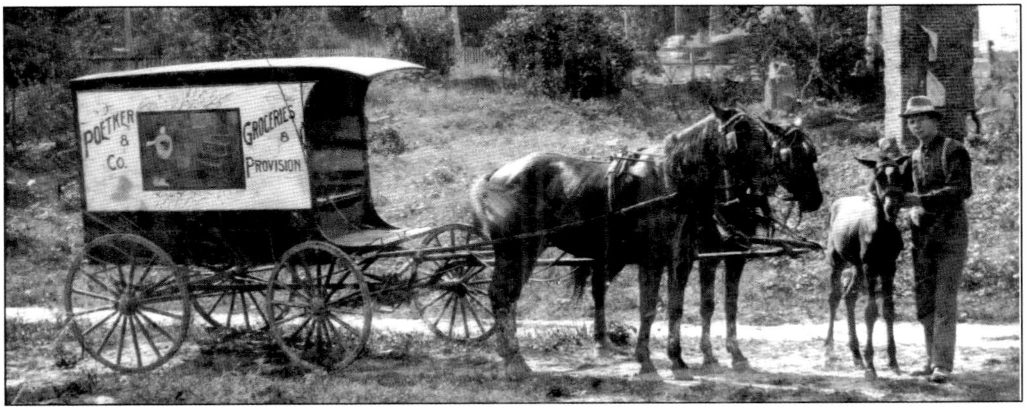

F. H. POETKER DELIVERY WAGON, 1910. F. H. Poetker was one of the leading businessmen in Huntingburg. The building he constructed is located at 319 East Fourth Street. According to Hugo C. Songer, the boy holding the colt is Poetker's son, Elmer. (Photograph courtesy of the Huntingburg Public Library.)

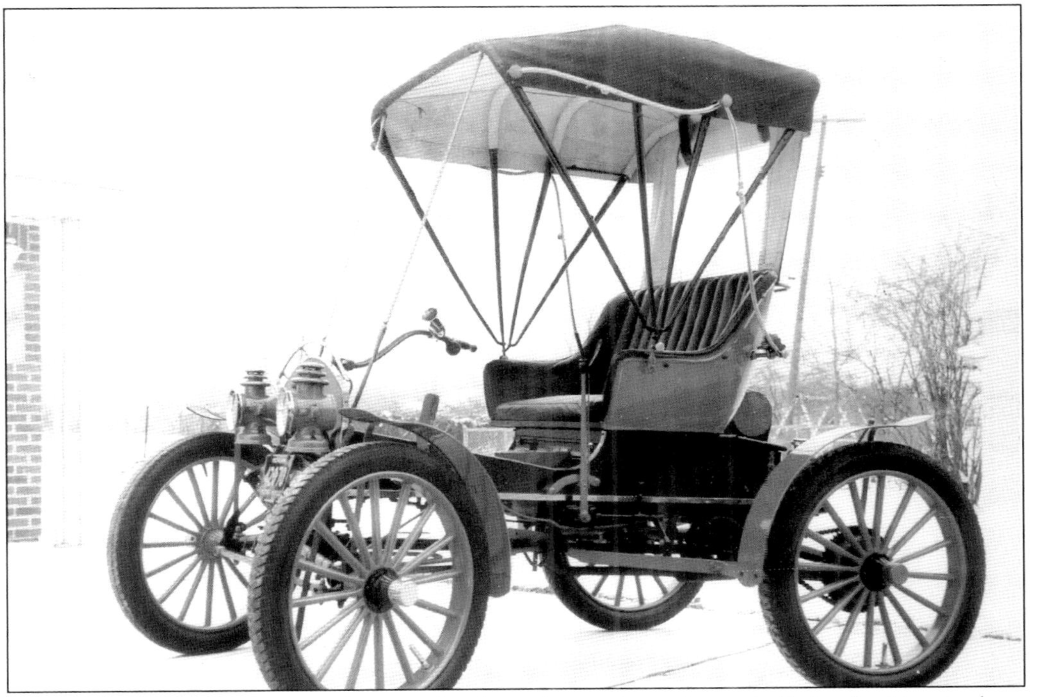

HUNTINGBURG BUGGY. Considered to be the only remaining buggy built by the Huntingburg Wagon Works, this buggy, constructed in 1901, is on display in the Huntingburg City Hall. According to Christine Prior, executive director of the Huntingburg Chamber of Commerce, Huntingburg Buggies were manufactured for just a few years before the manufacturer decided horses and carriages, not automobiles, were the wave of the future—a notion which ultimately proved wrong. Wallace Spencer Huffman, author of *Indiana-Built Automobiles*, writes that Indiana was one of the early leaders in automotive development. Indiana was regarded as the national leader in automobile production up until the 1930s, when Detroit became the technological and industrial giant. Over 88 cities and towns in Indiana either manufactured or assembled automobiles. (Photograph courtesy of the Huntingburg Public Library.)

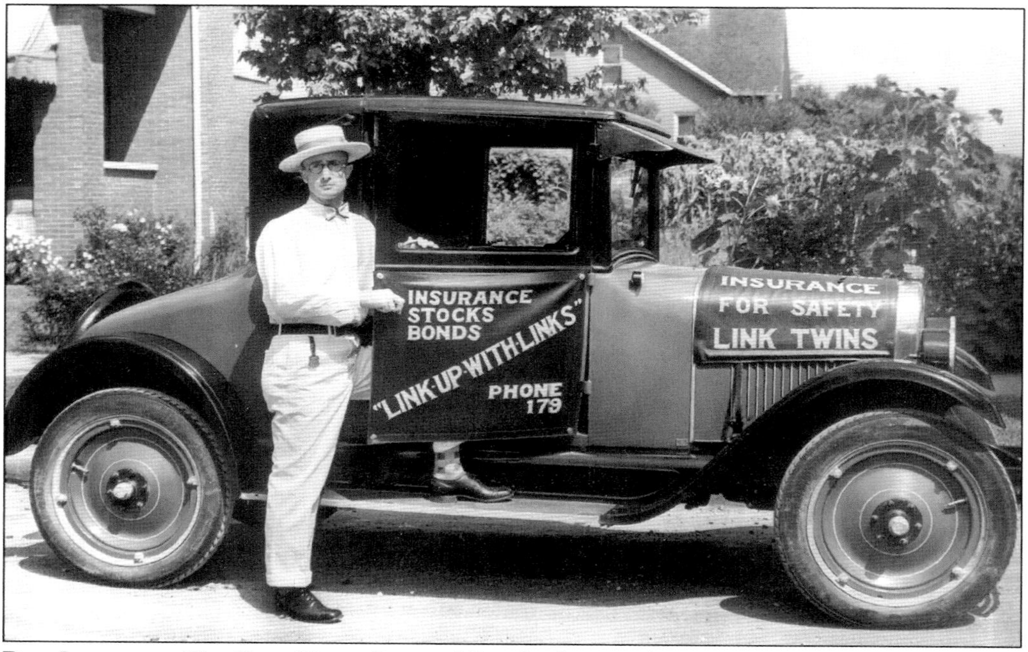

ROY LINK AND HIS CAR. Twins Roy and Ray Link owned an insurance company and were, judging by this and the accompanying photo, snappy dressers. (Photograph courtesy of the Huntingburg Public Library.)

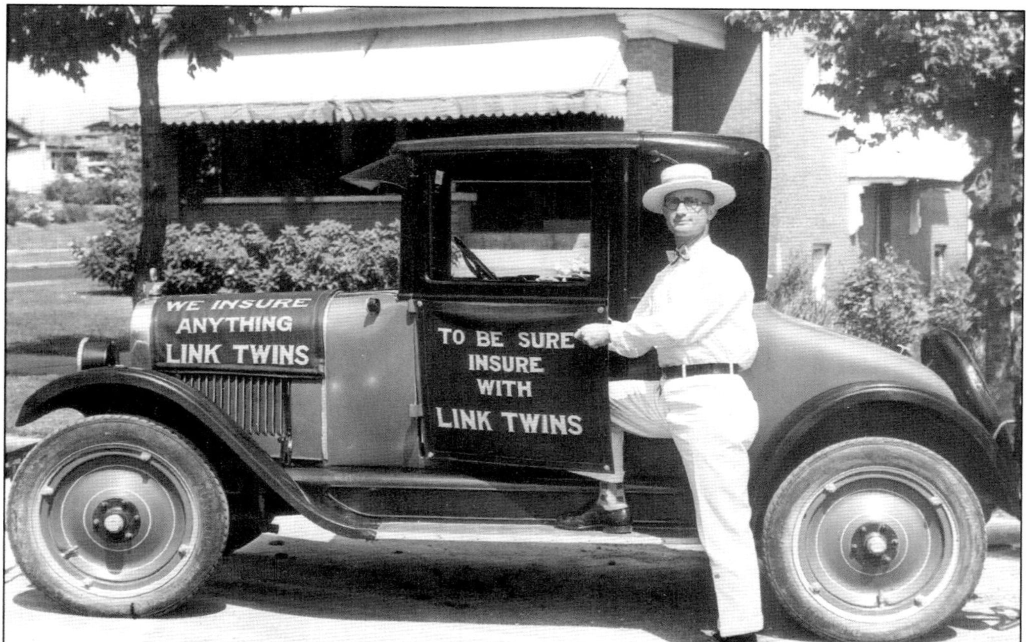

RAY LINK AND HIS CAR. This matching photograph shows Ray Link standing in front of the home of Cy Uebelhor on Van Buren Street in Huntingburg. (Photograph courtesy of the Huntingburg Public Library.)

Five

Church and School

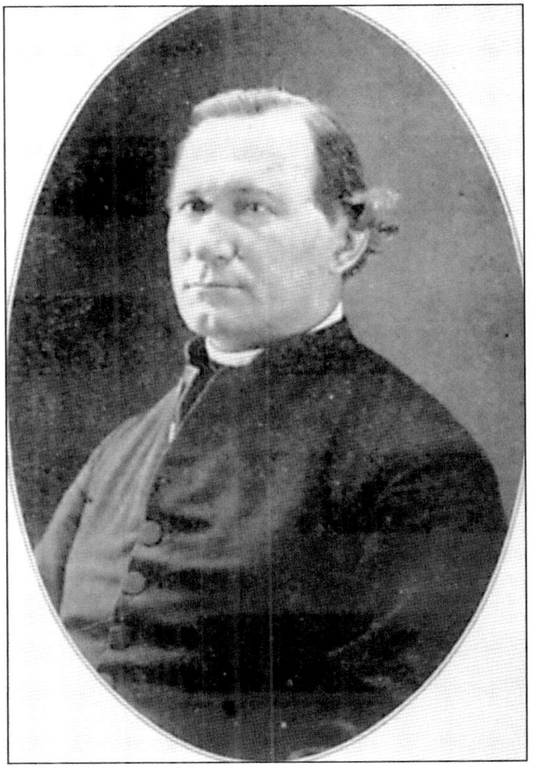

Father Joseph Kundek. Originally from Croatia, Father Joseph Kundek was the first Catholic priest in Dubois County and had a great impact on the area, founding several churches and becoming a respected community leader. He is still revered today. According to *The Castle on the Hill*, "Bishop Brute of Vincennes received Father Kundek and gave him charge of the almost unbroken mission field at Jasper, Dubois County, where the young missionary arrived on September 28, 1838. Besides being graced with a deep faith and a childlike piety, Kundek was a man of vision geared to energy; moreover, he had the happy faculty of seeing the bright side of things and of relishing the humorous twinkle in the eyes of events. At times, indeed, he showed a quick temper and a disregard for social conventionalities, but his attitude was straight-forward. Equally toward high and low. His zeal was unselfish and his energy unsparing of self." (Photograph courtesy of the Ferdinand Historic Society.)

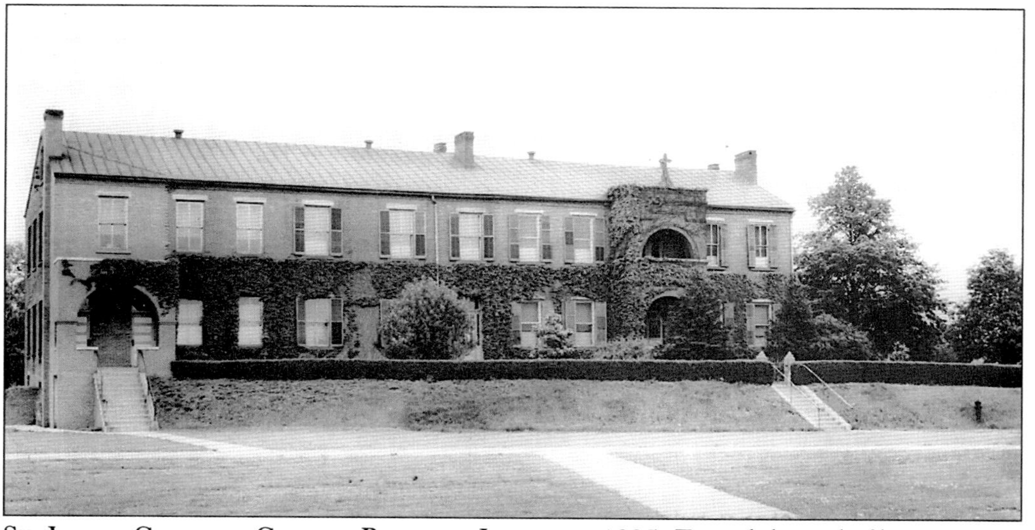

ST. JOSEPH CATHOLIC CHURCH RECTORY, JASPER, C. 1935. Toward the end of his pastorate, Father Joseph Kundek, who had lived in simple log cabins since his arrival in Jasper, approved the plans for a brick rectory to be built on the church property. Unfortunately, Kundek did not live to see its completion in 1858. The building sat on an elevated rise northwest of the present church. Behind the rectory was a garden and to the east was an orchard. The building and gardens were demolished in the late 1960s and replaced with a parking lot after a new rectory was built, north of the church. (Photograph courtesy of Ron Flick.)

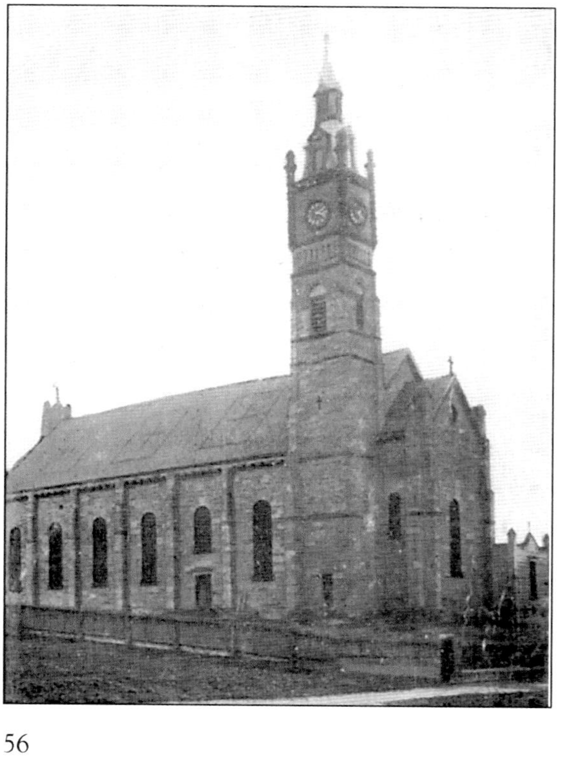

ST. JOSEPH CATHOLIC CHURCH, JASPER, C. 1920. Pictured here is a postcard of St. Joseph Catholic Church addressed to Mr. Paul Jasper and dated June 15, 11:30 p.m., 1921. This massive sandstone church, begun in 1867 by Fr. Fidelis Maute, replaced an earlier brick church built by Fr. Joseph Kundek, the first pastor. The church took decades to complete. (Photograph courtesy of the Jasper Chamber of Commerce.)

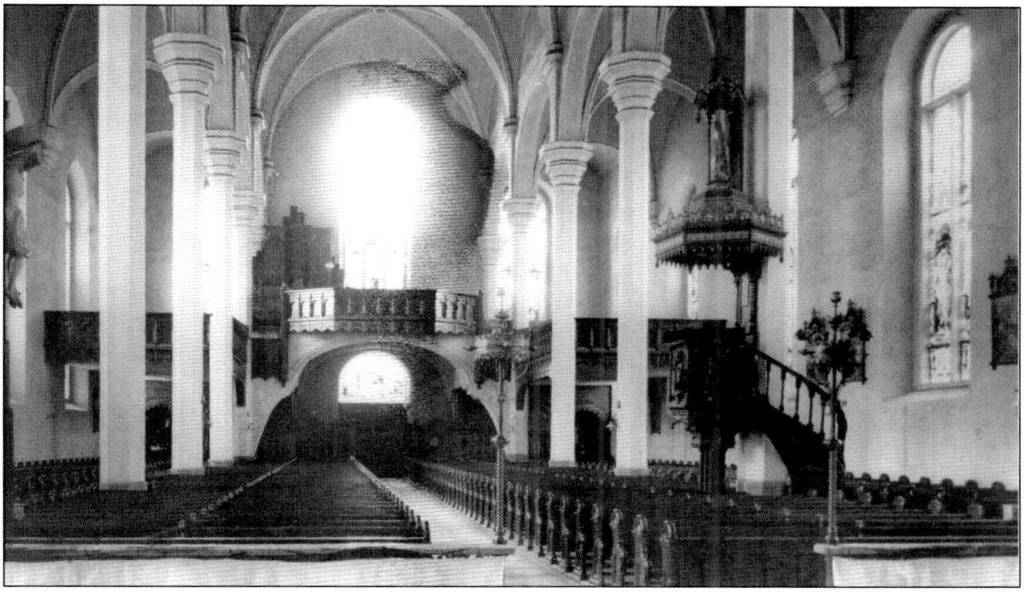

ST. JOSEPH CATHOLIC CHURCH INTERIOR, c. 1910. This view, looking from the altar to the rear of church, was taken prior to the frescoing done in the early 1920s. Note the beautifully-detailed pulpit, the entrance arch under the balcony at the single rear entrance, and the shrines at the rear corners. These are some of the items eliminated since modernization of the interior began in 1953. (Photograph courtesy of Ron Flick.)

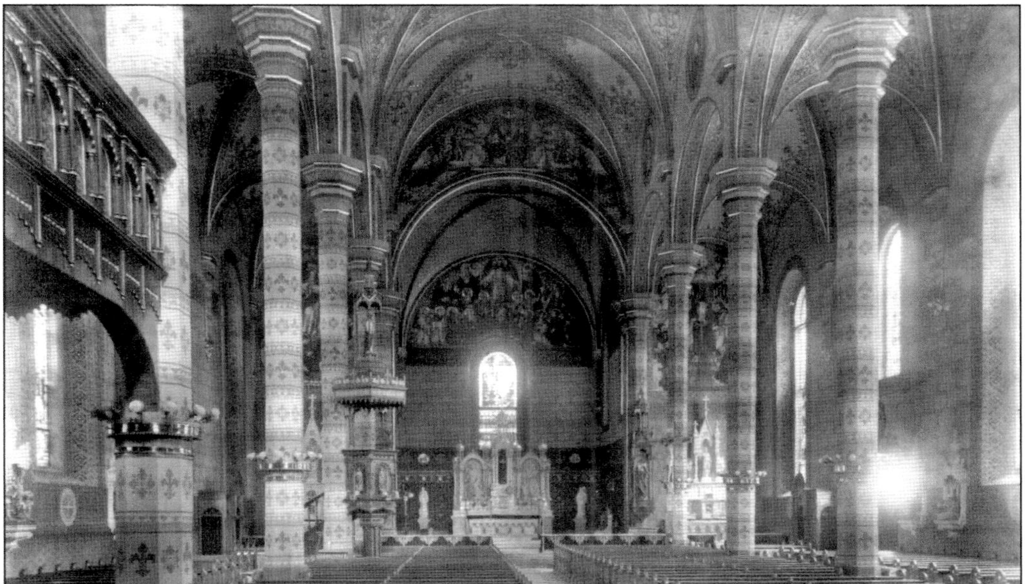

ST. JOSEPH CATHOLIC CHURCH INTERIOR, c. 1930. This view, looking from the rear of church to the front, was taken after frescoing of the interior was finished. Despite its dark appearance in the photograph, the actual color scheme included beautiful blue, green, red, and yellow hues. Note also that the original balconies protruded further out into the body of the church than they do today. (Photograph courtesy of Ron Flick.)

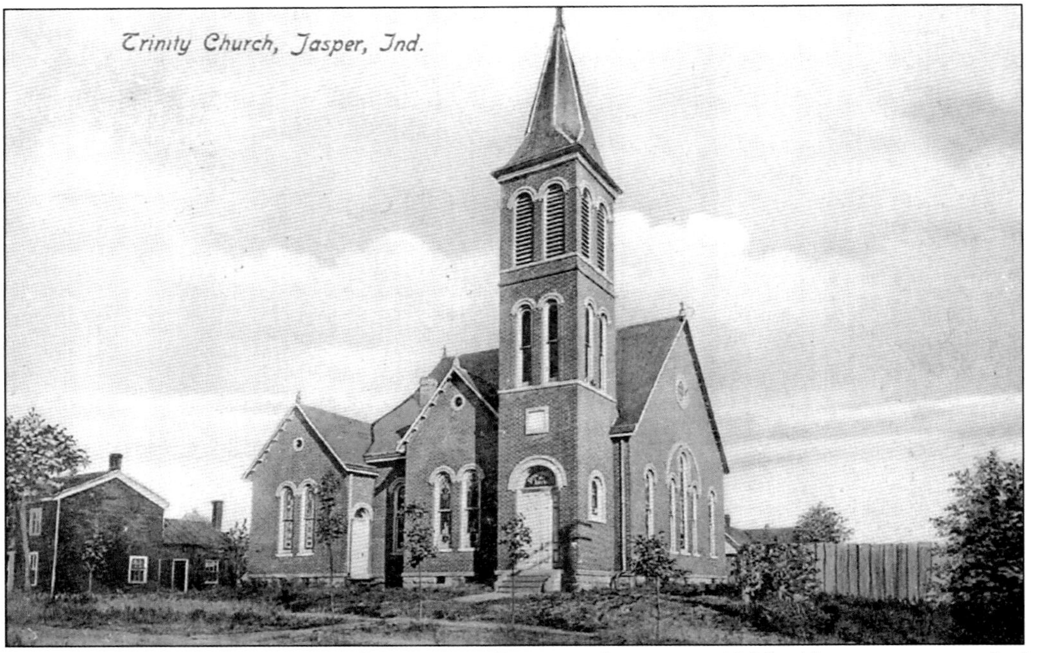

TRINITY GERMAN EVANGELICAL LUTHERAN CHURCH, JASPER, C. 1905. Above is a postcard of Trinity Church from Jasper, dated November 1907. Built in 1898 at Eighth and Clay Streets, the old church was torn down in the 1960s to make room for a more modern facility. The church is known today as the Trinity United Church of Christ. (Photograph courtesy of the Jasper Chamber of Commerce.)

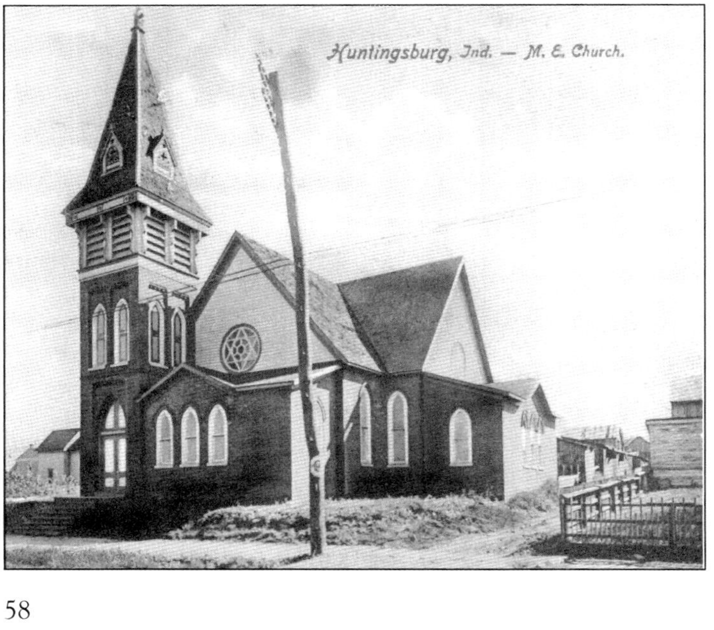

TRINITY METHODIST EPISCOPAL CHURCH, HUNTINGBURG, C. 1905. The Trinity Methodist Episcopal Church was built in 1894 on the south side of Fifth Street between Main and Jackson Streets. It is no longer standing. (Photograph courtesy of Tom Uebelhor.)

SALEM EVANGELICAL REFORMED CHURCH, HUNTINGBURG, C. 1925. Organized in 1842, today the Church is known as the Salem United Church of Christ. The church building was dedicated in 1890. The old parsonage to the right stood from 1887 to 1924. (Photograph courtesy of the Huntingburg Public Library.)

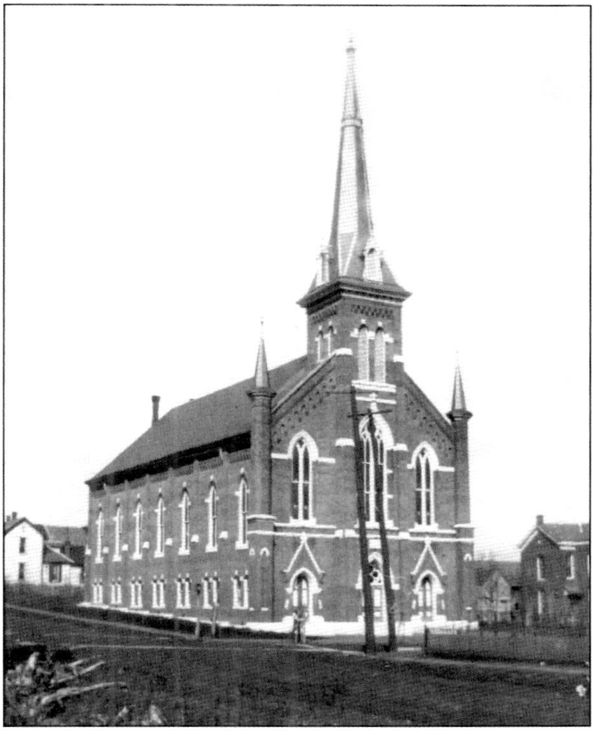

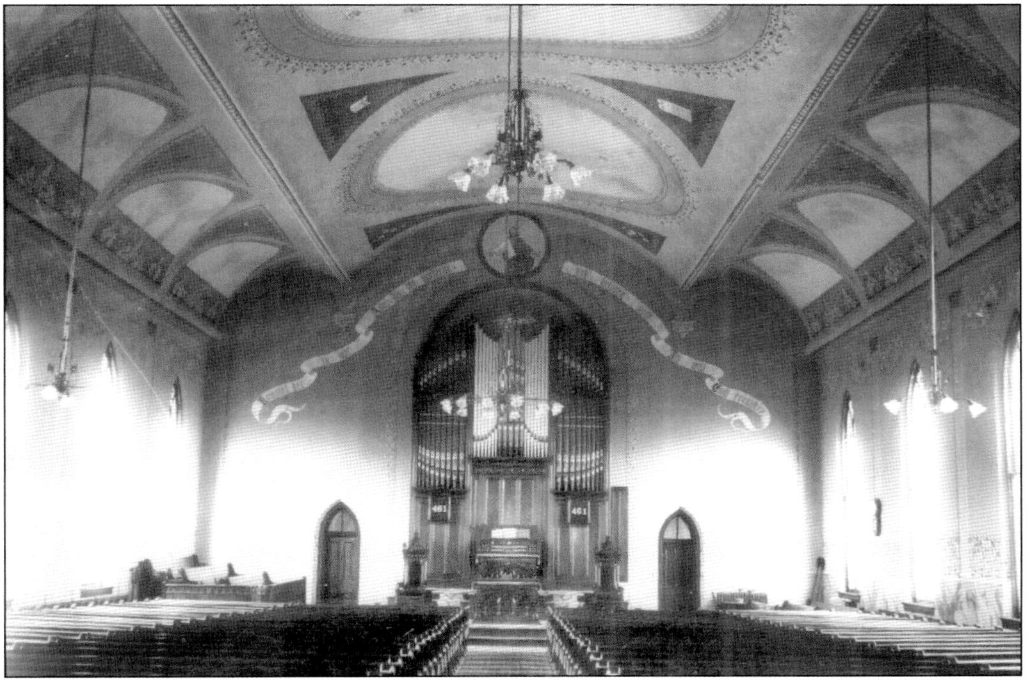

SALEM CHURCH INTERIOR, HUNGTINGBURG, C. 1905. The interior is a grand space with no columns to obstruct the congregation's view of the service. The photograph shows the interior as it looked from 1902 to 1921. (Photograph courtesy of the Huntingburg Public Library.)

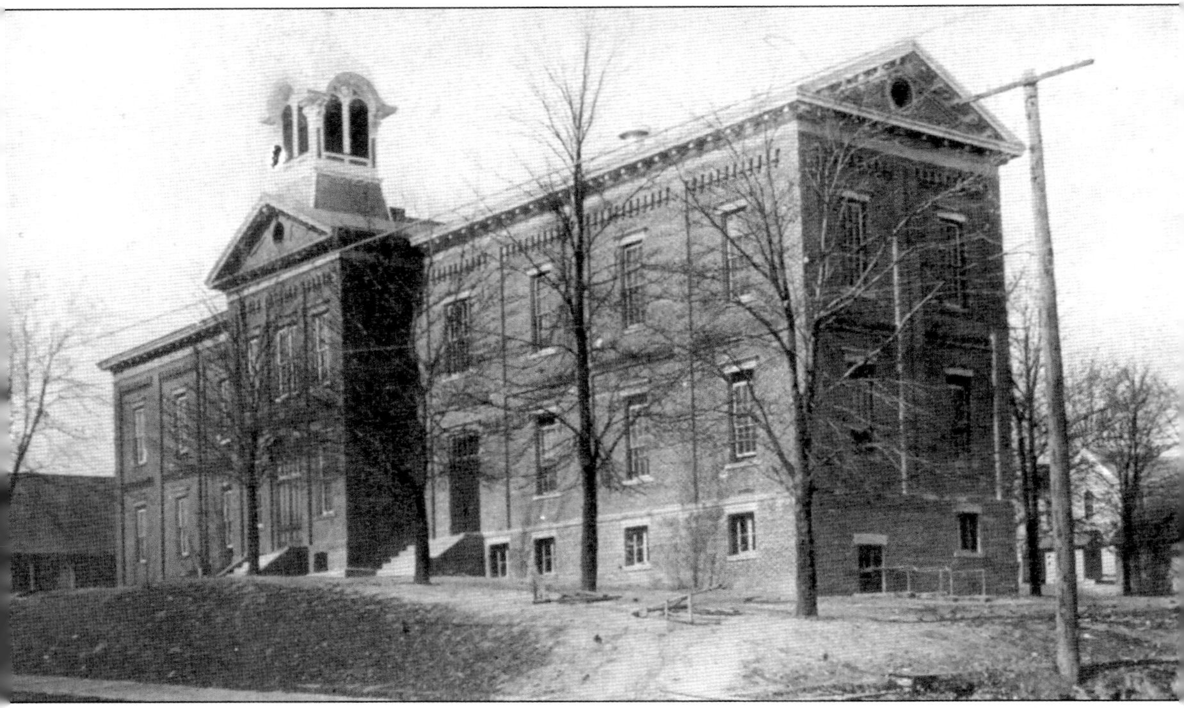

JASPER HIGH SCHOOL, JASPER, C. 1915. The public school in Jasper began in 1871, when a lot was purchased from Wendolin Bohnert on West Sixth Street, three blocks from the courthouse square. A brick schoolhouse, approximately 25 feet in width, was constructed the following year and first used in January 1873. The school primarily served the non-German Catholic population of the Jasper area. A west wing to the building was added in 1891. A high school curriculum was first taught in the school in 1898. Prior to that time, instruction ended after the eighth grade. In 1908, the east wing was added. The building then served as the public grade school and high school until 1936, when a new high school was erected on the same site. (Photograph courtesy of Don Flick.)

(opposite, bottom) **JASPER COLLEGE, C. 1910.** With more and more students enrolling at the school, Jasper College was expanded in 1905 with the addition of a large east wing. Designed once more by Michael Durlauf, the addition was crowned by a beautifully-detailed chapel on the upper floor. Inside were large study halls, dormitory rooms, classrooms, offices, and other facilities. In 1928, the name of the school was changed to "Jasper Academy." Because the school was drawing a considerable number of students from the Chicago area, the Benedictine leadership decided to relocate the school, in 1933, to Aurora, Illinois. For the first year after its closure, a portion of Jasper Academy served as headquarters for the new state police post, until their own building was constructed on the north side. The following year, the Sons of Divine Providence opened a home for disabled and retired men in the building. The building was demolished around 1970. (Photograph courtesy of John Fierst.)

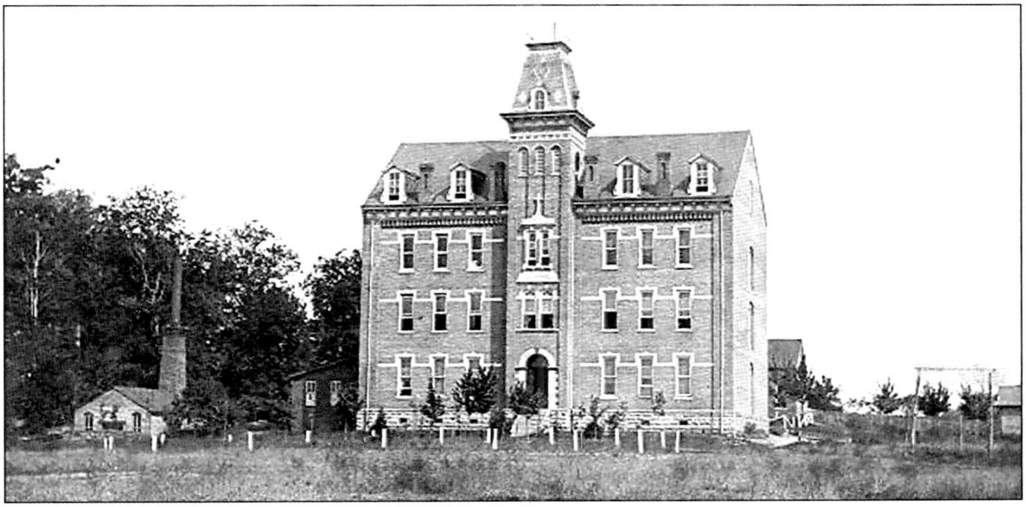

JASPER COLLEGE, 1898. After fire destroyed the buildings at St. Meinrad Abbey, Seminary, and College in 1887, a group of businessmen petitioned the Benedictine abbot of St. Meinrad to allocate the college portion of the complex to Jasper. The "College" served young men of high-school age only. For its first year, classes were held in the rectory at nearby St. Joseph Church. The following year, in 1890, the handsome new home of Jasper College opened its doors to students. The building was designed by architect and stone mason Michael Durlauf, and superbly built by Jasper contractor Anthony M. Hochgesang. It featured a two-story entrance hall with surrounding balcony, and a mansard-roofed tower. (Photograph courtesy of John Fierst.)

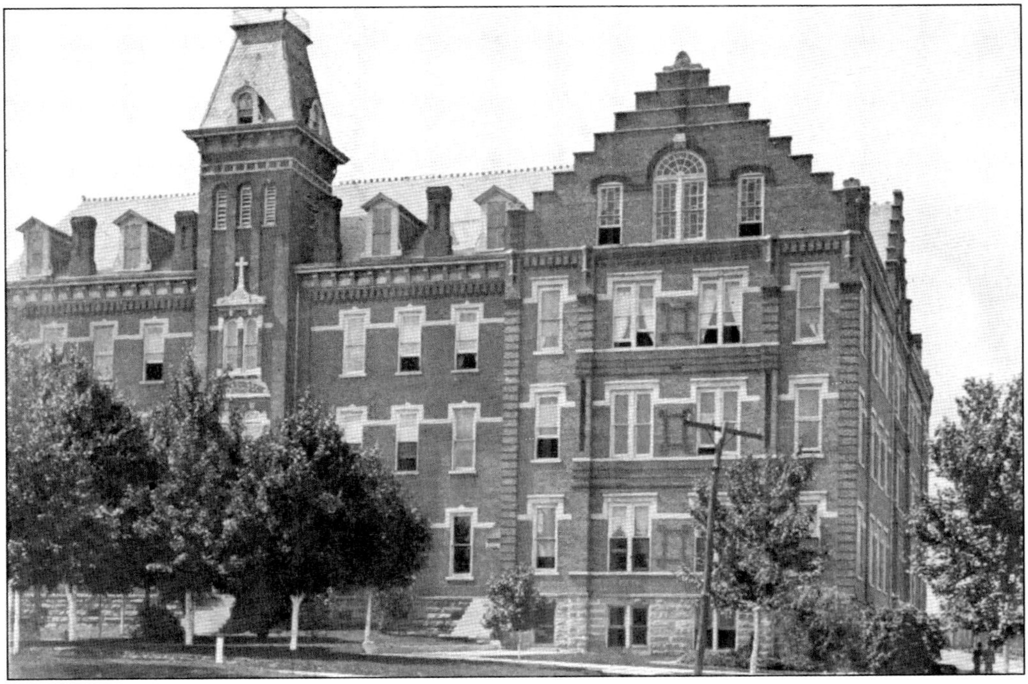

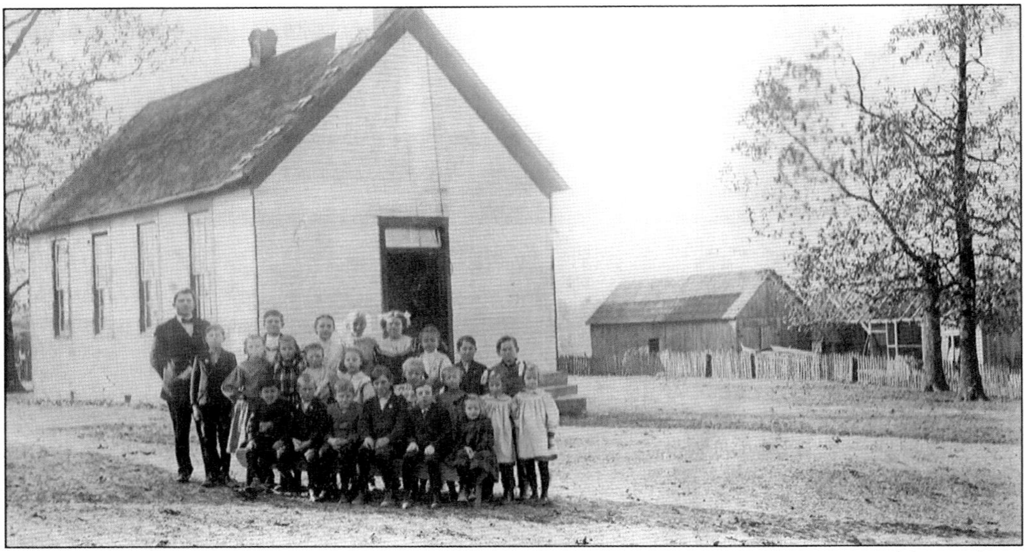

WARNSMAN SCHOOL, OLD JASPER ROAD, NEAR HUNTINGBURG, 1908. Pictured here, from left to right, are: (seated) Karl Rummel, Elmer Hammelman, Albert Lohman, Lawrence Christopher, Frank Lehmkuhler, and Metelda Weissner Vandervier; (second row) Earl Rauscher, Florence Hammelman Taylor, Edith Weissner, Julia Spitzer Davis, Grace Niehaus Weisheit, Flora Lohman Sunderman, Lydia Hammelman Rauscher, and Jeanette and Mildred Rauscher; and (back row) George Fisher (teacher), Martin Lohman, Lilly Rummel Heitman, Laura Warnsman, Norma Christopher Hilgeman, Ida Lohman Langford, Lawrence Bretz, and Athel Hilgeman. (Photograph courtesy of the Museum of Huntingburg.)

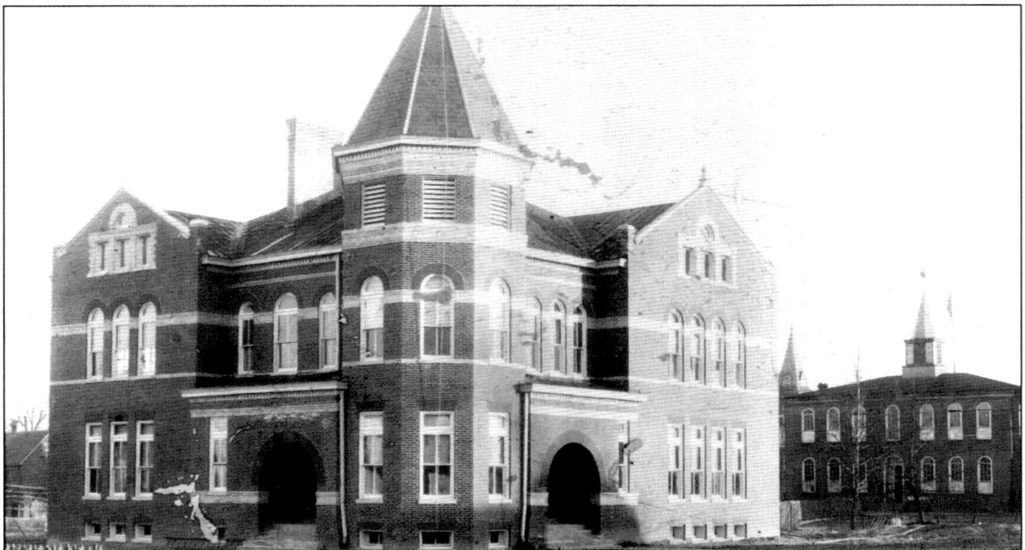

HUNTINGBURG HIGH SCHOOL, C. 1900. This building, located at the southeast corner of Sixth and Main Streets, was Huntingburg's second high school, built in 1898. It replaced the first high school shown on the right. The first school would later be torn down and replaced with the city's third high school in 1907. The "second" high school then became a grade school. (Photograph courtesy of the Huntingburg Public Library.)

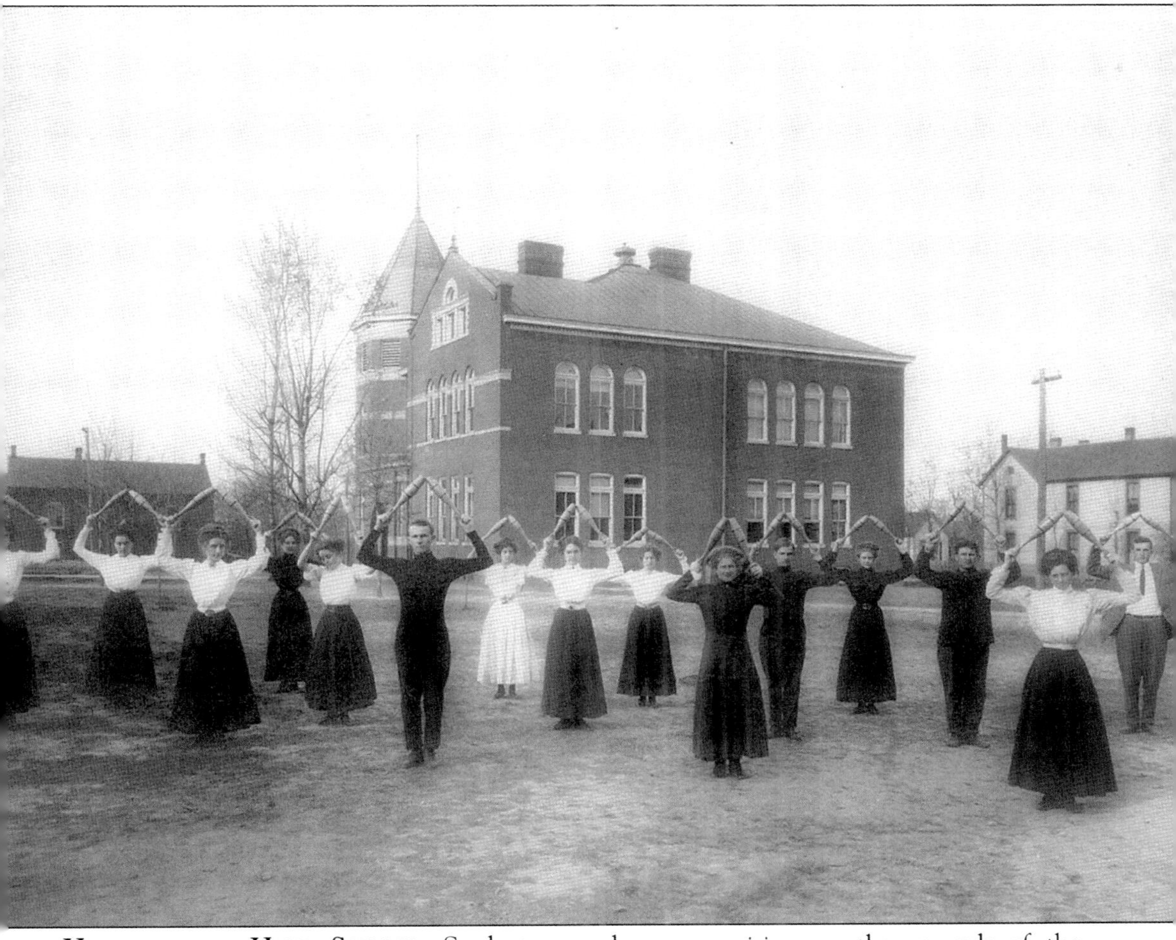

HUNTINGBURG HIGH SCHOOL. Students are shown exercising on the grounds of the Huntingburg public schools. On these grounds was later built the high school's first gymnasium, which is now a youth center. (Photograph courtesy of the Museum of Huntingburg.)

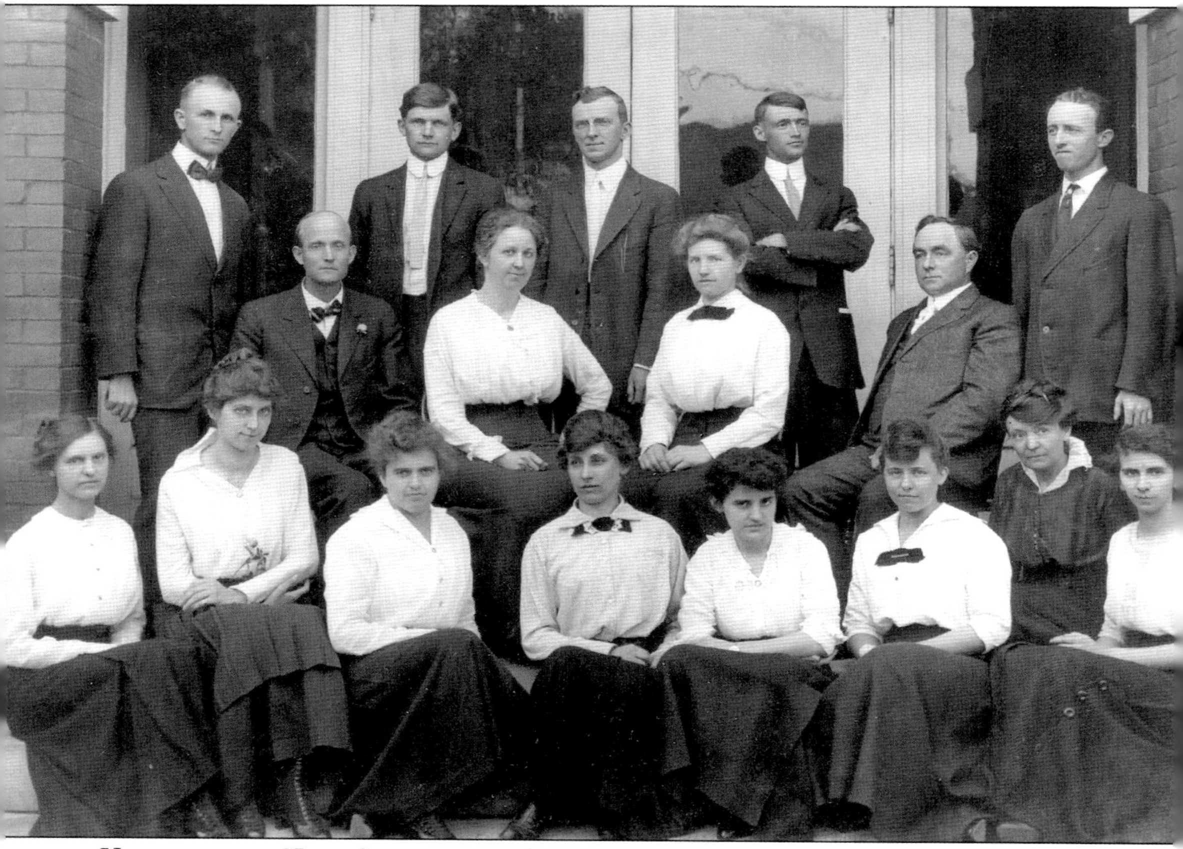

HUNTINGBURG HIGH SCHOOL AND GRADE SCHOOL FACULTY, 1915. Pictured here, from left to right, are: (front row) Meta (Schlessing) Rauscher, Ariel (Anderson) Partenheimer, Lucille (Briscoe) Partenheimer, Mabel Sutton, Amanda (Bamberger) Milbourn, Clementine (Carpenter) Ellsworth (mother of Tom and Mary Ellen Ellsworth), Anna Behrens, and Helen (Gumz) Partenheimer; and (second row) Louis Wagner, Lydia (Poetker) Steinkamp, Lydia Partenheimer, Superintendent N. F. Hutchison; (top row) Cecil Katterjohn, Albert Fenneman, Oscar Koenig, Lee A. Meyer, and principal Harry Parks. (Names courtesy of Judge Hugo C. Songer's *The History of Huntingburg*. Photograph courtesy of the Huntingburg Public Library.)

Six

HOSPITALITY

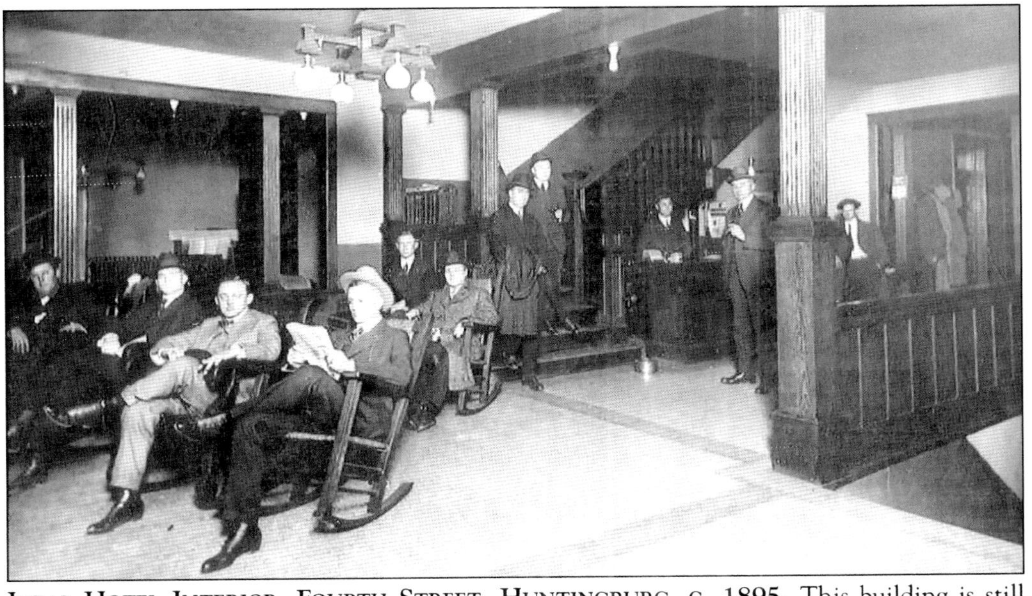

IDEAL HOTEL INTERIOR, FOURTH STREET, HUNTINGBURG, C. 1895. This building is still standing, downtown across the street from the Museum of Huntingburg. (Photograph courtesy of the Museum of Huntingburg.)

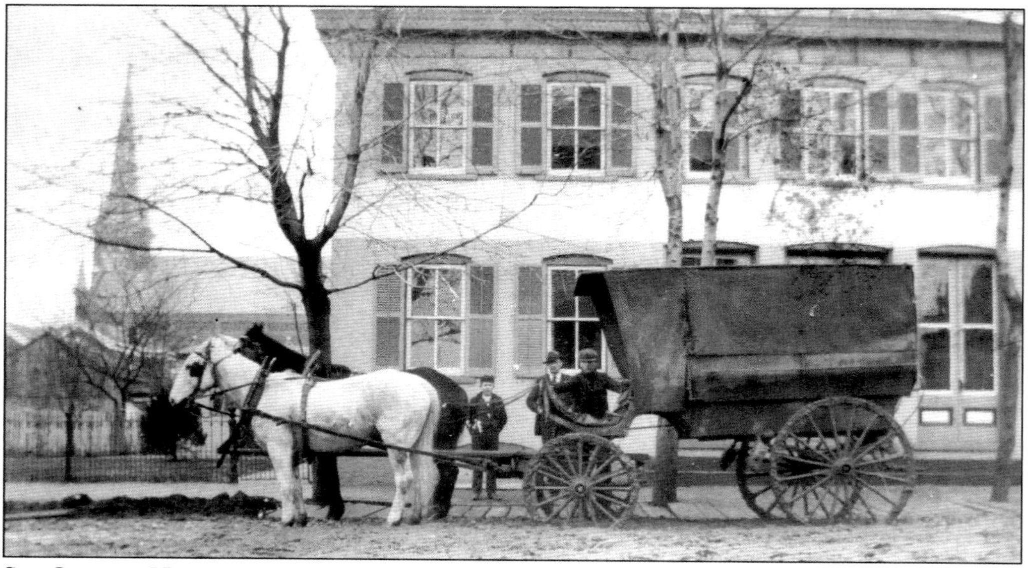

St. George Hotel, Geiger Street, Huntingburg. In front, according to records at the Huntingburg Public Library, is the St. George hack which took visitors to and from the railroad depot. The Huntingburg Bank was once located in a room at the St. George, but as the bank expanded, it moved to a building next door. There was also a livery & feed stable next door. The St. George was razed in 1936. Charles Moenkhaus, proprietor of the St. George, was born in Louisville, Kentucky, on March 18, 1860. He was one of seven children born to William Moenkhaus and Fredrica Ramsbrok, who were from Germany. Charles and his family moved to Huntingburg when he was a child. (Photograph courtesy of the Huntingburg Public Library.)

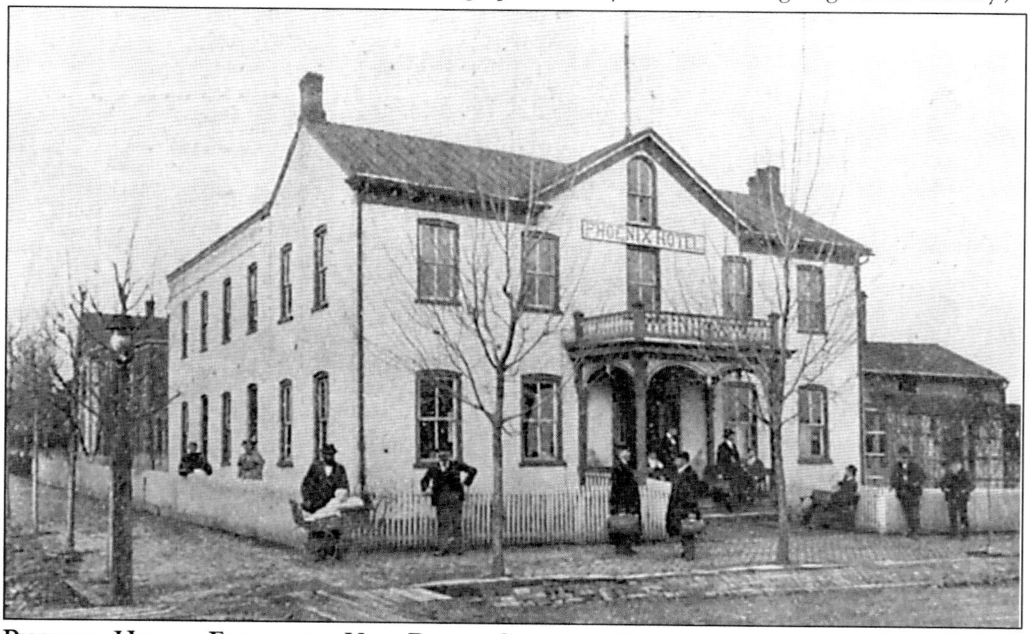

Phoenix Hotel, Fifth and Van Buren Streets, Huntingburg, 1896. According to *Hoosier Vignettes* by R. H. Menke, Huntingburg's first library was in the west annex of the hotel. (Photograph courtesy of the Huntingburg Public Library.)

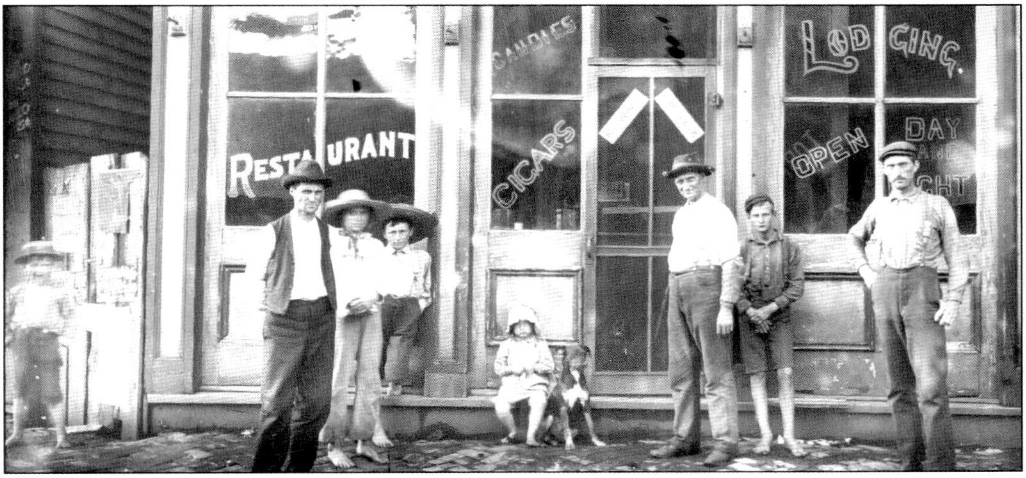

ROHLEDER'S RESTAURANT, HUNTINGBURG. Affectionately known as the "Bloody Bucket," this establishment was located opposite the Southern Railway Depot in Huntingburg. (Photograph courtesy of the Museum of Huntingburg.)

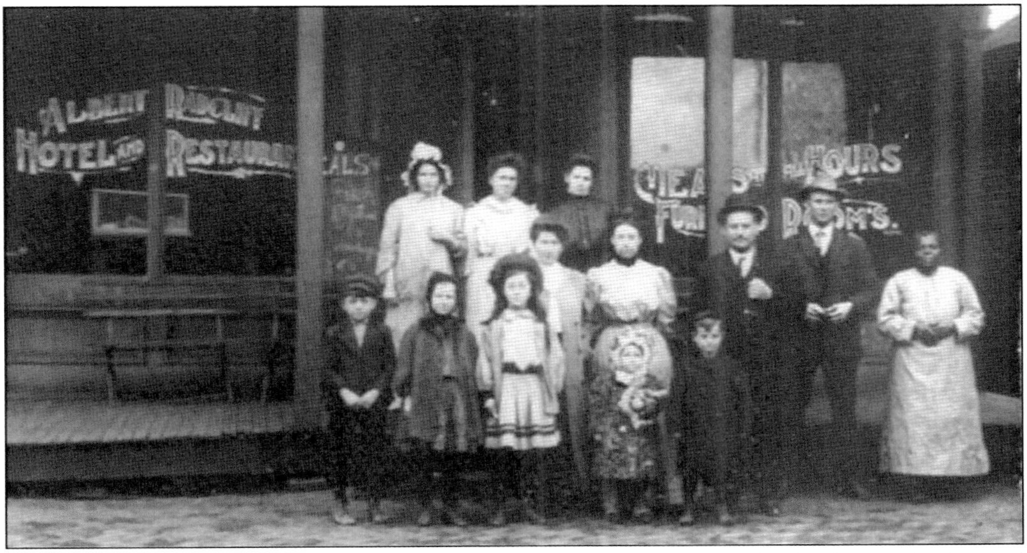

ALBERT RADCLIFF HOTEL AND RESTAURANT, HUNTINGBURG. The Radcliff was also located across the railroad tracks from the Southern Railway Depot in Huntingburg. According to the November 22, 1960, *Daily Herald* (provided by Loma Hartke), the people in the photograph, from left to right, are: (front row) Russell Radcliff, Mrs. Lillie McMillan Dearing, Hazel Lovejoy McAtee, Lorraine Radcliff W. Siebe, and Edward Radcliff; (second row) unidentified, Mrs. Albert Radcliff, Albert Radcliff, Paul Rohlender, and "Aunt" Martha Houston; and (back row) unidentified. At one time, William J. "Peggy" McMillan, father of Lillie Dearing, owned the 27-room hotel, which was known as the Koldura Hotel. The article goes on to state, "When E. S. "Jack" Parks, father of Mrs. Rohleder, first came to Huntingburg as an employee of the Southern Railway Company, he stayed at the hotel. Failing health caused the McMillans to dispose of their hotel and it was operated by the Radcliffs, Charlie Adams and Mrs. Alice Williams." (Photograph courtesy of the Museum of Huntingburg.)

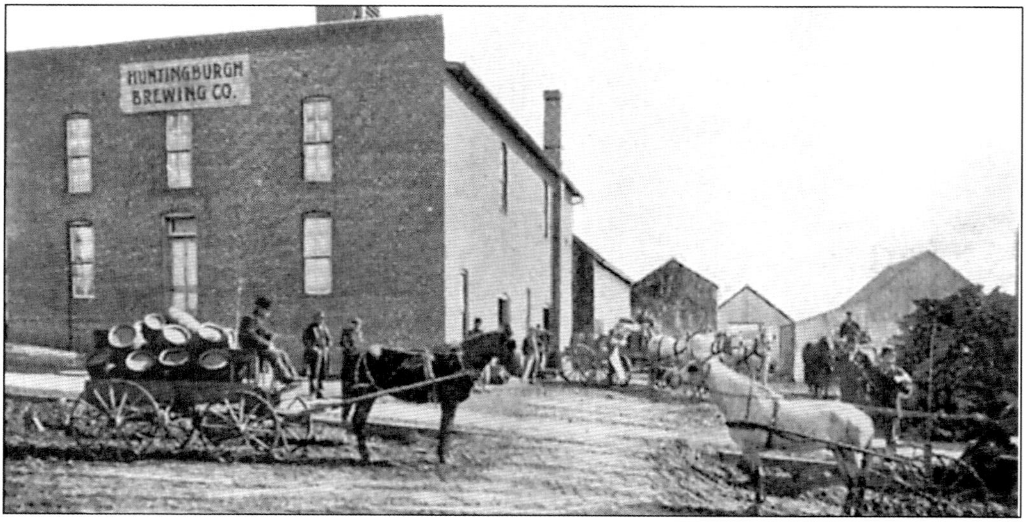

THE HUNTINGBURG BREWING COMPANY, HUNTINGBURG, C.1895. The brewing company first opened in 1894 at First and Main Streets under the ownership of Andreas and Henry Fritch and Charles and Henry Moenkhaus. Two years later, Charles Moenkhaus, who also owned the St. George Hotel, was the sole owner. The brewery's specialty was common or cream beer, which was two percent alcohol. Though the brewery hit hard times during Prohibition, according to Christine Prior, executive director of the Huntingburg Chamber of Commerce, moonshiners flourished, producing "Dubois Dew." (Photograph courtesy of the Huntingburg Public Library.)

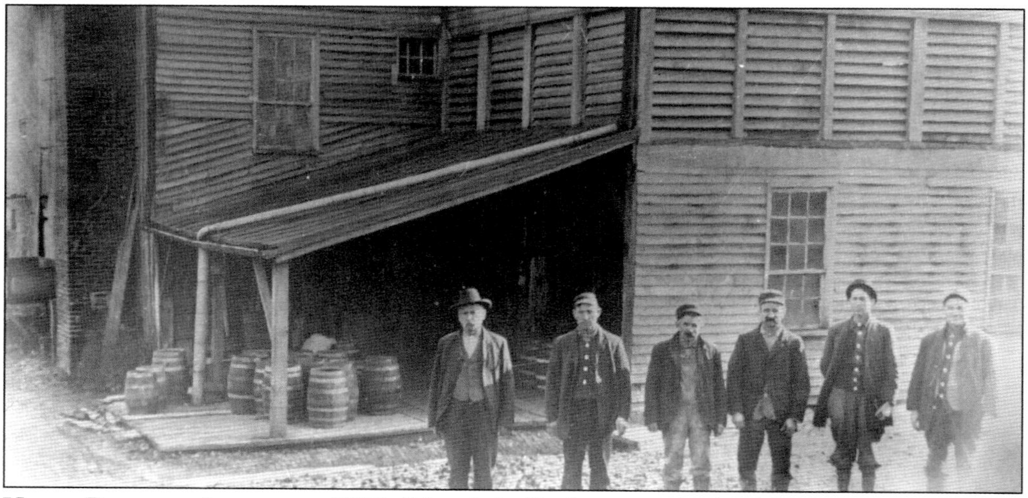

HABIG BREWERY, JASPER, C. 1905. Edward A. Hochgesang, the local brick manufacturer and masonry contractor, purchased an existing brewery soon after the end of the Civil War. From October of 1869 to November of the following year, Hochgesang built a new brick brewery building on the lot bounded by Eleventh and Twelfth Streets and Main and Jackson Streets. In 1884, after Mr. Hochgesang's death, his widow, the former Cecilia Habig, sold the business to her brother, Anton Habig, and his brother-in-law and partner, Martin Eckstein. The brewery was known as the Excelsior Brewery during this time period, and the fine-quality beer it produced was labeled "Jasper Common Draft Beer." In the decades that followed, the business was passed down to Anton's son, Frank. Later, the Jasper Public Library was constructed on the site. (Photograph courtesy of the Habig family.)

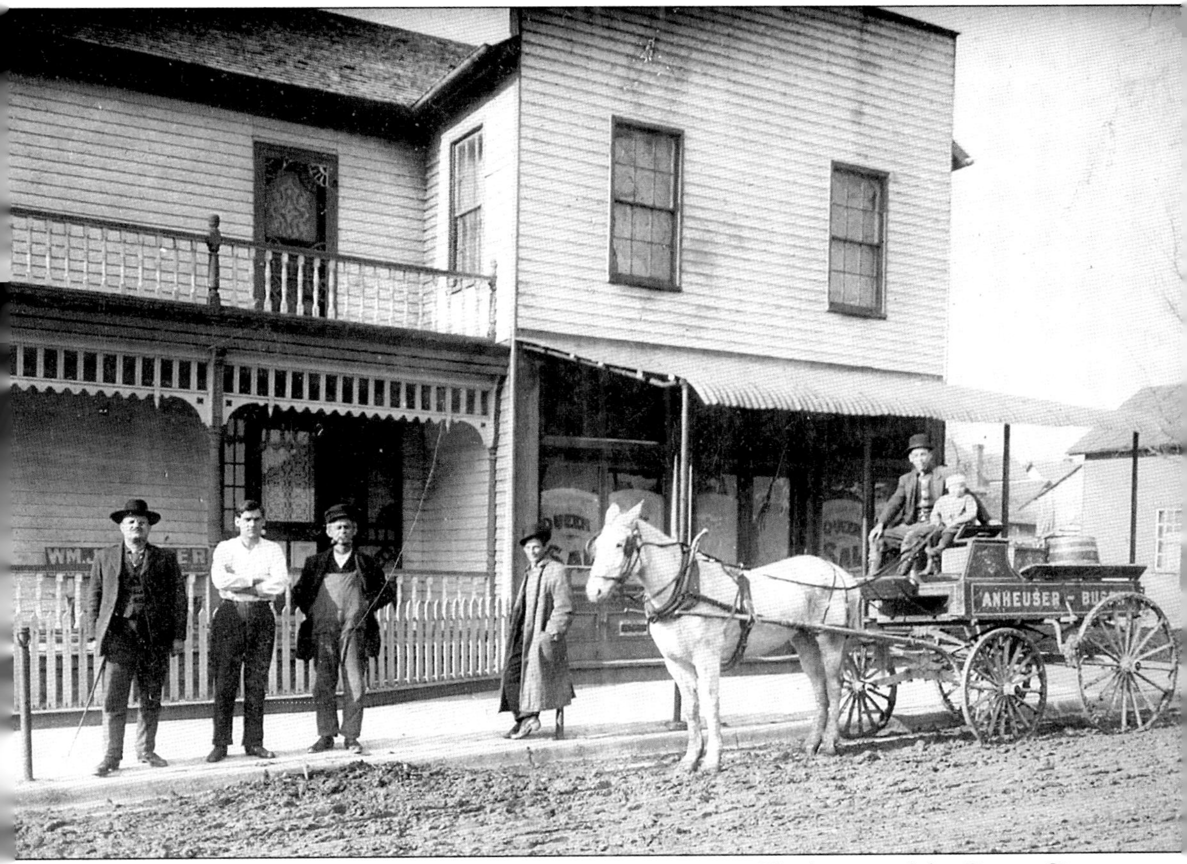

QUEEN CITY SALOON, 1115 MAIN STREET, JASPER, C. 1915. The history of the Queen City Saloon began in 1872, when Cornelius Hurst constructed a boarding house and saloon on the southwest corner of Twelfth and Main in Jasper. Because this was on the northern outskirts of town at the time, the saloon was originally known as the "First and Last Chance Saloon." In 1882, A. J. McNerney became owner and renamed the business the "Queen City Saloon." The next owners were the Habig and Eckstein families, who also operated the brewery across the street. Subsequent owners of the Queen City included the Gerber, Knapp, Kunkel, Gutgsell, and Haas families. In 1928, William Giesler, who would eventually own numerous taverns in Jasper, purchased the business and placed two of his sons in charge. One of the sons, Cyril "Snap" Giesler, bought out his father in 1940 and changed the name of the bar to "Snap's Café." Snap retired in 1989, after 60 years in business. Subsequent owners kept Snap's open until 1999, when Ron and Debbie Flick purchased the property, restored the building, and changed the name back to the Queen City Café. The restaurant lasted only a little more than a year, however. Three subsequent restaurants lasted only briefly, as well. Recently, the business has been reopened as Snap's Steakhouse. (Photograph courtesy of Anthony Habig.)

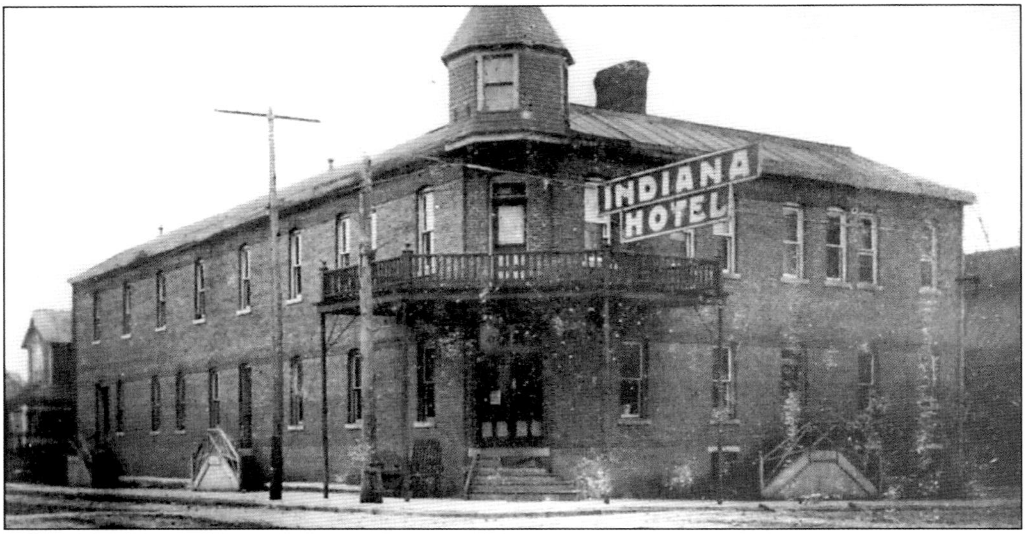

INDIANA HOTEL, FIFTH AND JACKSON STREETS, JASPER, C. 1905. James Condict built a wood-frame hotel on the southwest corner of Fifth and Jackson Streets and operated it from 1845 to 1853. The next owners were Esquire Rose and Martin Friedman. Fred Neudeck purchased the business just after the Civil War and maintained it for a quarter century, selling it to T. K. Dougherty, a son-in-law of Martin Friedman, in 1893. During these many years, the building was enlarged and remodeled numerous times, somewhat haphazardly, until it finally burned to the ground on Easter Sunday morning in 1902. Soon after, James Haller purchased the property and erected the larger, brick structure shown in the photograph. In 1911, Haller traded the hotel for the bakery across the street. As the decades passed, the hotel lost its luster, eventually becoming sleeping rooms for the transient and falling into decay. It was torn down in the early 1990s to provide more parking for the downtown. (Photograph courtesy of the Jasper Chamber of Commerce.)

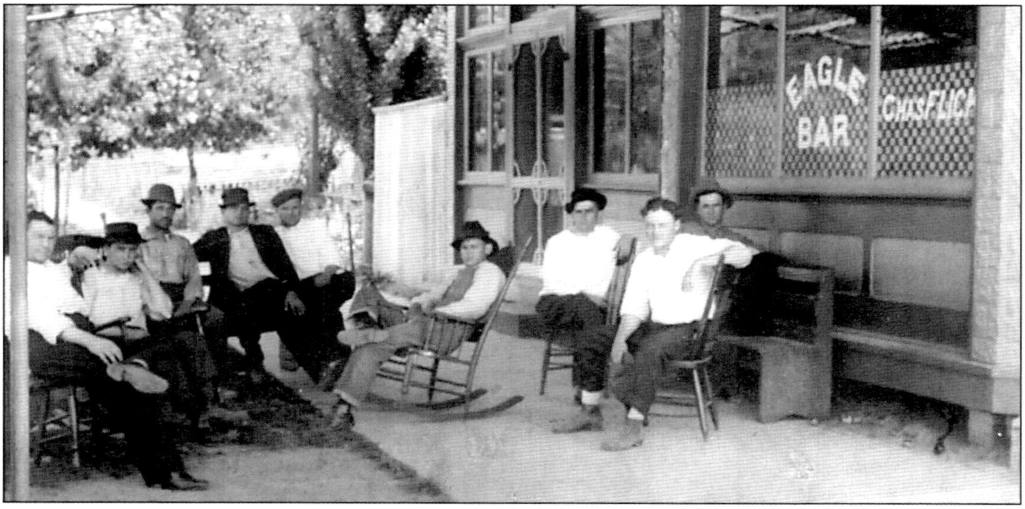

EAGLE BAR, THIRD AND MAIN STREETS, JASPER, C. 1915. The Eagle Bar was owned and operated by Charles Flick, shown seated at the far left. The business was located on the northeast corner of Third and Main Streets, adjacent to the Flick residence and the home of Charles's in-laws, the Schubles. The buildings are still standing, but have been covered over with brick and stone. (Photograph courtesy of Lil (Flick) Blemker.)

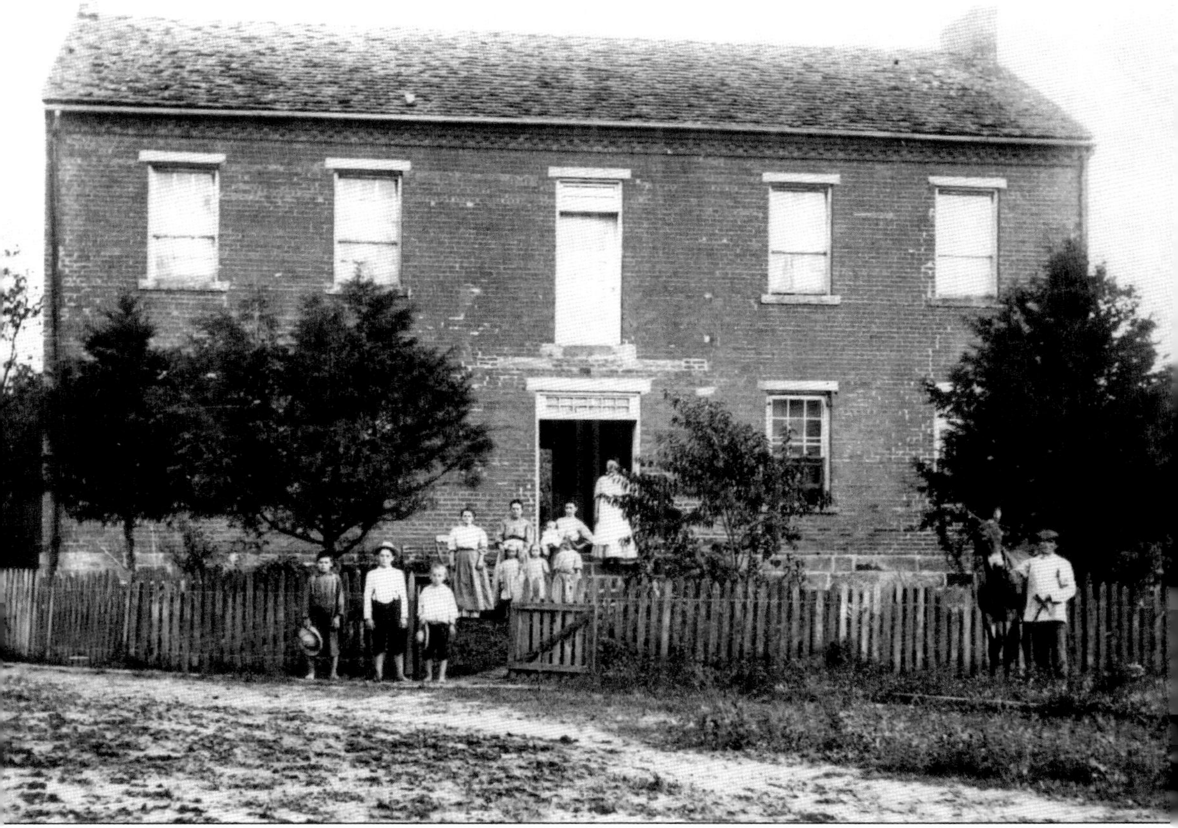

GREENTREE INN, JASPER, C. 1900. John and Margaretha Opel, who had immigrated to America from Bavaria in 1840, constructed a large brick home southeast of Jasper sometime in the 1850s. An article in one of the very first editions of the *Jasper Courier*, dated November 17, 1858, stated: "Among the new buildings, that of Mr. John Opel on the Troy road is one of the best. It is a fine large two story brick, embracing a store room and residence. It is built in a most substantial manner with a massive stone foundation and has a very superior cellar." During the ensuing years, the structure, known as the Opel or Greentree Inn, became a popular gathering spot for events, including annual Fourth of July celebrations. A large ballroom on the second floor was used for dances and other celebrations. At the time the photograph was taken, the Bockelman family lived in the home. Pictured here are Othmar Bockelman, Urban Burger, Oscar Burger, Minnie Bockelman, Mary Burger, Laura Burger, Anna Burger, Martha Jerger, Laura Jerger, Leona Bockelman Eckstein, Cecilia Bockelman Eckerle, and Lawrence Bockelman. In 1977, Joe and Judy Rohleder purchased the aging house from Richard and Helen Hochgesang and began a painstaking restoration of the property. Today the beautiful home is listed on the National Register of Historic Places. (Photograph courtesy of Joe and Judy Rohleder.)

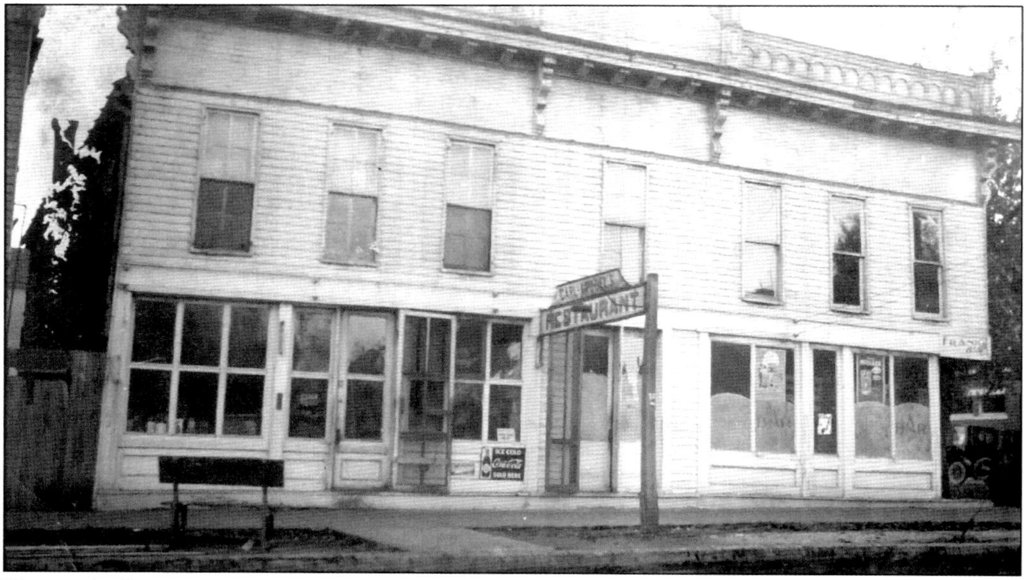

KRODEL'S RESTAURANT AND FRANK'S BAR, JASPER, C. 1915. The two photographs on this page are of the same building at Sixth and Jackson Streets during different periods of time. Before its demolition, the building had a long and varied history. As suggested by Arthur Nordhoff in his superb compilation, *Pictures from the Past* (1966), the building was originally two separate structures, which were connected at a later date. The east and west portions had different owners and occupants from the mid-1870s until 1909, when the entire building came under the ownership of Gerhard Johannemann. The Johannemanns were the landlords at the time the first photograph was taken. Carl Krodel leased the east half for his restaurant, while Frank Knapp rented the west half for his tavern, known as Frank's Saloon or Frank's Bar. In 1929, Frank Seng acquired ownership of the building and eventually the bar and restaurant came under the same management. James Whelan operated the business from 1924 to 1927, after which Edward Yaggi became proprietor. The Yaggi family purchased the building from Seng in 1936 and named their business Yaggi's Café. In 1949, a new brick building was built behind the frame building on Jackson Street and the old structure was removed for a small parking lot. (Photograph courtesy of John Fierst.)

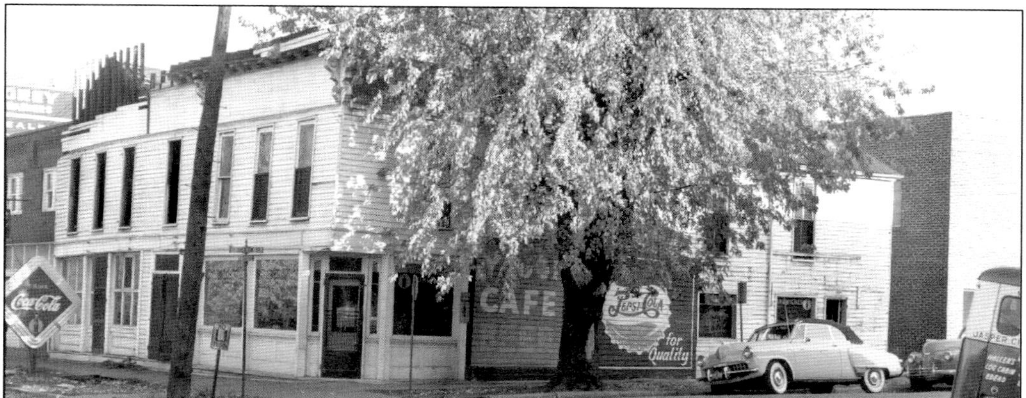

YAGGI'S CAFÉ, JASPER, 1949. This photograph was taken as the old Yaggi's Café was being dismantled for demolition. The new brick building sits to the right, behind the old building. Yaggi's is still at the same site after these many years. (Photograph courtesy of John Fierst.)

SCHNITZELBANK RESTAURANT AND BAR, 409 THIRD AVENUE, JASPER, C. 1945. The history of the Schnitzelbank dates back to 1908, when Michael Hochgesang and his brother-in-law, James Bates, co-owners of the Hochgesang Brickyard, erected a small, brick building on the Troy Road (now Third Avenue) during the summer of that year. The September 11, 1908, *Jasper Courier* documented the opening of the new tavern: "James J. Bates on Monday was granted a liquor license by the Board of Commissioners and on Tuesday opened up his saloon on the Troy road a short distance from Eckert's mill and will be known as the Little Kentucky Saloon." Exactly one year later, Bates sold the business to another Hochgesang in-law, Anthony Streicher, husband of Albert Hochgesang's daughter Clara. In 1933, after the end of Prohibition, a subsequent owner, Ed "Toots" Haller renamed the business the "Schnitzelbank," a German word meaning "carving bench." In 1961, Larry and Betty Hanselman became proprietors. Larry's grandfather was Lawrence Hochgesang, brother to Albert Hochgesang. Ten years later, a new era in the history of the Schnitzelbank began with the construction of a new and larger building. Today, members of the Hanselman family still own and operate the restaurant. (Photograph courtesy of Larry and Betty Hanselman.)

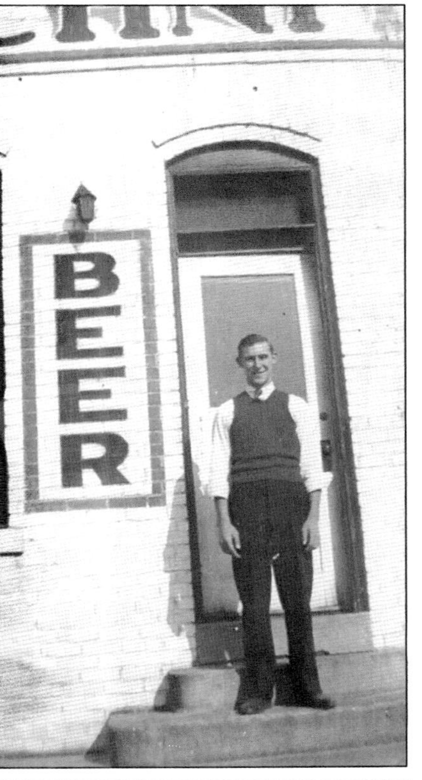

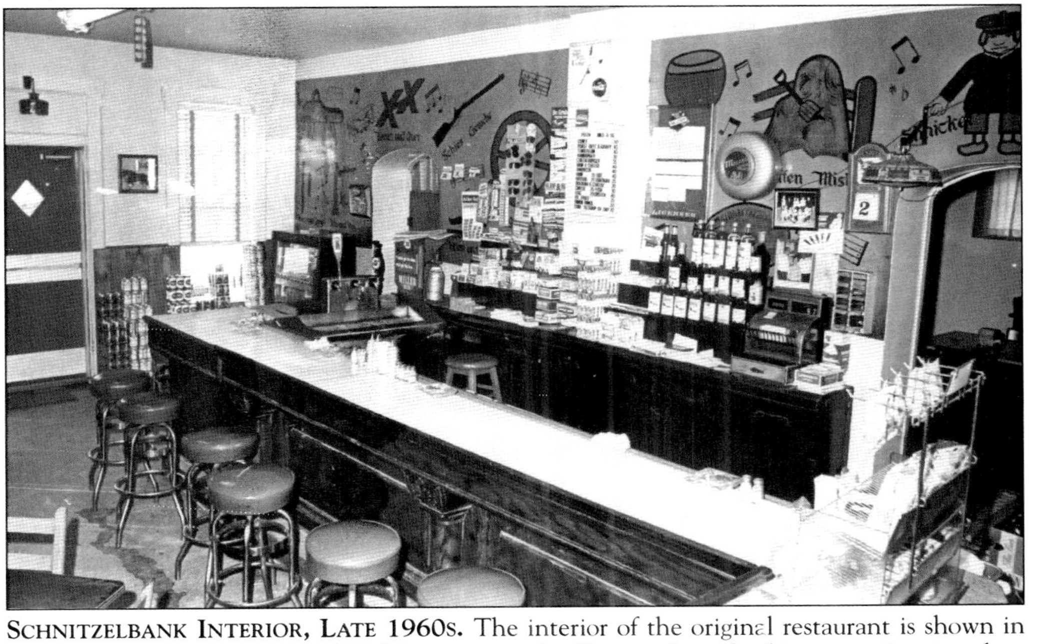

SCHNITZELBANK INTERIOR, LATE 1960S. The interior of the original restaurant is shown in this photograph. The Schnitzelbank song, a popular German beer-drinking tune, is painted on the walls with words and graphics. A signboard on the wall lists the complete menu at the time, including tenderloins for 40 cents. (Photograph courtesy of Larry and Betty Hanselman.)

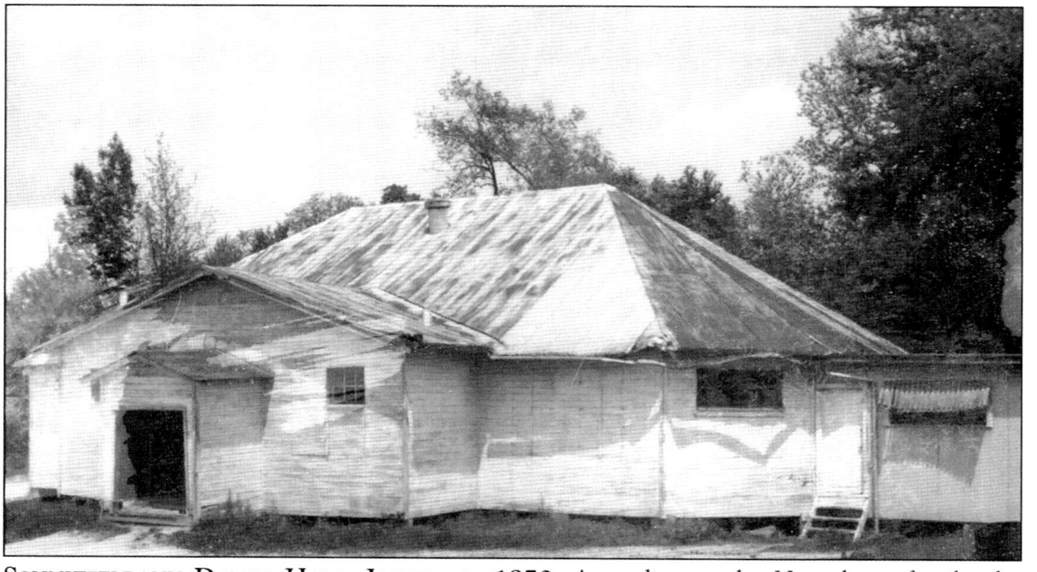

Schnitzelbank Dance Hall, Jasper, c. 1970. According to the Hanselman family, the Schnitzelbank dance hall was constructed in 1936 as a chicken house. The wood-frame building sat a distance off the highway, behind the original restaurant building. It was a popular spot for dances and get-togethers for many years. Later it was the first facility used by the St. Vincent de Paul Society. As the photograph indicates, it fell into quite a state of disrepair prior to its demolition. (Photograph courtesy of Larry and Betty Hanselman.)

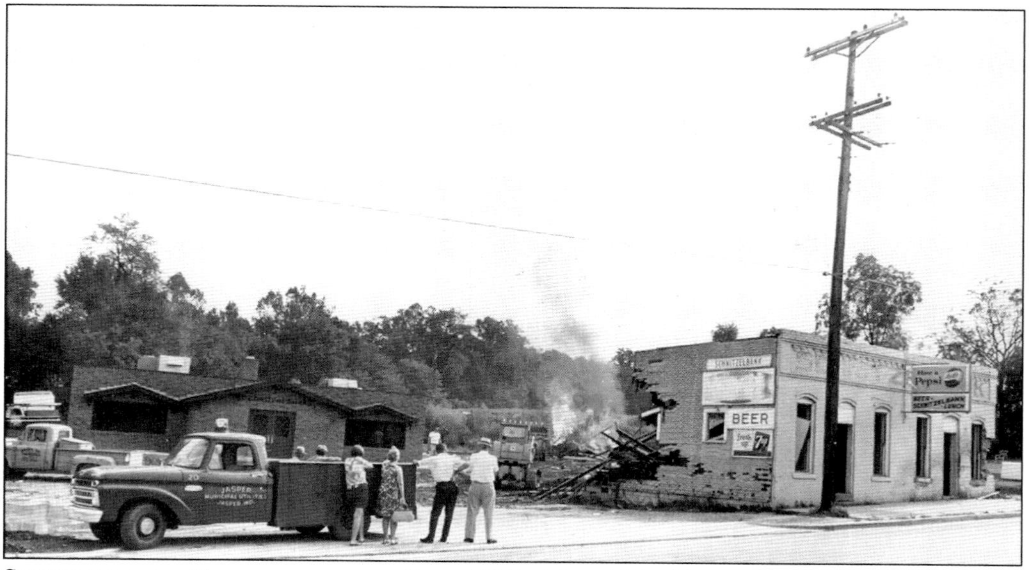

Schnitzelbank Restaurant and Bar, 1971. The old building is shown being torn down, as the new Schnitzelbank sits ready for business. Subsequent additions to the restaurant were constructed in 1973 and 1988, including the now-famous Glockenspiel tower. The Hanselman family also added a hotel and a catering building adjacent to the restaurant in the 1990s. (Photograph courtesy of Larry and Betty Hanselman.)

Seven

FUN AND CELEBRATION

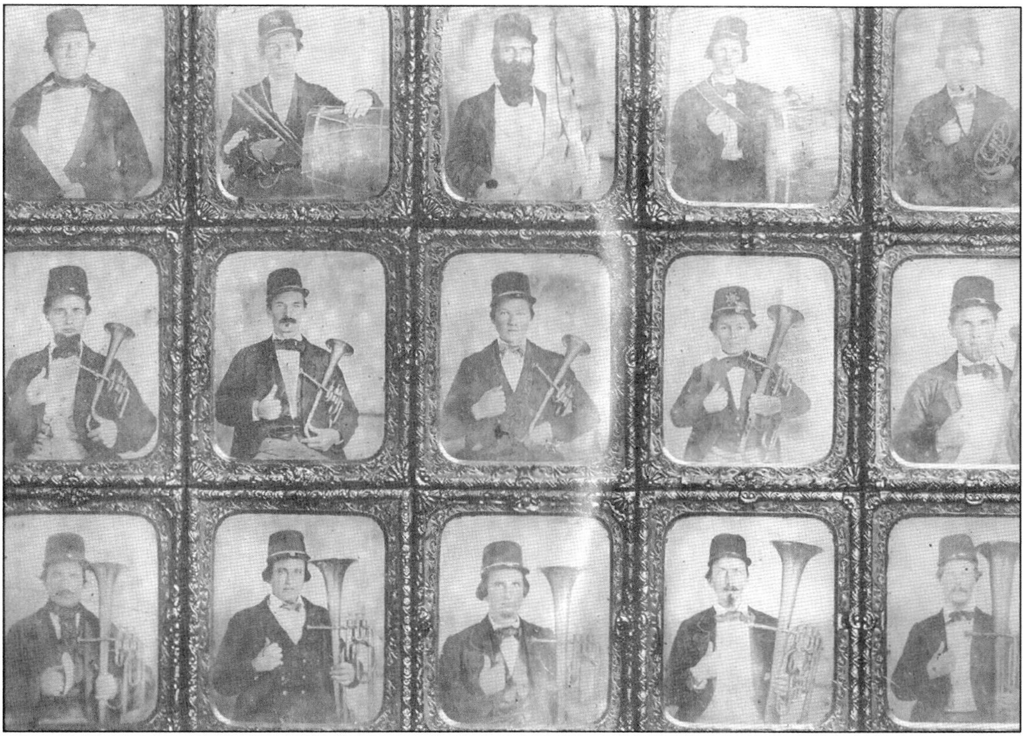

HUNTINGBURG BRASS BAND, 1861. According to Huntingburg historian Loma Hartke, at the time this photograph was taken, most towns and cities didn't have high school bands; instead, they had municipal bands. Pictured here, from left to right, are: (front row) Mike Dittmer, Conrad Hoewener, Louis Krebs, Jacob Fromm, and Henry Mauntel; (second row) Ernst Pickhardt, William Pickhardt, J. F. Meinker, Henry Berger, and Emil Ewig; and (back row) William Helfrich, Moses Bauermeister, Francis Delphus, Chas. Inderieden, and Fred Moenkhaus. (Photograph courtesy of Margaret Rothert Gatling and the Museum of Huntingburg.)

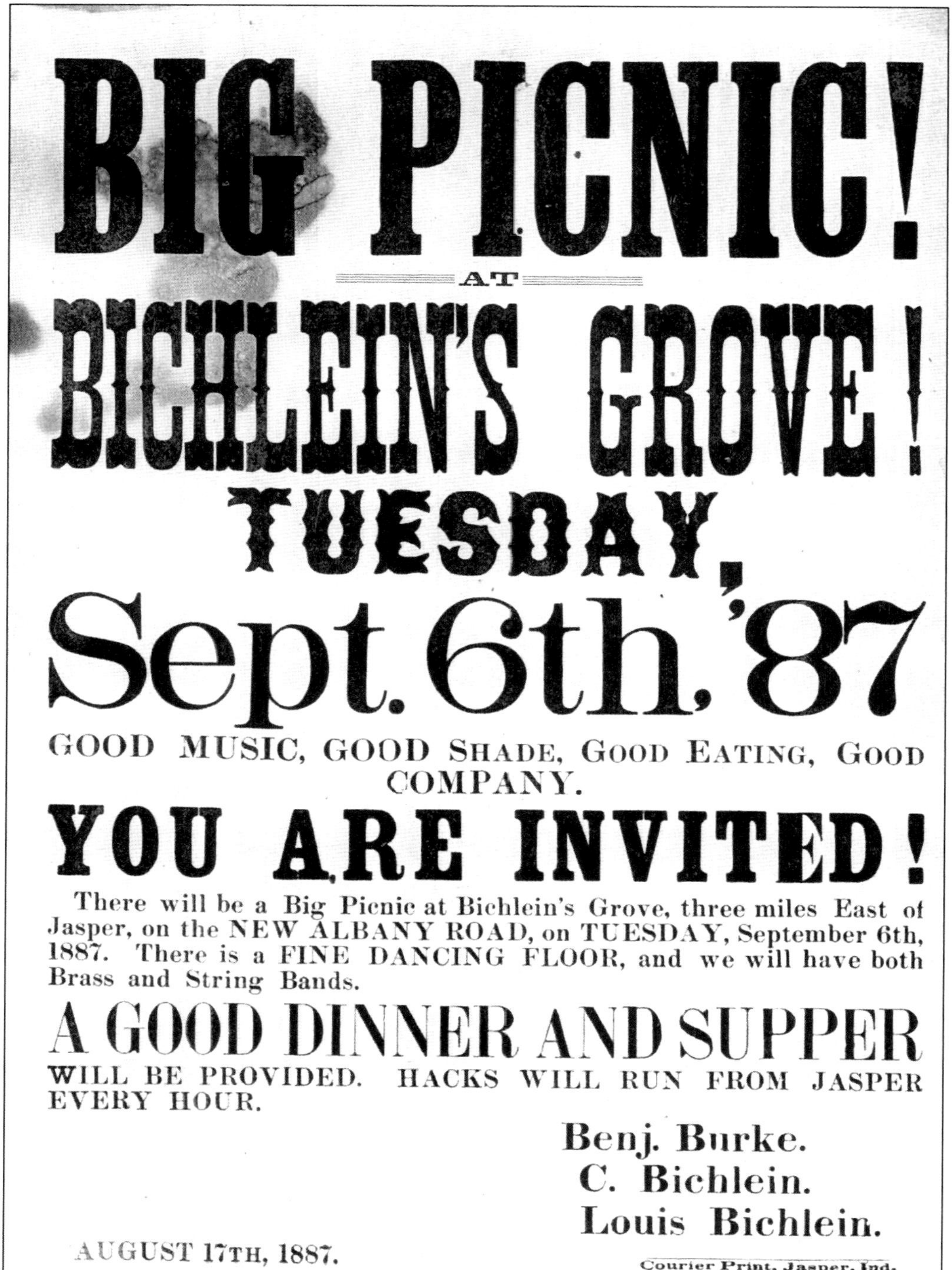

PICNIC ADVERTISEMENT, SEPTEMBER 1887. This was a loose advertisement printed by the *Jasper Courier*, announcing a picnic at Buechlein's Grove, east of Jasper. (Photograph courtesy of Ambrose Buechlein.)

KASTNER HALL DANCE CARD, AUGUST 1894. Shown is 24-year-old Charles Flick's dance card from a Cakewalk and Dance held on August 9, 1894, at Kastner's Opera House at Fourth and Mill Streets in Jasper. The dances had names such as Tucker and Home, York, Varsorianna, Waltz Quadrille, Mazourka, and Redowa. The name entered as dance partner for nearly all of the dances was Katie Schuble, who was only 16 years old at the time. Charles would marry young Katie six months later and would purchase Kastner's Hall within the next ten years. (Photograph courtesy of Lil [Flick] Blemker.)

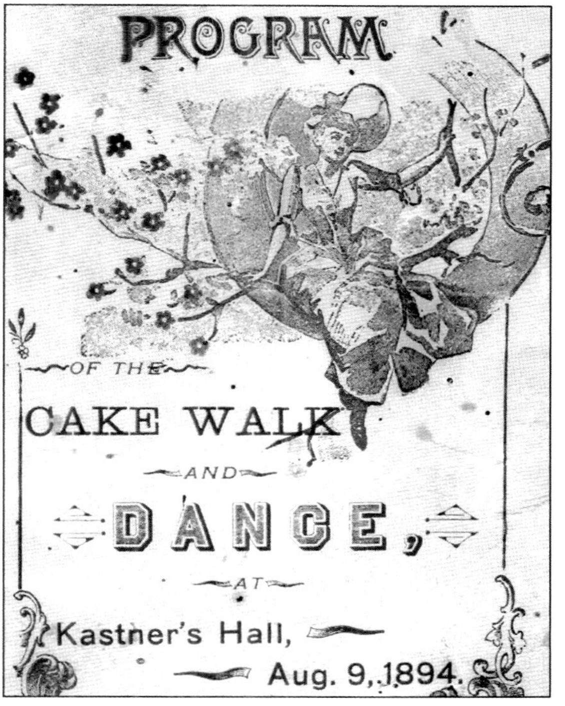

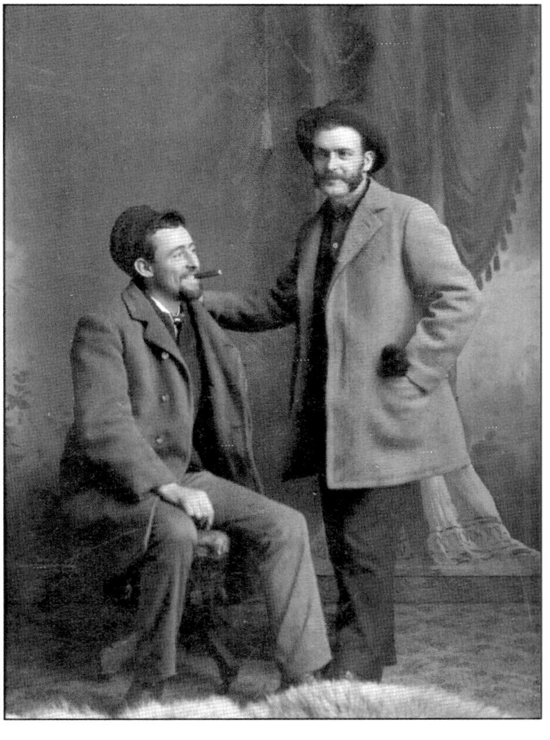

FLICK FRIENDS. Pictured here are two gentlemen friends of Charles and Katie Flick. (Photograph courtesy of Lil [Flick] Blemker.)

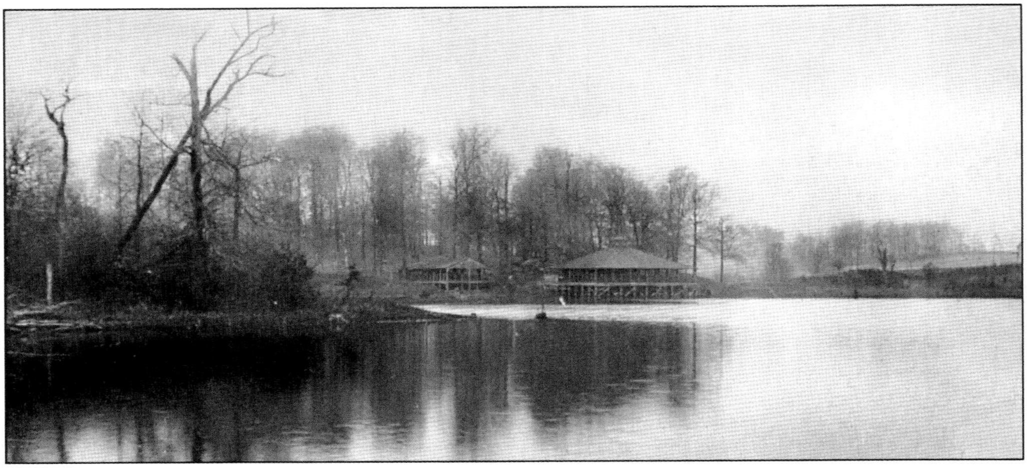

CALUMET LAKE, JASPER, C. 1910. Calumet Lake is located off North Mill Street on Jasper's northeast side. In May 1899, a group of local businessmen chartered the Calumet Lake Corporation for the purposes of creating a man-made lake in Jasper to be used for recreational purposes. Construction of the lake began immediately and was completed the next year. The open air pavilion and other structures were built and motorized boats obtained. The lake became a popular recreation spot throughout the year. In 1916, the lake was drained and the ground became farmland. In 1937, former mayor John Lorey's son, Edward Lorey, who one day would be mayor as well, built a home on the property. Three years later, the lake was re-filled, and a dance hall was erected. Lorey also constructed a hotel on the hill adjacent the lake. In the years that followed, Calumet Lake became a popular entertainment venue. In 1956, Lorey sold the dance hall and lake to Ed and Rosie Rees, who operated the business for many years. (Photograph courtesy of Ron Flick.)

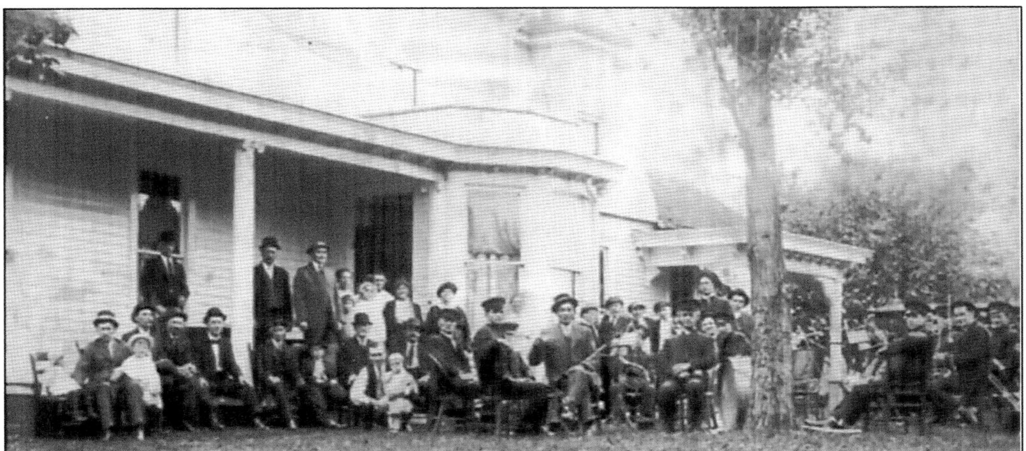

THE STAR BAND AND FRIENDS, JASPER. The Star Band of Jasper entertained at local celebrations and family gatherings. Here they are shown at the William Traylor residence at Seventh and Mill Streets. Philip Kunkel, a neighbor who owned the home to the west, is the man standing third from left. The Traylor home eventually became what is today the Becher-Kluesner Funeral Home. (Photograph courtesy of Jerry Birge and Marlene Bingham.)

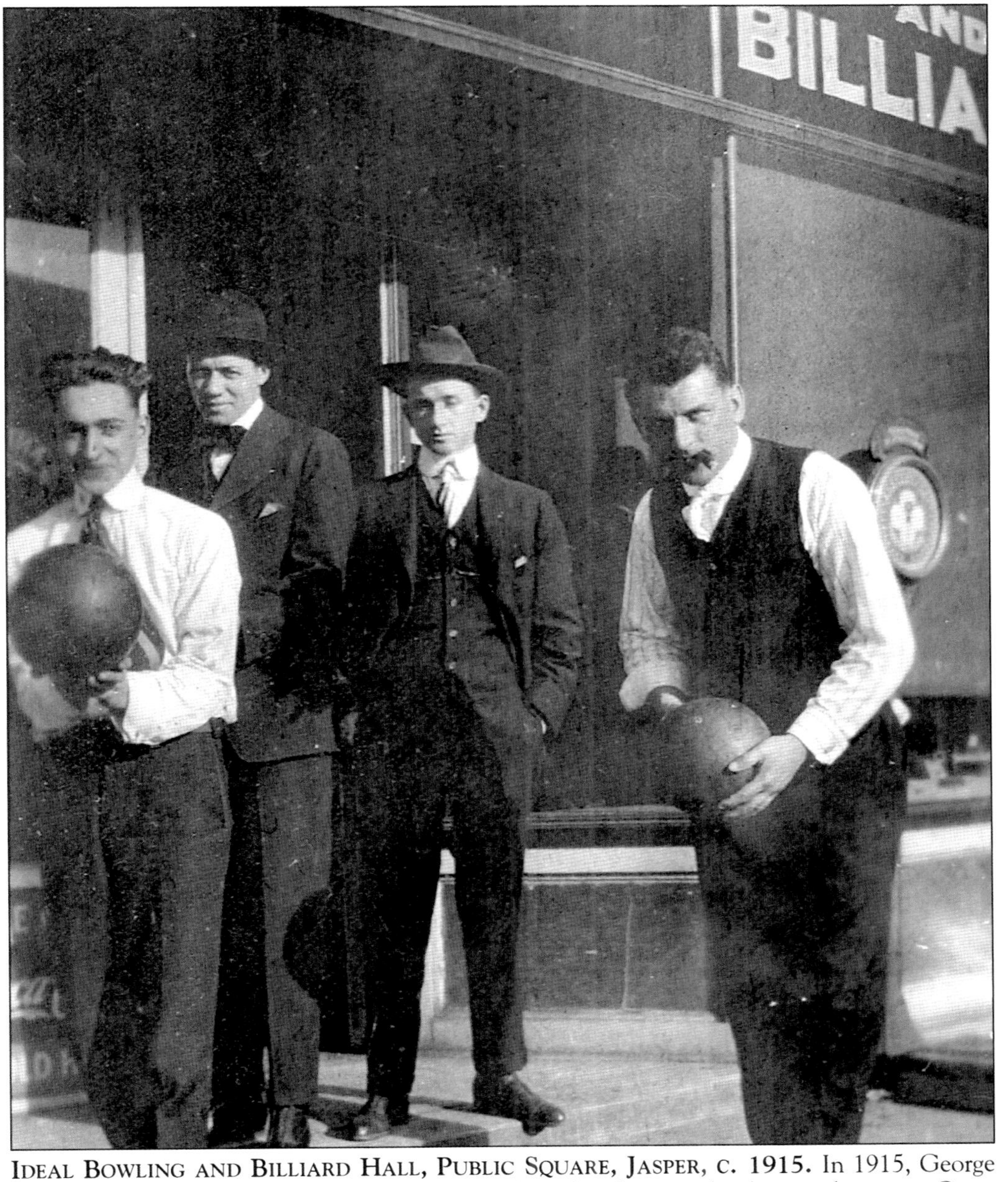

IDEAL BOWLING AND BILLIARD HALL, PUBLIC SQUARE, JASPER, C. 1915. In 1915, George Gerber and A. W. Flick, shown with bowling balls in the photograph, along with partner Omer Kuebler, opened a bowling and billiard hall on the southeast side of the Public Square. The billiard hall occupied the first floor, with the bowling alley located above. After its opening, the building became a raucous gathering place for drinkers and gamblers. A. W. sold his interest in the building in 1918. Eight years later, George converted the building to an automobile showroom and repair shop. In 1935, Henry Buchart and Robert and Edwin Gerber opened the Gerbo Bowling Lanes in the building. From 1946 to the late 1960s, the building was the location of Vic's Appliance Store, after which it housed the central computer system for the Dubois County Bank. In 1982, the building was purchased by the Siebert family and became part of their retail clothing store. (Photograph courtesy of Ron Flick.)

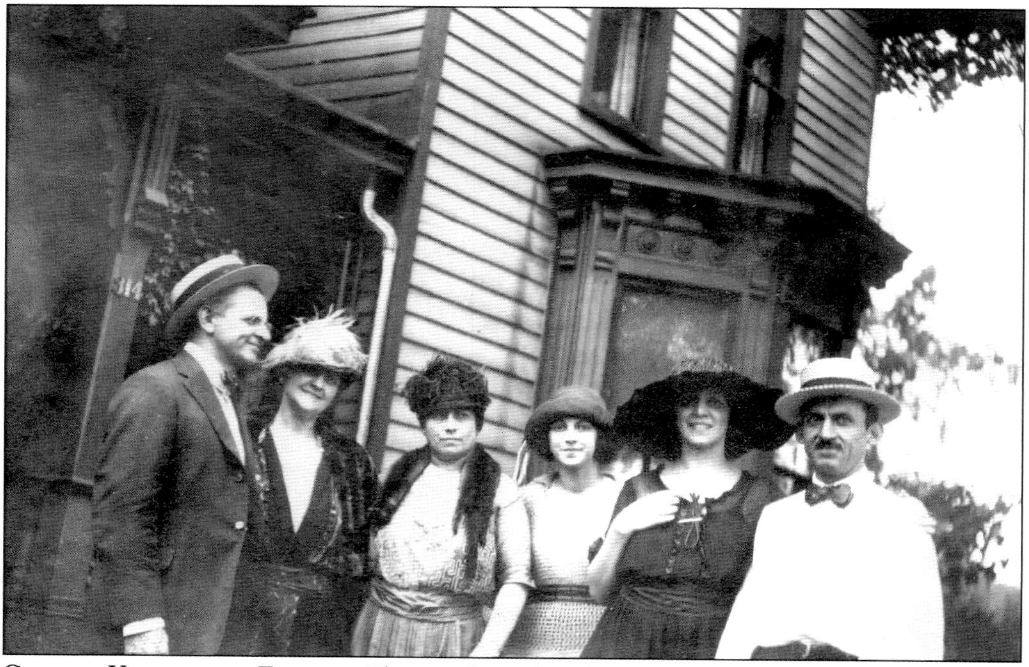

CHARLIE KREMPP AND FRIENDS. The people in this photograph, from left to right, are Charlie Krempp, Minnie, K. Clara, Margaret, Louise, and Conrad. Louise was Charlie's wife. Note that everyone is wearing a hat. (Photograph courtesy of John Fierst.)

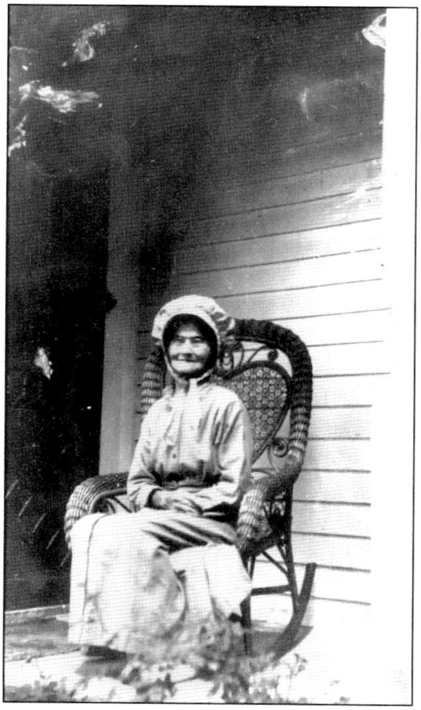

ROSA (ROELLE) FRIEDMAN, C. 1920. Rosa Roelle was born in Luzerne, Switzerland, and immigrated to America with her parents when she was four years old. Rosa married George Friedman in 1858, three years before he entered service during the Civil War. The couple had nine children. They lived on a farm two miles east of Jasper prior to the war, and then after the war, built a beautiful country home west of town, shown in Chapter Eight. After George's death in 1891, Rosa moved to a large residence at Seventh and McCrillus Streets in Jasper. Rosa died in 1925. (Photograph courtesy of John Fierst.)

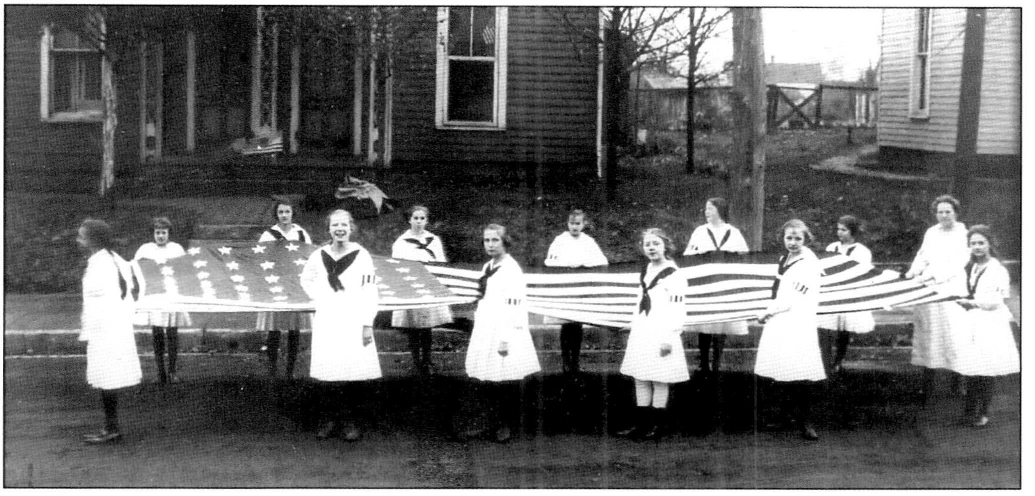

BETSY ROSS CIRCLE, FIRST FLAG DEDICATION, C. 1917. The flag shown was the first to hang from a pole at the intersection of Fourth and Main Streets. Pictured, from left to right, are the following: *(front row)* Alice Dufendach, Margaret (Finke) Cather, Gertrude Renner, Louise Greener, Louise (Strolin) Boyde, Alma (Flein) Hoing; and *(back row)* Frances (Meissner) Mulvey, Marie Lovall, Geneva (Milton) Eishoff, Charlotte Shurig, Helen (Seay) Vogl, Hannah (Uhl) Switzer, and Mrs. Frank Forth. (Photograph courtesy of the Huntingburg Public Library.)

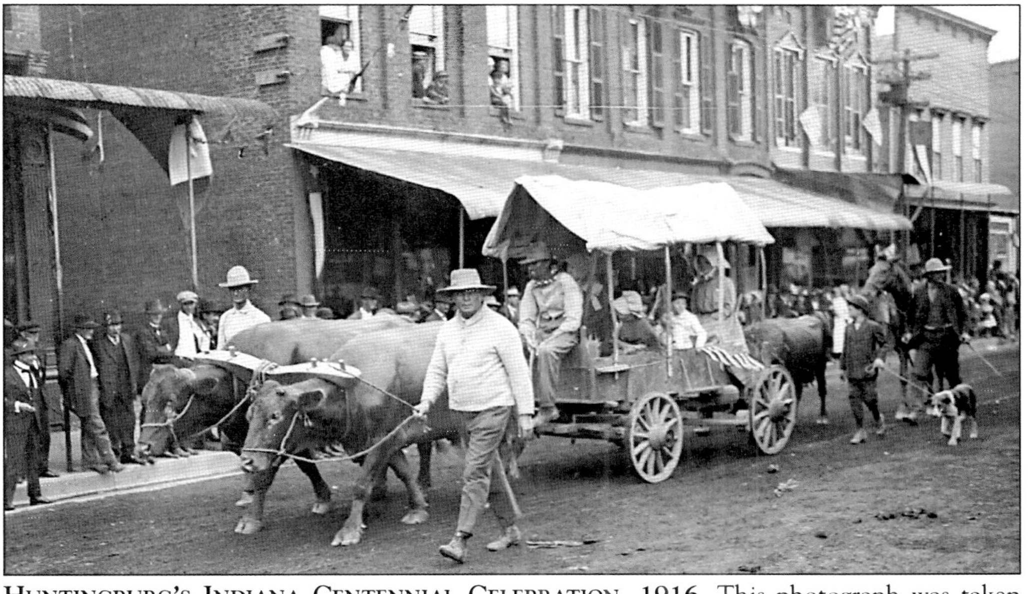

HUNTINGBURG'S INDIANA CENTENNIAL CELEBRATION, 1916. This photograph was taken during a parade celebrating Indiana's Centennial. The view is on Fourth Street. According to the Indiana State Library, the Dubois County Centennial celebration was held September 22, 1916, in Huntingburg. The festivities began with a dance for the gifts of nature in which 350 people participated. The following episodes in history were included in the pageant: "Granting the Vincennes tract of land to the French," "Raising the American flag on Vincennes soil," "the Arrival of the McDonald Family," "the Buffalo Trace Incident," "Dubois receives patent for land," "Last Journey of Captain Dubois," and "Events in the Early History of Dubois County." (Photograph courtesy of the Huntingburg Public Library.)

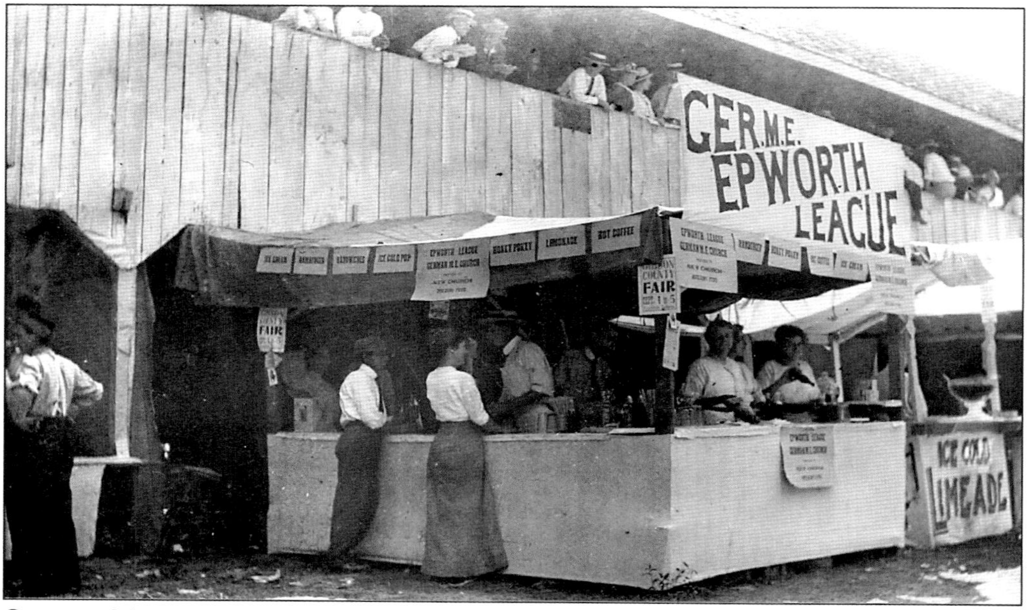

GERMAN METHODIST EPISCOPAL EPWORTH LEAGUE FOOD STAND, 1914. The caption on this photograph reads, "The place to get your Hokey Pokey, 2 for 5." It was taken at the Dubois County Fair on August 13, 1914. According to *Hoosier Vignettes* by R. H. Menke, Herb Meyer sold a flavored sugar ice sandwich served in wax paper at this stand. Menke describes it as a forerunner of the popsicle. (Photograph courtesy of the Huntingburg Public Library.)

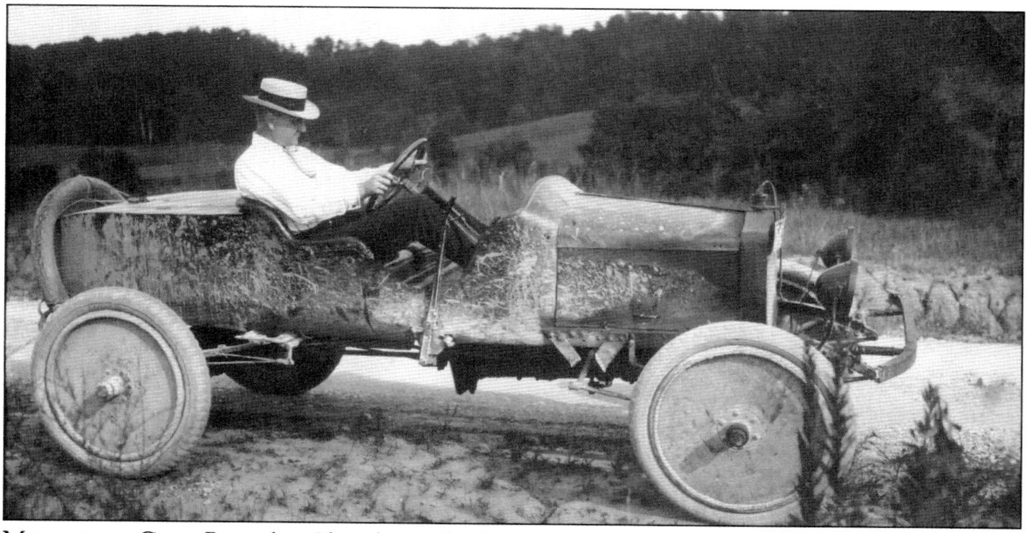

MAN WITH CAR. Romulus Chambers, chief clerk at the Southern Railway station in Jasper, enjoys a spin in his automobile on the muddy roads of Dubois County.

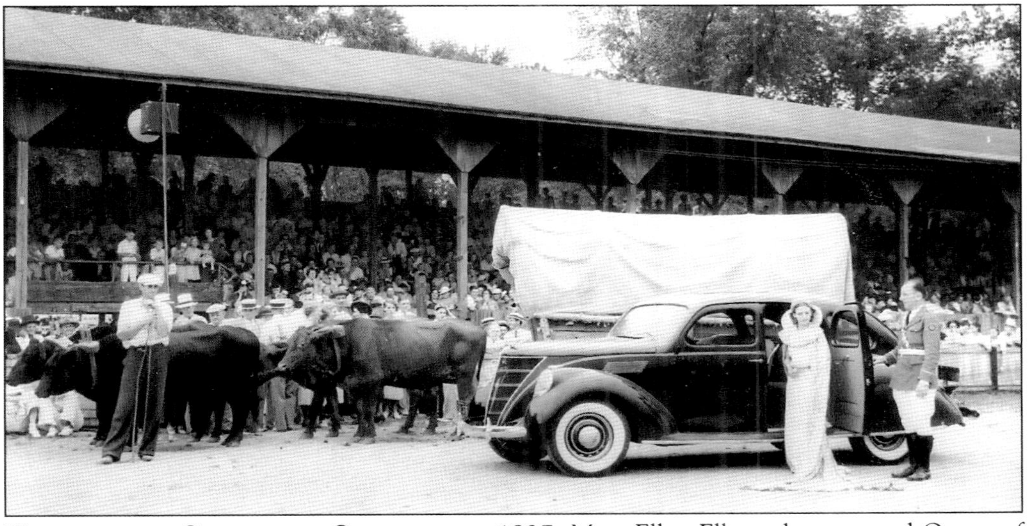

HUNTINGBURG CENTENNIAL CELEBRATION, 1937. Mary Ellen Ellsworth was voted Queen of the Huntingburg Centennial in 1937. Mary Ellen, a 1937 graduate of Huntingburg High School, attended Hanover College in Hanover, Indiana. According to her brother, Tom Ellsworth of Huntingburg, she was one of 14 to be recommended for C.P.T. Flight Training in the fall of 1940 and received her private pilot's license in February 1941. She married Carl Schultz and the couple lived in Huntingburg. Also pictured in the photograph, holding the car door open, is Orville Kemp, who later would be mayor of Huntingburg. Orville is the great-uncle of Gail Kemp, the current mayor of the city. (Photograph courtesy of the Huntingburg Public Library.)

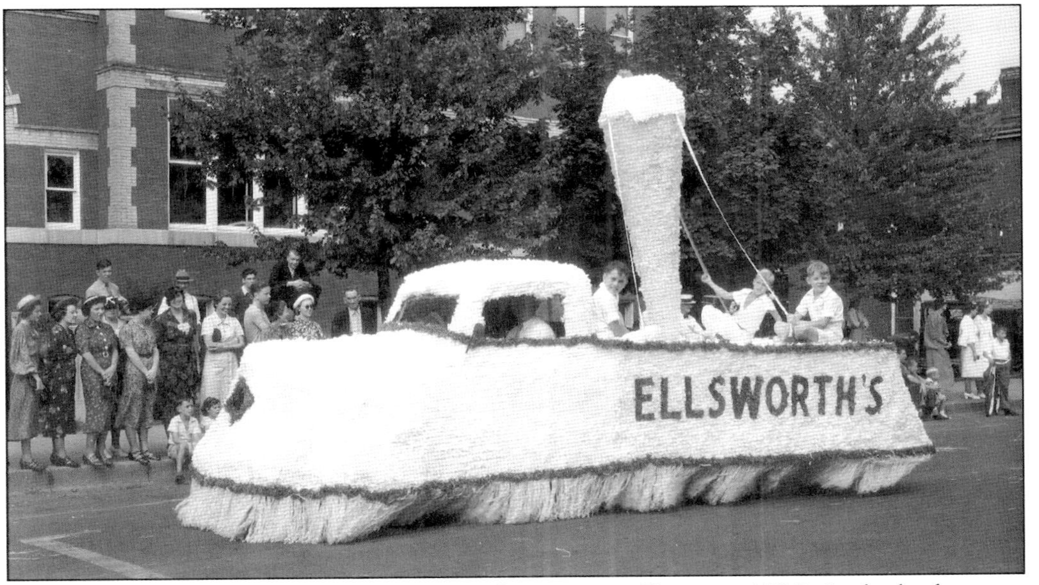

ELLSWORTH DAIRY FLOAT, HUNTINGBURG CENTENNIAL PARADE, 1937. In the back corner is Tom Ellsworth, age 9, who is the brother of Mary Ellen Ellsworth, elected queen of the Centennial. The dark-haired boy in front is Tom's cousin Joe Ellsworth, who was killed while serving his country in World War II, as was Tom's brother, Bill Ellsworth, who went down in his B-24 bomber in 1942 over Hankow, China. The other boy is Joe's brother, Jim Ellsworth. (Photograph and information courtesy of Tom Ellsworth.)

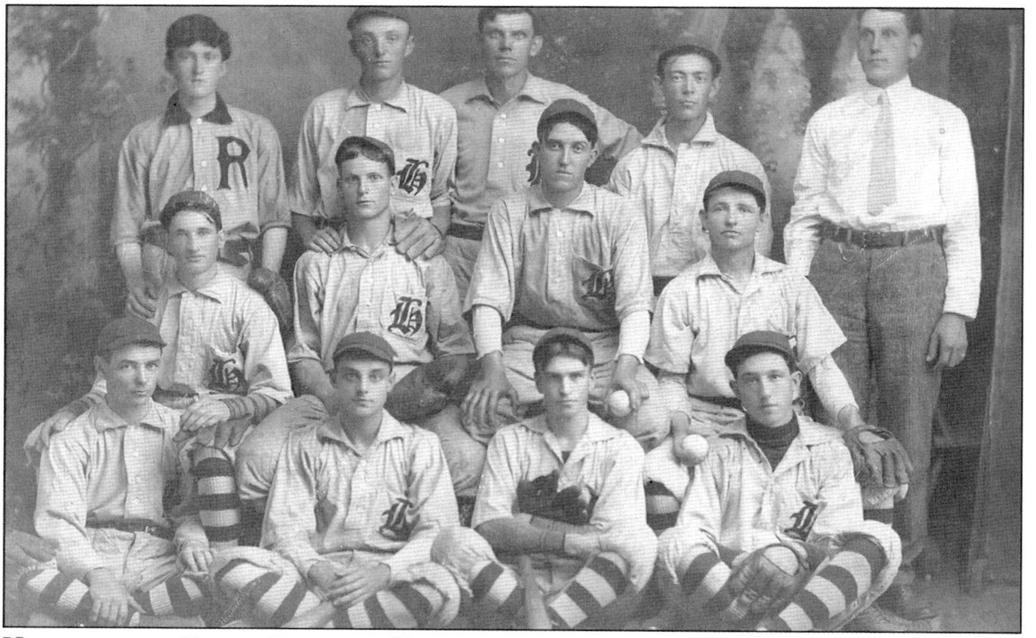

HUNTINGBURG BABIES BASEBALL TEAM, C. 1905. Pictured are the Huntingburg Babies of 1905, champions of Southern Indiana, Kentucky, and Illinois. (Photograph courtesy of the Museum of Huntingburg.)

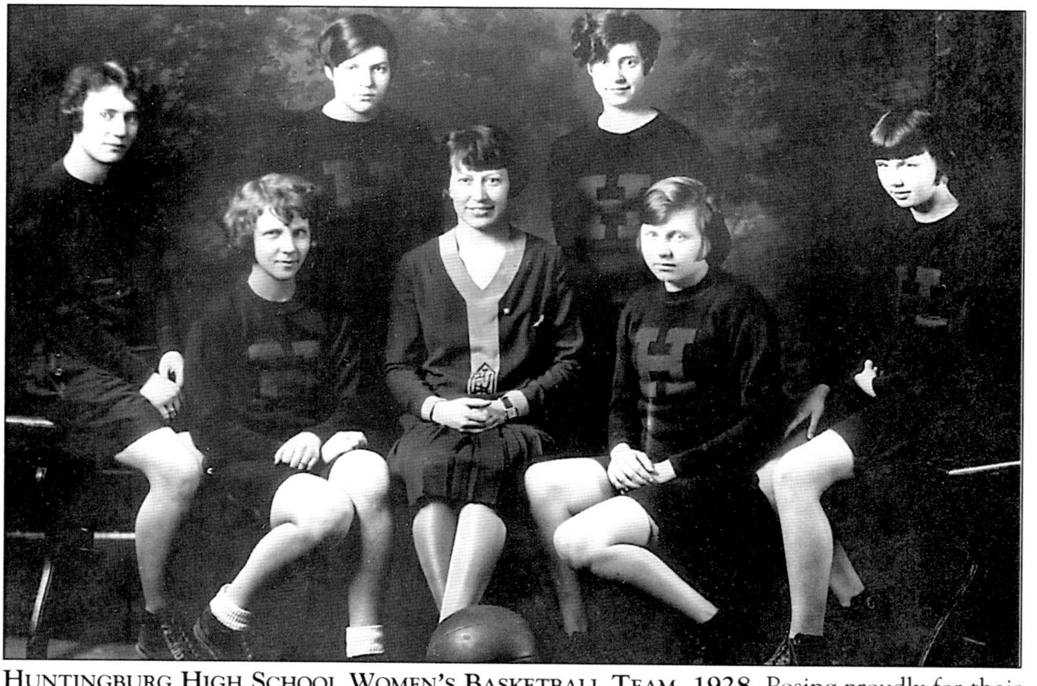

HUNTINGBURG HIGH SCHOOL WOMEN'S BASKETBALL TEAM, 1928. Posing proudly for their team photograph, from left to right, are: *(front row)* Ruth Gerlach, Coach Mildred Douglas, and Louise Statts; and *(back row)* Louanna Niehaus, Lois Helmerich, Martha Hermann, and Vera Katterhenry. (Photograph courtesy of the Huntingburg Public Library.)

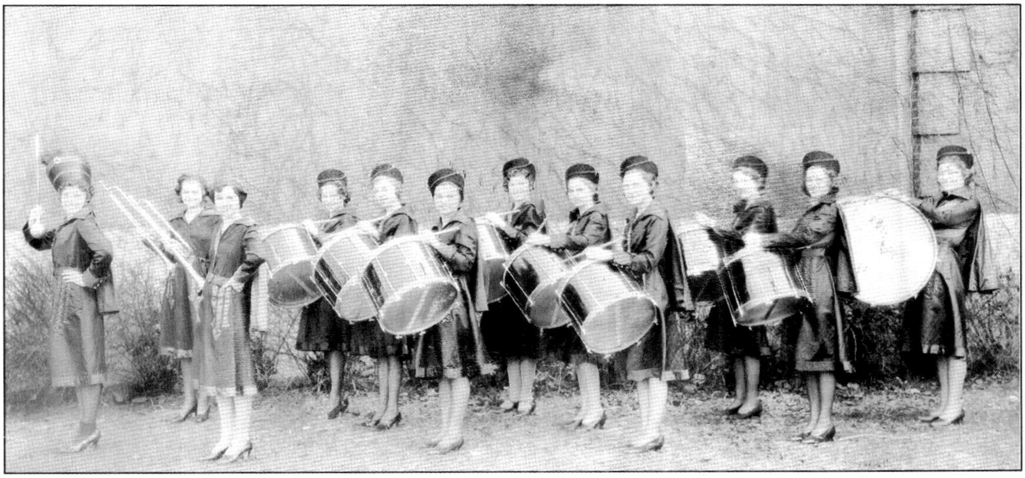

HUNTINGBURG HIGH SCHOOL DRUM CORPS, 1932. Pictured here, from left to right, are: Martha Landgrebe (drum majorette), Thelma Heitman and Vera Rauscher (buglers), O'Dean Rickelman, Frances Milton, Nadine Fink, Louella Ketterhenry, Juanita Goldman, and Marjorie Main (bass drum). (Photograph courtesy of the Museum of Huntingburg.)

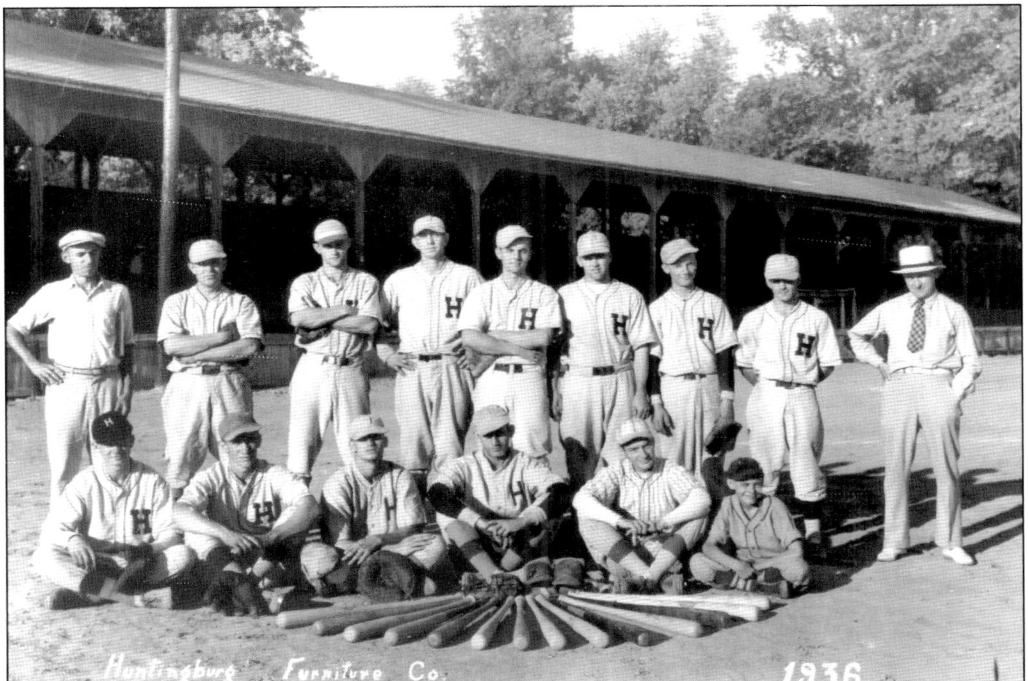

HUNTINGBURG FURNITURE BASEBALL TEAM, 1936. Shown is the Huntingburg Furniture Company baseball squad in 1936. Baseball was big in this part of Indiana, and the Huntingburg's League Stadium, which was built in 1894, has been the backdrop for three Hollywood movies; two of them are *A League of Their Own*, starring Tom Hanks and Madonna, and *Soul of the Game*, a made-for-television movie. But the vintage stadium isn't just a Hollywood prop; baseball is played there each summer. (Photograph courtesy of the Huntingburg Public Library.)

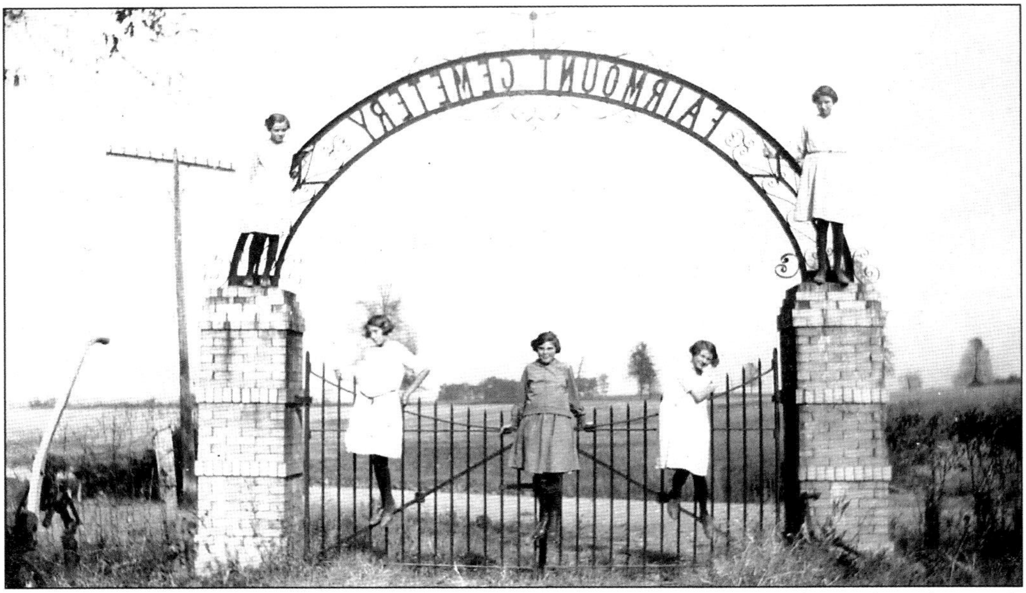

GIRLS PLAYING AT FAIRMOUNT CEMETERY GATE. Fairmount Cemetery, located on the south edge of Huntingburg, features many beautiful monuments and tombs.

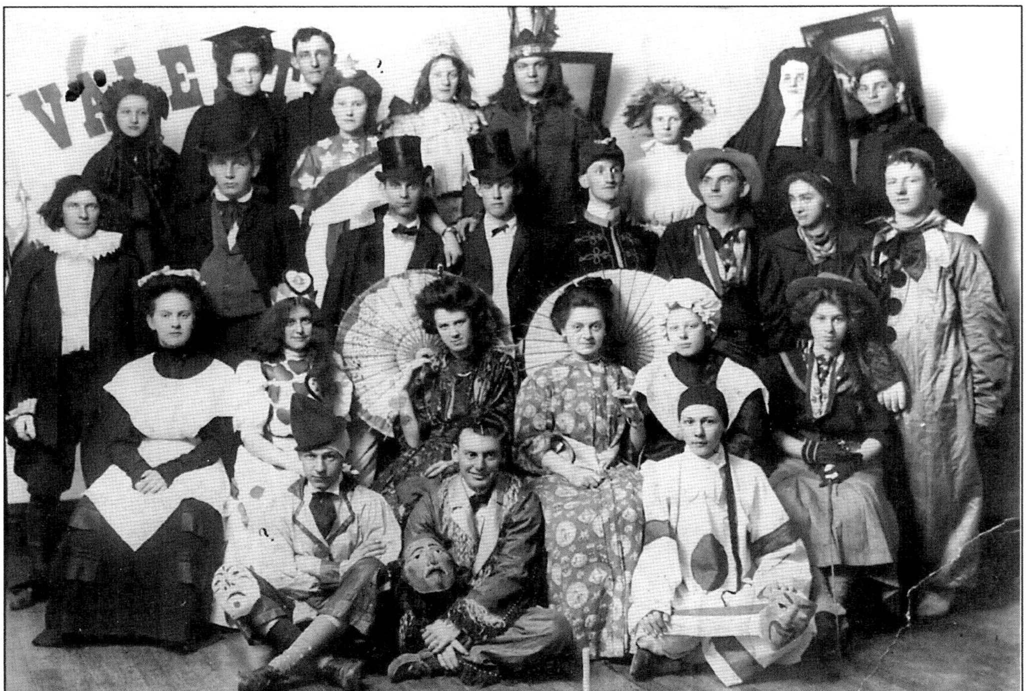

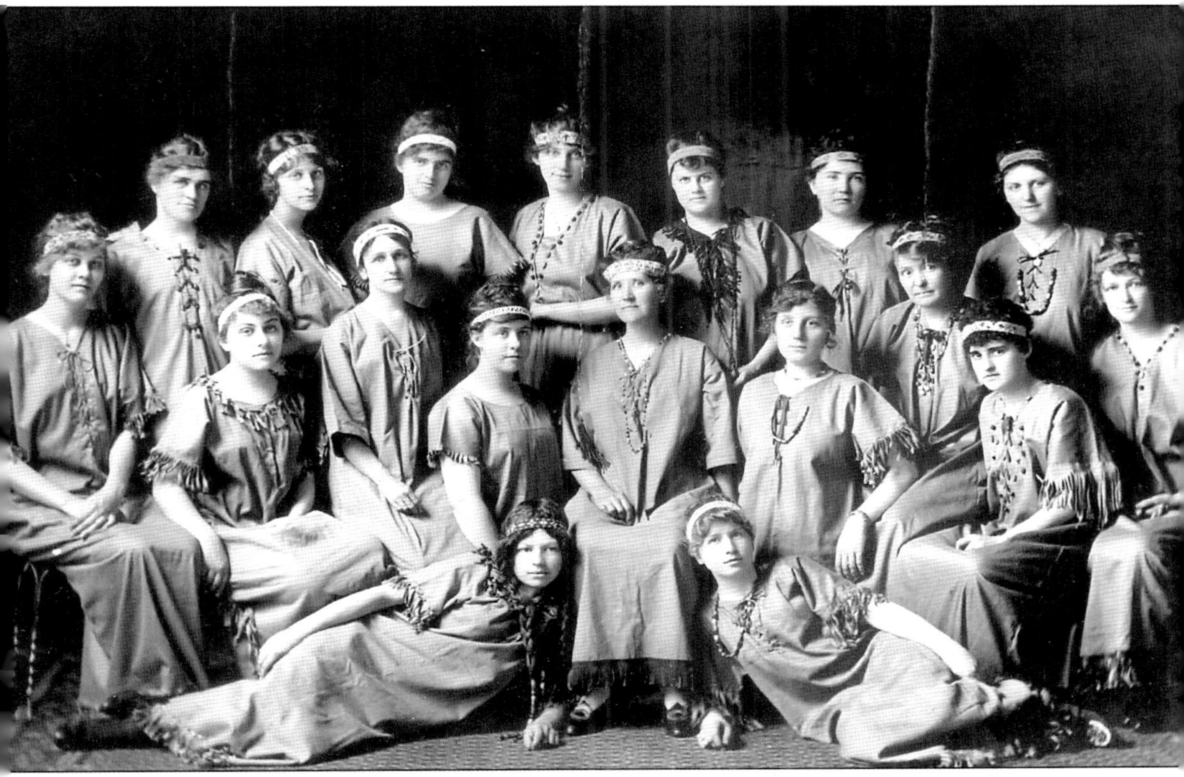

CAMPFIRE GIRLS. The Camfire Girls were not associated with scouting, but rather were affiliated with the fraternal society known as the Improved Order of Red Men. (Photograph courtesy of the Huntingburg Public Library.)

(*opposite, bottom*) **ACIREMA CLUB, 1909.** This photograph was taken during the 1909 Valentine dance of the Huntingburg Acirema Club. Pictured here, from left to right, are: (front row) Hildret Bamberger, Ed Landgrebe, and Edwin Schwartz; (second row) Neil Greenlaw, Lillian Fay, Jessie Thomas, Jessie Greenlaw, August Ginglebach, and Edythe Katterjohn; (third row) Albert Partenheimer, Martin Richard, Carl Koerner, Leslie Selby, Carl Schwartz, Bill Partenheimer, Till Kincehll, and Fred Heich; (fourth row) Beatrice Schwartz, Mabel Schmutzler, and Dalla Pickhardt; and (back row) Grace Williams, John Eggers, Mathilda Gingelbach, Mike Geiss, Amanda Bamberger, and Sam Partenheimer. Acirema is America spelled backwards. (Photograph courtesy of the Huntingburg Public Library.)

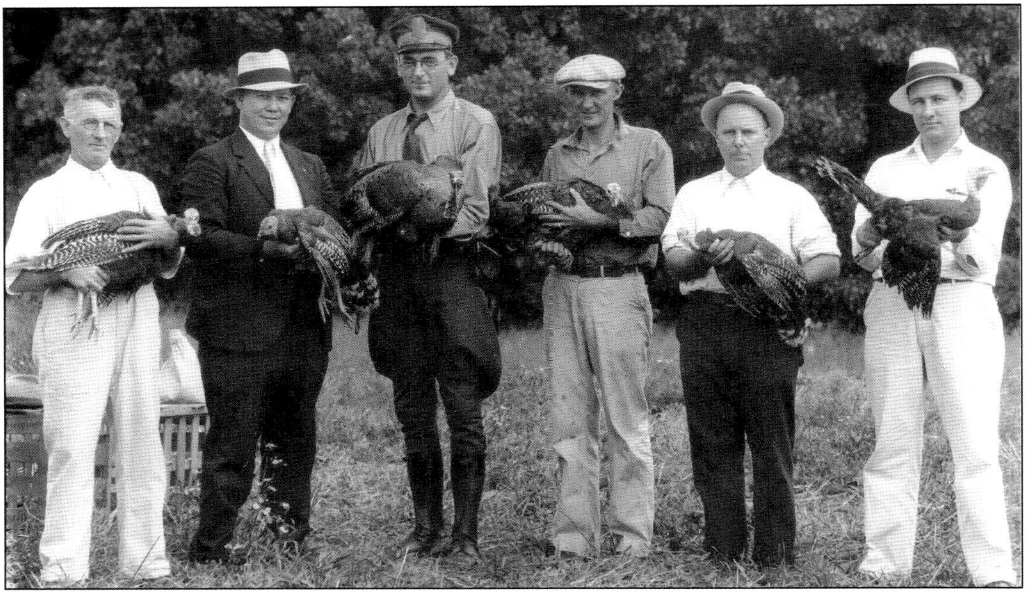

PATOKA ROD AND GUN CLUB, C. 1945. Pictured above, from left to right, are Frank "Jack" Helmerich, Al Woeter, unidentified conservation officer, Jesse Rauscher, Norman Bretz, and Hilbert Schmutzler. These men, holding wild turkeys, were involved with a program to release animals into the wild to perpetuate the species. Other animals released included quail and deer. (Photograph courtesy of the Museum of Huntingburg.)

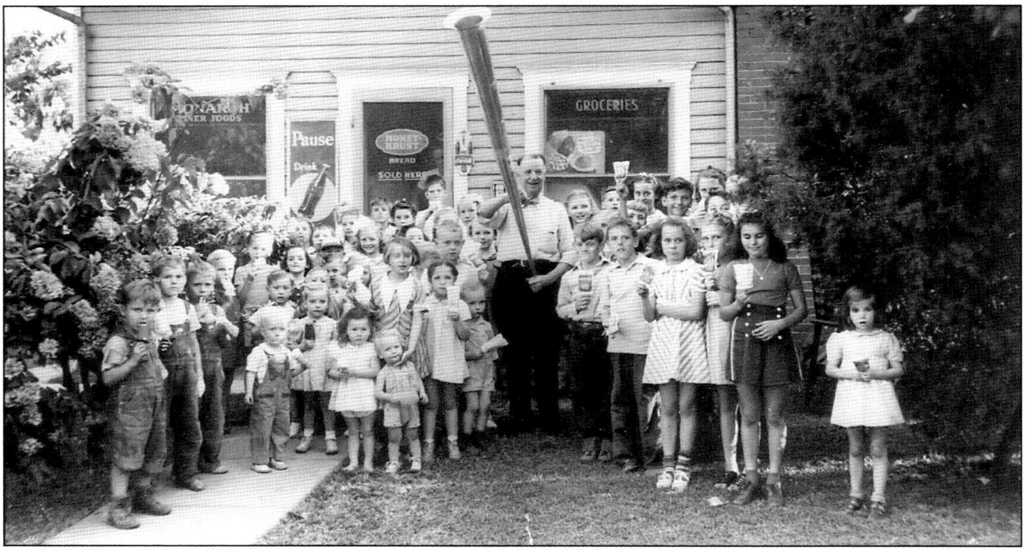

LOUIS POETKER AND ENTOURAGE. Louis Poetker, vice president of the First National Bank, was known as the Pied Piper of Huntingburg. He would often lead the children of Huntingburg down the street as he played his horn and gave away candy. The horn that he is holding can be seen at the Old Town Hall, built in 1886, at 309 North Geiger in Huntingburg. According to Christine Prior, executive director of the Huntingburg Chamber of Commerce, Louis's father owned a grocery store which was located in the building. Today, the Old Town Hall is home to the Huntingburg Chamber of Commerce. (Photograph courtesy of the Huntingburg Public Library.)

Eight

HOME SWEET HOME

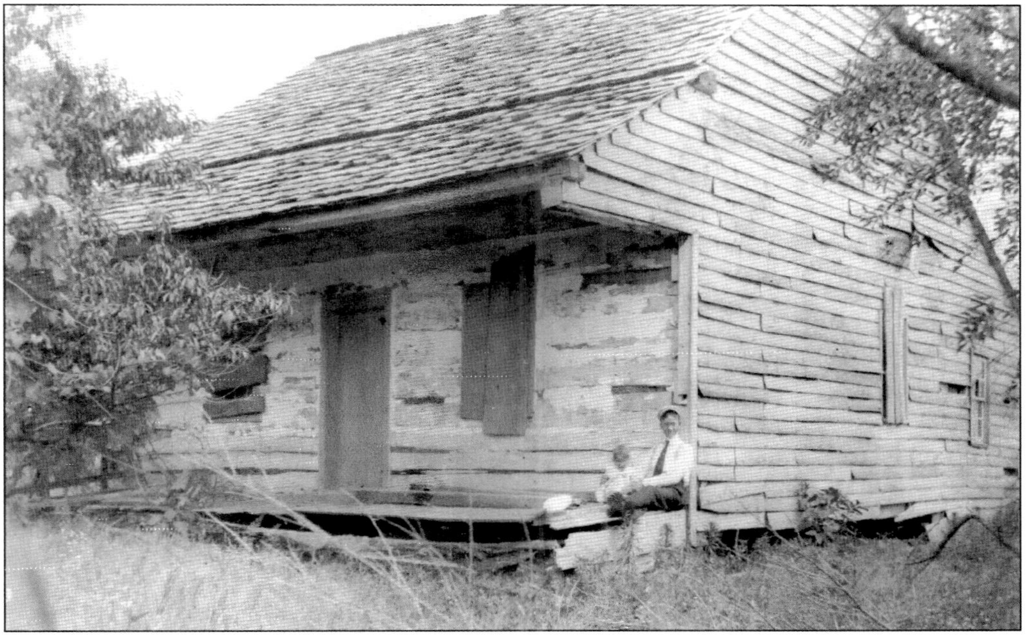

FRIEDMAN LOG CABIN, JASPER, C. 1900. The Joseph and Mary Friedman family of Ulm, Baden, was one of many early pioneer German families from the Wagshurst, Baden, area to settle in Jasper. County records indicate that Joseph purchased land east of Jasper in 1837, after having previously lived in Pennsylvania and Ohio. The family's German-style log cabin home, which featured a cantilevered, non-supported front porch roof, was located near what is now 330 South Meridian Road. The Friedmans were the parents of nine children. Three sons, Martin, Joseph M., and George, became prominent Jasper businessmen. Martin Friedman was the second owner of the Indiana Hotel at Fifth and Jackson Streets and a tobacco dealer; he also operated a drug store for many years. George and the younger Joseph were involved in the early woodworking industry in Jasper, owning several mills. The photograph, taken many years after the log cabin was built, shows two young boys, identified as Louis and Harold. It was published in the *Jasper Herald* on September 19, 1902, accompanying a lengthy article about the Friedman family. (Photograph courtesy of John Fierst.)

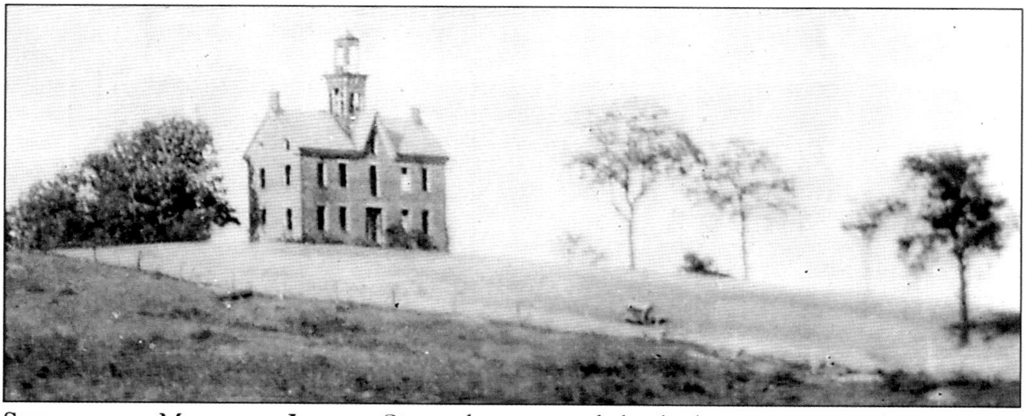

STEPHENSON MANSION, JASPER. Situated on one of the highest points on the northeast side of Jasper, the Stephenson Mansion held a commanding view of the young town when it was constructed in 1881. The *Jasper Courier* described it in glowing terms: "It is one of the handsomest and most substantial residences in Southern Indiana, and is an evidence of the growing taste and culture of the community. It contains 12 large and pleasant rooms and is surmounted by an observatory, from which a scope of country miles in extent can be seen." Dr. Edward Stephenson, the owner, was born in 1823 and came to Dubois County in 1845 to practice medicine. His wife, the former Missouri Edmonston, was the daughter of one of Jasper's earliest pioneer settlers, B. B. Edmonston. Dr. Stephenson not only practiced medicine, but was also the Dubois County Treasurer for five terms. (Photograph courtesy of John Fierst.)

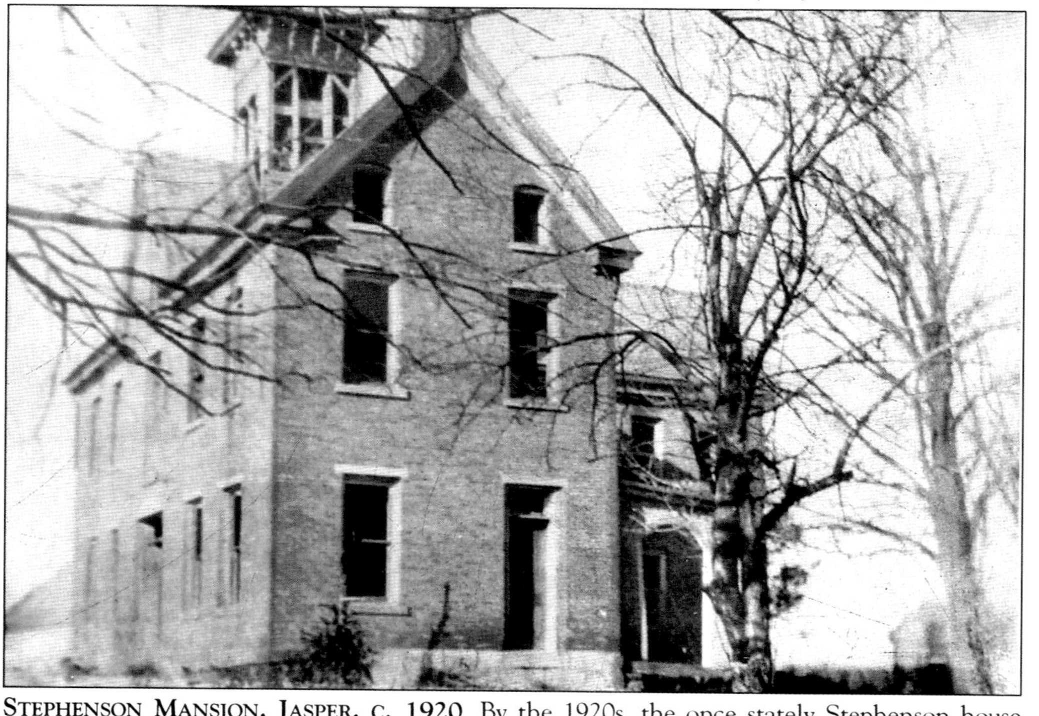

STEPHENSON MANSION, JASPER, C. 1920. By the 1920s, the once stately Stephenson house had been abandoned for some years and the residence was finally demolished by property owner Joseph Gutzweiler, who utilized some of the building's bricks in the construction of the Gutzweiler Building/Tivoli Theater on the Public Square in 1924. (Photograph courtesy of John Fierst.)

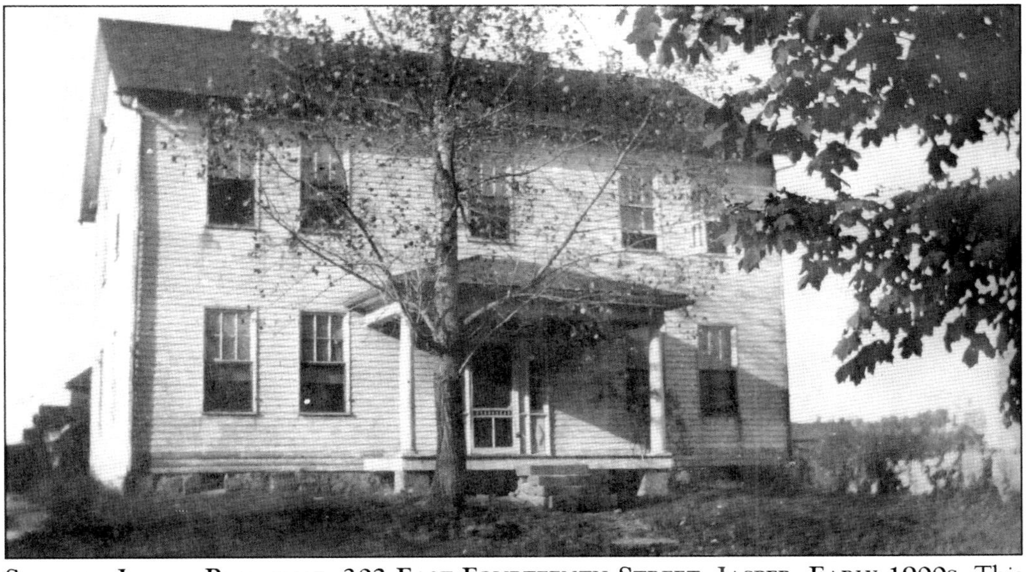

STRIEGEL-JERGER RESIDENCE, 302 EAST FOURTEENTH STREET, JASPER, EARLY 1900S. This simple two-story frame residence once stood on the northeast corner of Fourteenth and Jackson Streets. A brick duplex currently occupies the lot. (Photograph courtesy of John Fierst.)

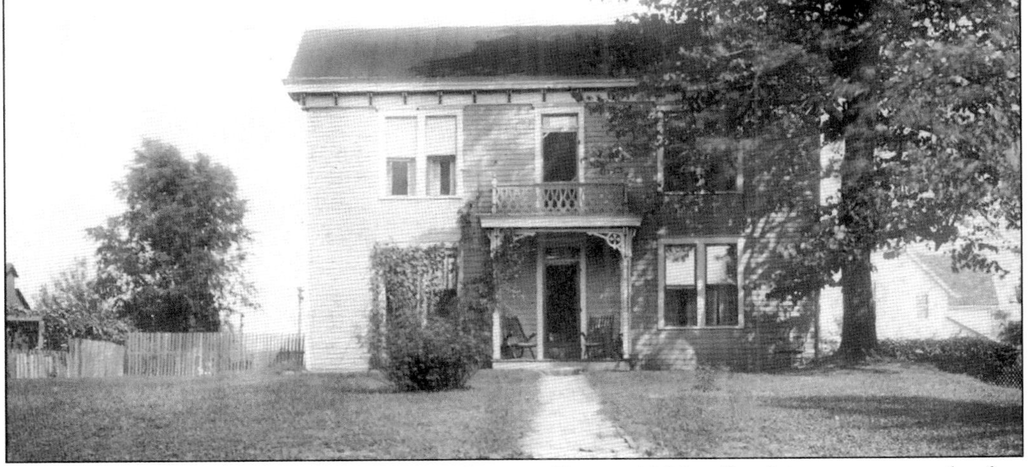

RESIDENCE, TENTH AND MAIN STREETS, JASPER, EARLY 1900S. On this property sat the first Sisters of Providence convent. The house in the photograph was built in the late 1800s, perhaps by Joseph Friedman Sr. Gustave Gramelspacher and his first wife lived in the home, followed by Conrad Marks and Joseph Sturm. Both Gramelspaher and Sturm later built grander residences on lots adjacent to this home. (Photograph courtesy of John Fierst.)

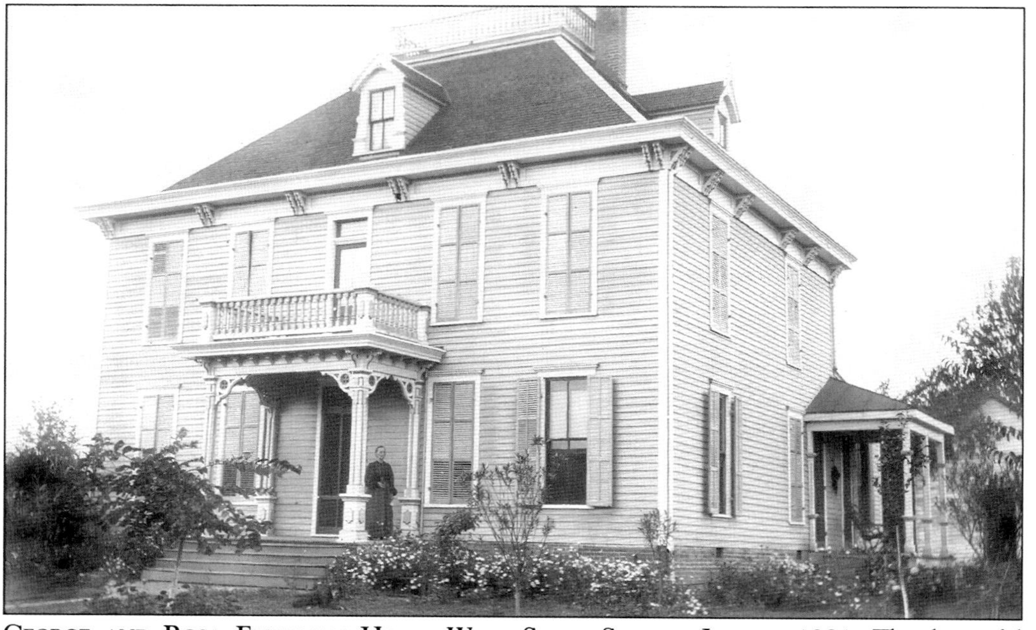

GEORGE AND ROSA FRIEDMAN HOME, WEST SIXTH STREET, JASPER, 1891. This beautiful country home was built by George and Rosa (Roelle) Friedman on the western outskirts of town, beyond the "Y" in Jasper, on what was then called the Petersburg Road. After George's death in 1891, Andrew Kremp, the local soft drink manufacturer, purchased the home and 40 acres for $2,500. The house was torn down many years ago. (Photograph courtesy of John Fierst.)

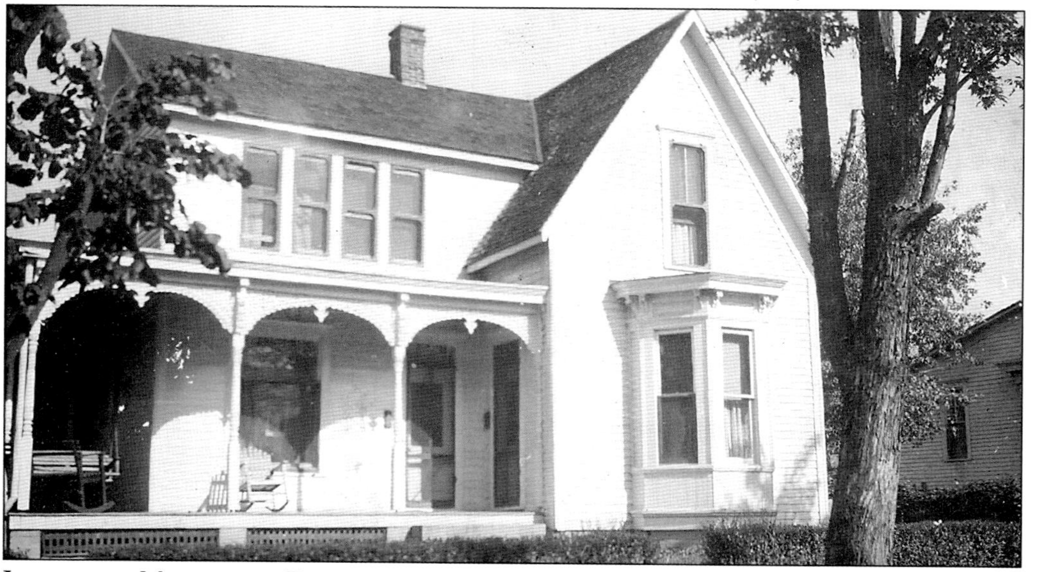

JOSEPH AND MAGDALENA FRIEDMAN HOME, EAST SIXTH STREET, JASPER, C. 1920. This home was built in 1884 by Joseph and Magdalena (Krempp) Friedman, two years after their marriage. The lot cost $65, while the home cost $750. Joseph was the son of George and Rosa Friedman. In his early years, Joseph was bookkeeper for the family's mill business. The photograph of the home was taken many years after the Friedmans had moved out. The residence was home to a number of other families before its demolition. (Photograph courtesy of John Fierst.)

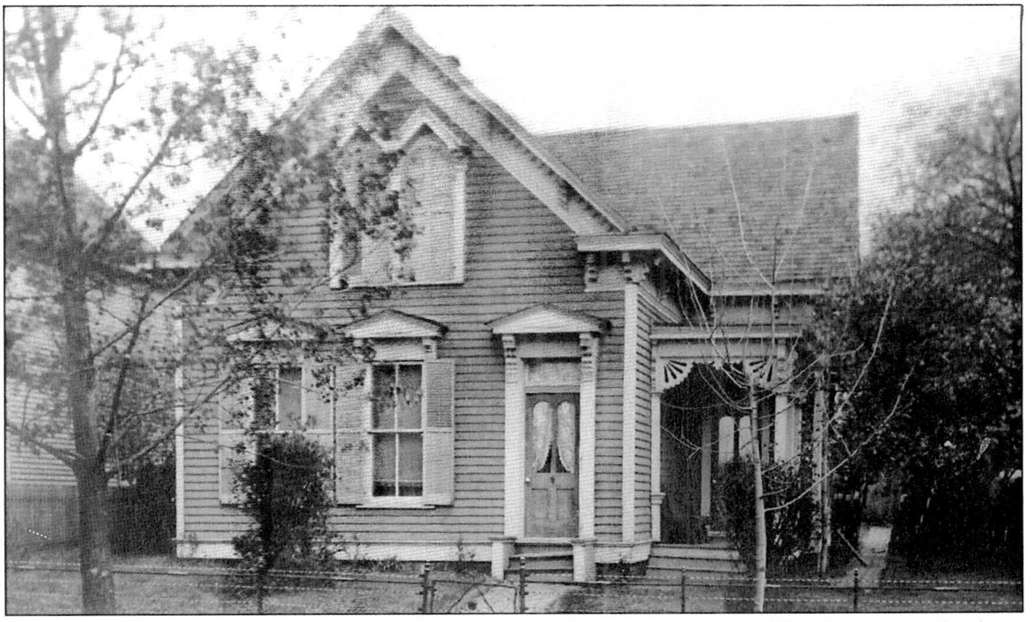

STOUT-FRIEDMAN RESIDENCE, 712 MILL STREET, JASPER, C. 1900. This home was built in the mid-1880s by John Stout, a partner in the Gramelspacher and Stout Planing Mill. In 1890, Joseph and Magdalena (Krempp) Friedman bought the Stout residence for $1,100 and lived there for only two years, until their large, two-story home was built at Sixth and Mill Streets. For many years, the residence was home to the Hoffman family. Later, it became the Gallery framing shop. The house was restored in the mid-1990s by Ron and Debbie Flick. Today, it is the office for Big Brothers-Big Sisters of Dubois County. (Photograph courtesy of John Fierst.)

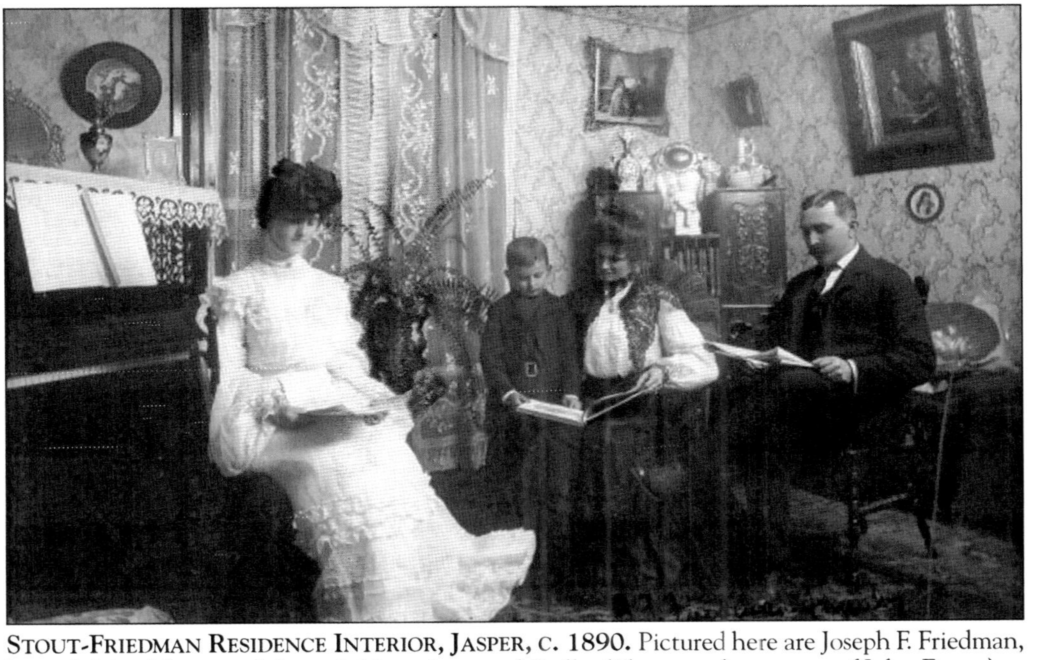

STOUT-FRIEDMAN RESIDENCE INTERIOR, JASPER, C. 1890. Pictured here are Joseph F. Friedman, his wife Magdalena, and their children, Ivan and Stella. (Photograph courtesy of John Fierst.)

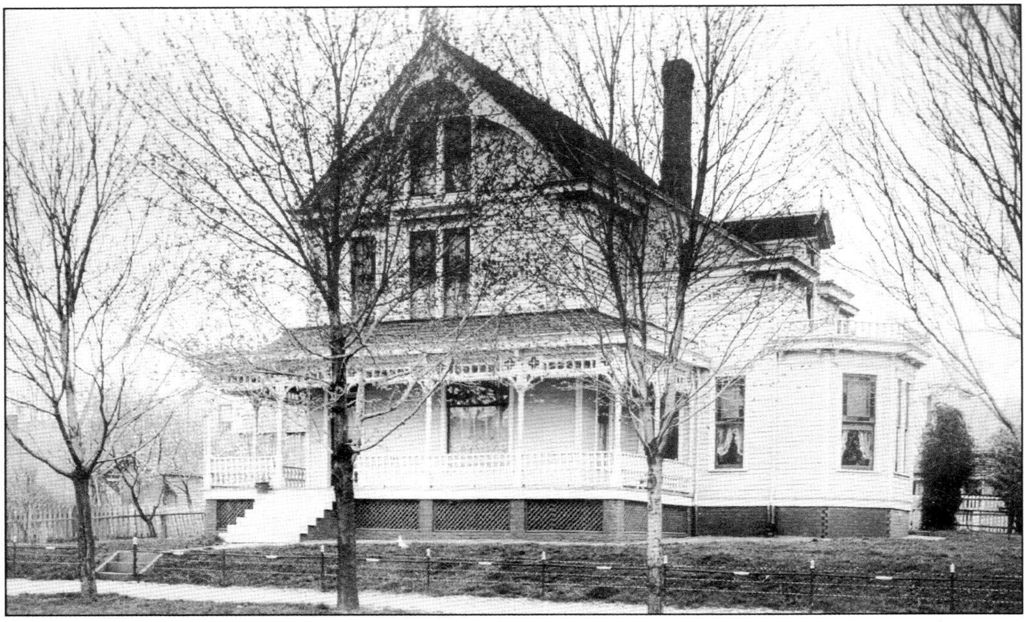

JOSEPH AND MAGDALENA FRIEDMAN RESIDENCE, EAST SIXTH, JASPER, C. 1905. Shown is the Joseph and Magdalena (Krempp) Friedman home on the northwest corner of Sixth and Mill Streets, constructed in 1892. The Friedmans' two previous residences are shown on the preceding pages. This house was torn down in the early 1960s and replaced by a drive-in bank branch. (Photograph courtesy of John Fierst.)

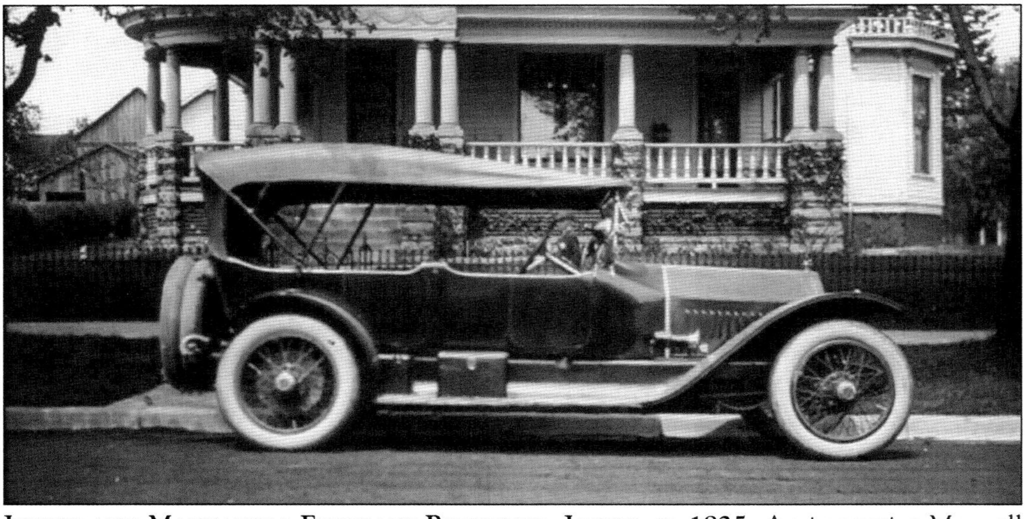

JOSEPH AND MAGDALENA FRIEDMAN RESIDENCE, JASPER, C. 1925. An impressive Maxwell automobile sits parked in front of the handsome Friedman residence on East Sixth Street. In the background can be seen the stone porch, added to the home in 1909 by master architect and stone mason, Michael Durlauf. (Photograph courtesy of John Fierst.)

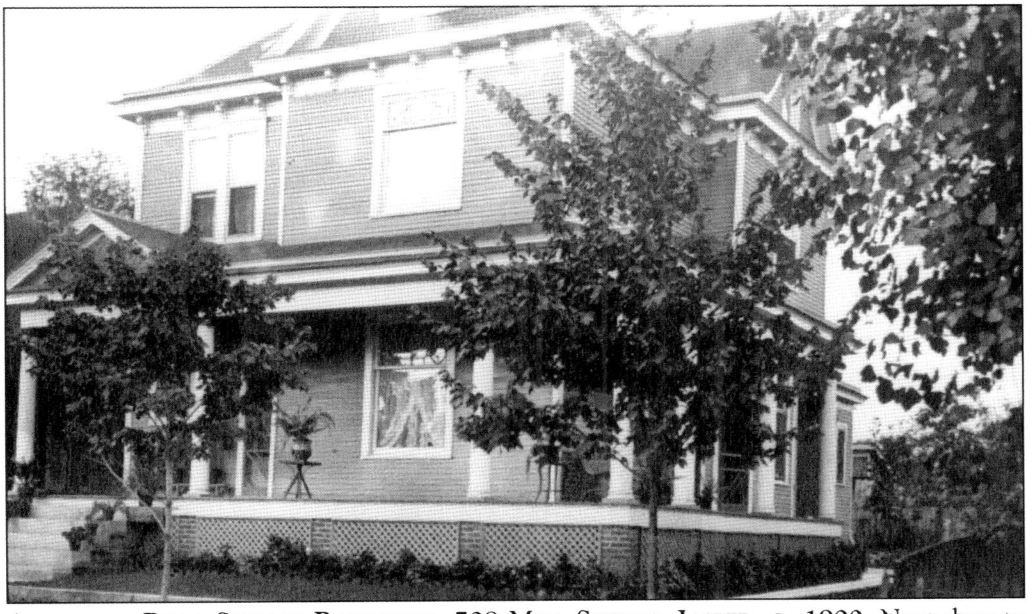

Alois and Rosa Schaaf Residence, 708 Mill Street, Jasper, c. 1900. Next door to the Stout-Friedman residence, shown on the previous page, is the Alois Schaaf residence, constructed in 1907. The house is still standing, but the porch has been modified and aluminum siding obscures much of the nice woodwork. (Photograph courtesy of Ron Flick.)

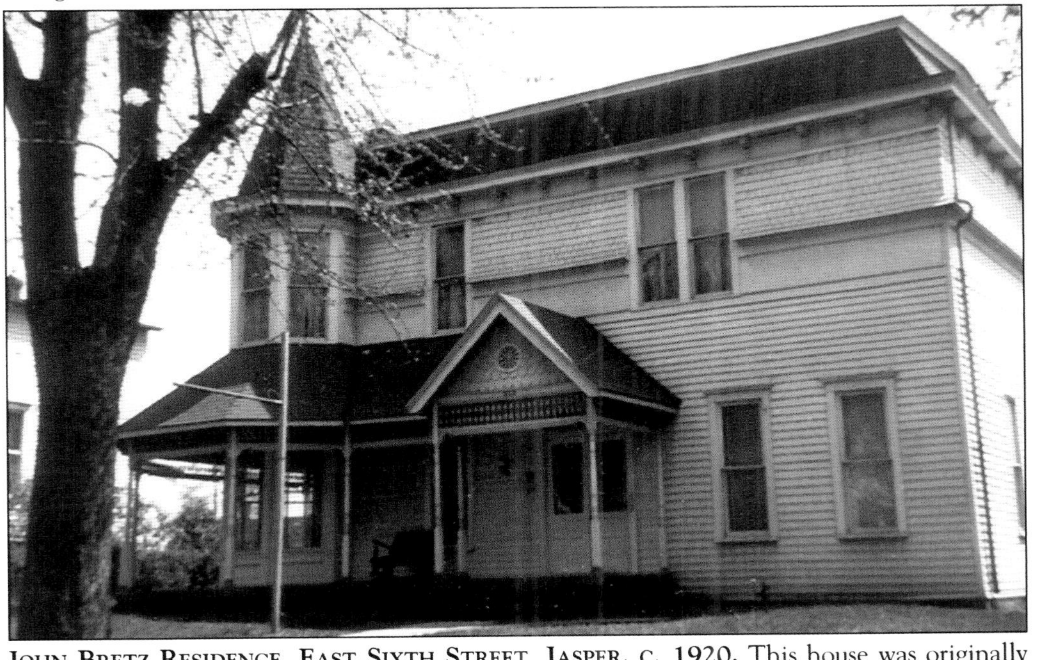

John Bretz Residence, East Sixth Street, Jasper, c. 1920. This house was originally built in 1881 as a one-story home for the John Bretz family. The home was enlarged in 1893 with the addition of the second floor, tower, and wrap-around porch. Unfortunately, the home has been demolished and the site is now the location of the Jasper police and fire station. (Photograph courtesy of John Fierst.)

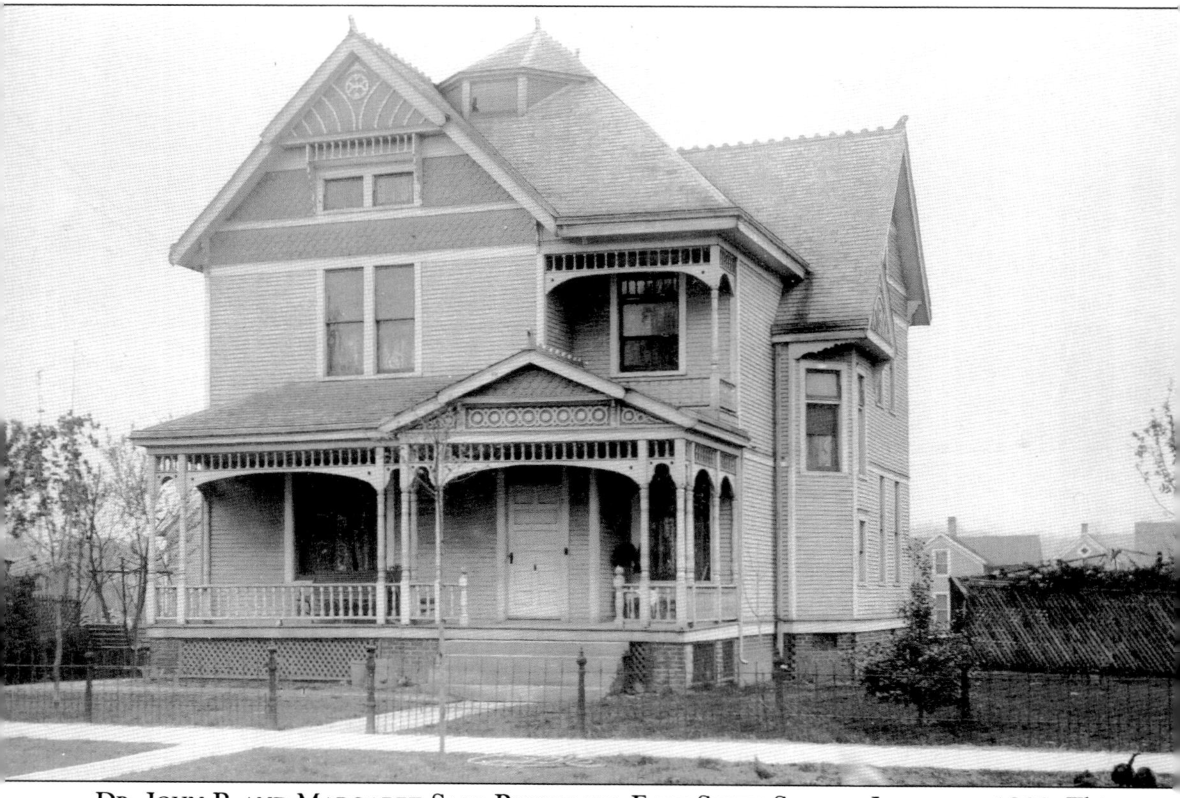

Dr. John P. and Margaret Salb Residence, East Sixth Street, Jasper, c. 1900. This residence was built in the year 1900 by local physician, J. P. Salb. Dr. Salb graduated from the Medical College of Indiana at Indianapolis in 1880 and set up practice in Schnellville, where he met and married Margaret Betz. The couple moved to Jasper in 1885, where, in addition to his medical practice, he ran a drug store for a number of years. Dr. Salb had a large family and, according to Jasper historian John Fierst, at least five of them became doctors. Unfortunately, this beautiful house is no longer standing. (Photograph courtesy of John Fierst.)

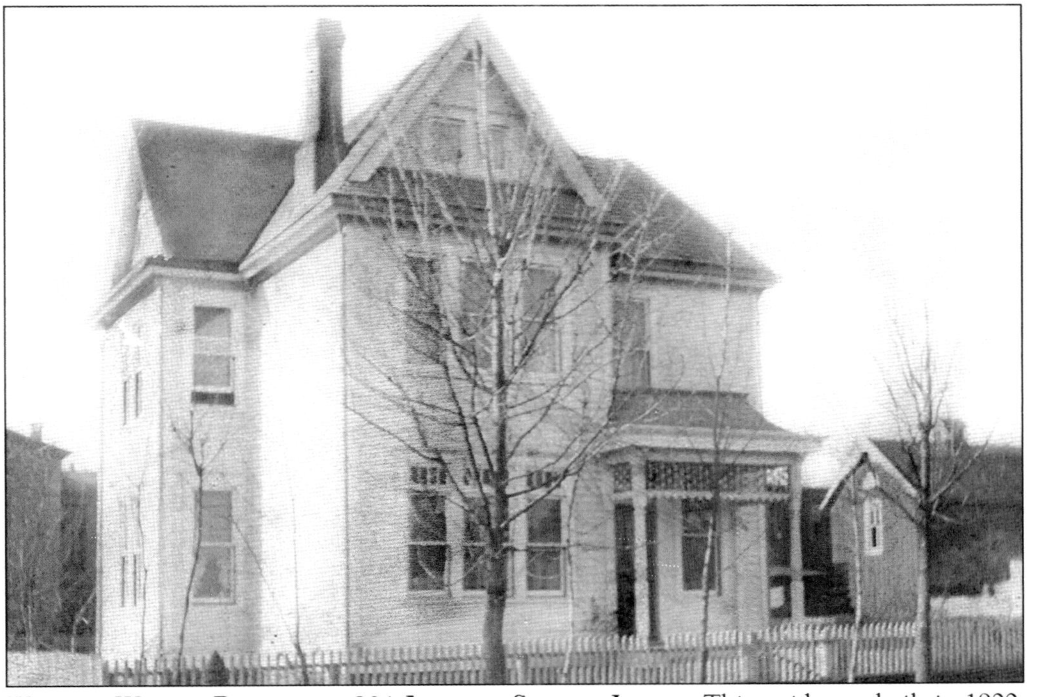

William Wilson Residence, 801 Jackson Street, Jasper. This residence, built in 1900, sat on the lot where Wilson's Flowers is now located. In the background is the William Krodel Building, on Main Street, and the barn/garage behind the Andrew Berger residence on Ninth Street. (Photograph courtesy of John Fierst.)

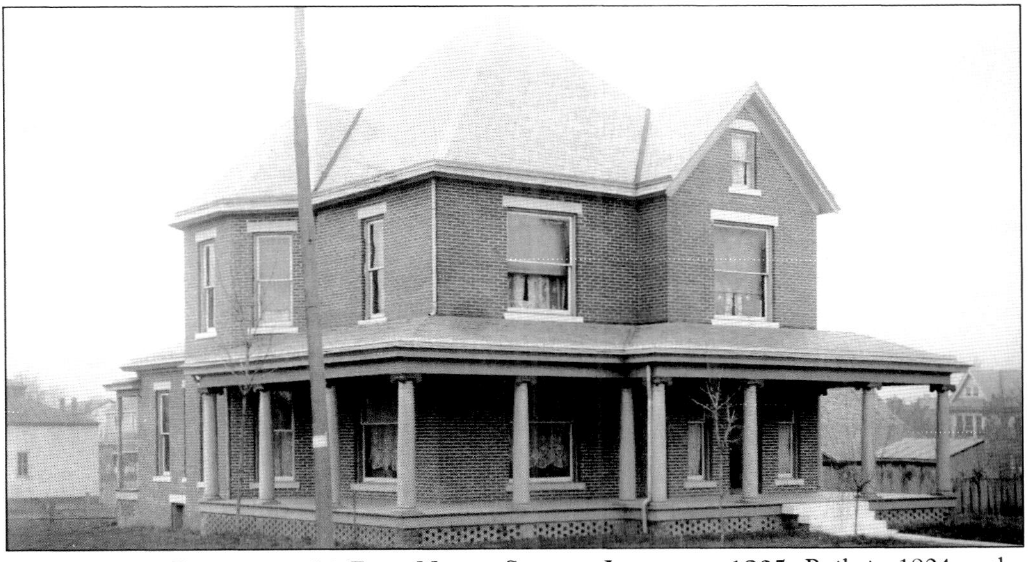

Louis Joseph Residence, 21 East Ninth Street, Jasper, c. 1905. Built in 1904 at the southwest corner of Ninth and Mill Streets, the residence was the family home of Louis Joseph, who was a director with the Jasper Furniture Company, which later became the Jasper Desk Company. It is currently the Ivy Manor flower and gift shop. In the background, to the right, is the Wilson Residence, shown in the photograph above. (Photograph courtesy of John Fierst.)

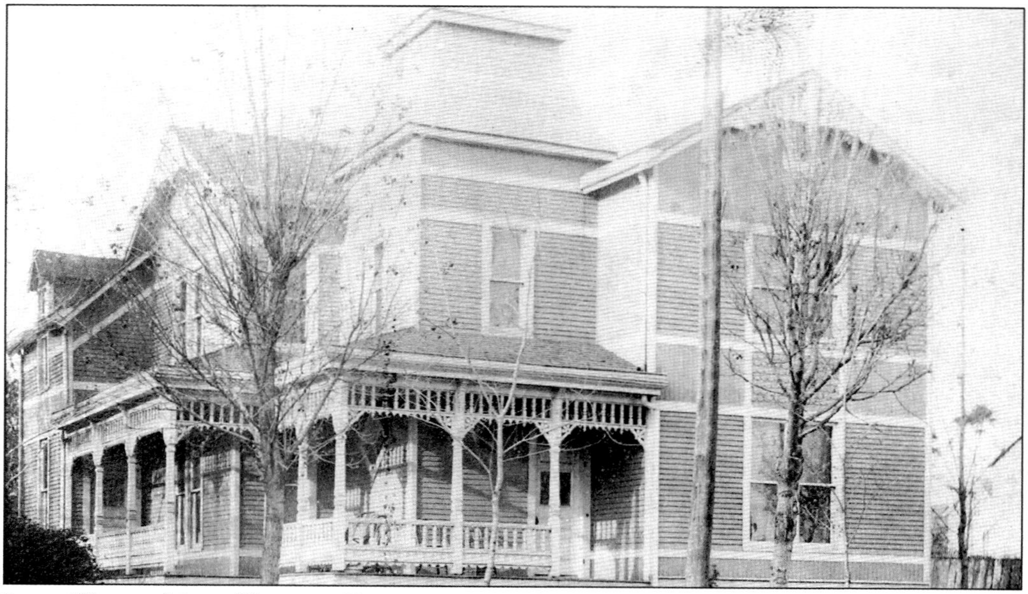

JOHN W. AND MARY KUEBLER RESIDENCE, 106 EAST NINTH STREET, JASPER, C. 1905. The two-story frame residence for John W. and Mary Kuebler was constructed in 1899 by Jasper contractor John M. Schmidt. Kuebler sold the house in 1910, shortly after the untimely death of his wife. Two subsequent owners lived in the home only briefly; then the Robert Nordhoff family purchased the residence in 1923. Ron and Debbie Flick purchased the property in 1989 and began a complete restoration of the home. (Photograph courtesy of Bob Kuebler.)

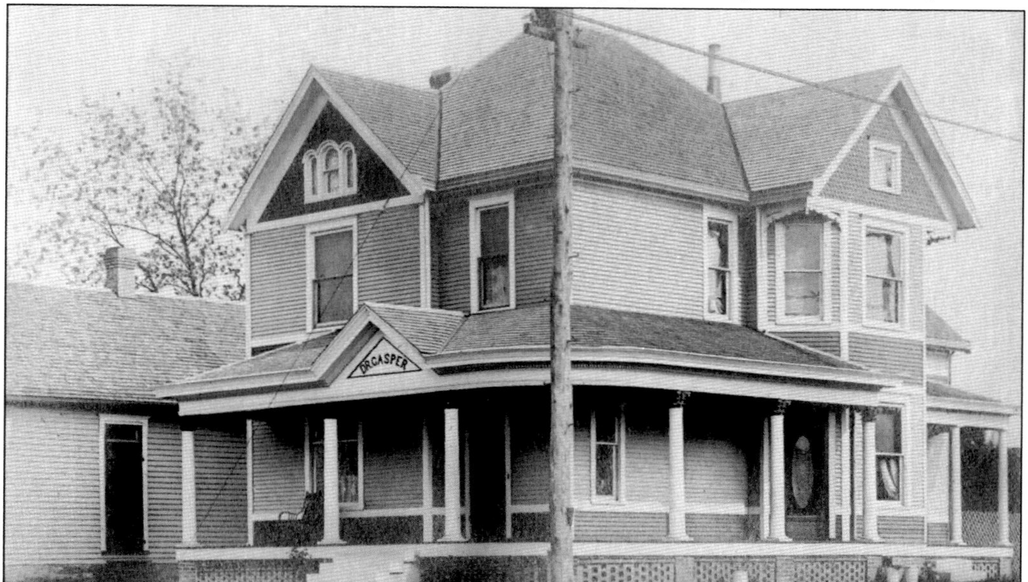

DR. JOHN AND DORA CASPER RESIDENCE, 115 WEST TENTH STREET, JASPER, C. 1910. This residence was built in 1908 for Dr. Joseph Casper by skilled Jasper contractor Andy Berger. Dr. Casper lived in the home only until 1912, at which time the Joseph and Caroline Fierst family purchased the property. A member of the family, Joe Fierst, still lives in the beautiful, well-preserved home. (Photograph courtesy of Joe Fierst.)

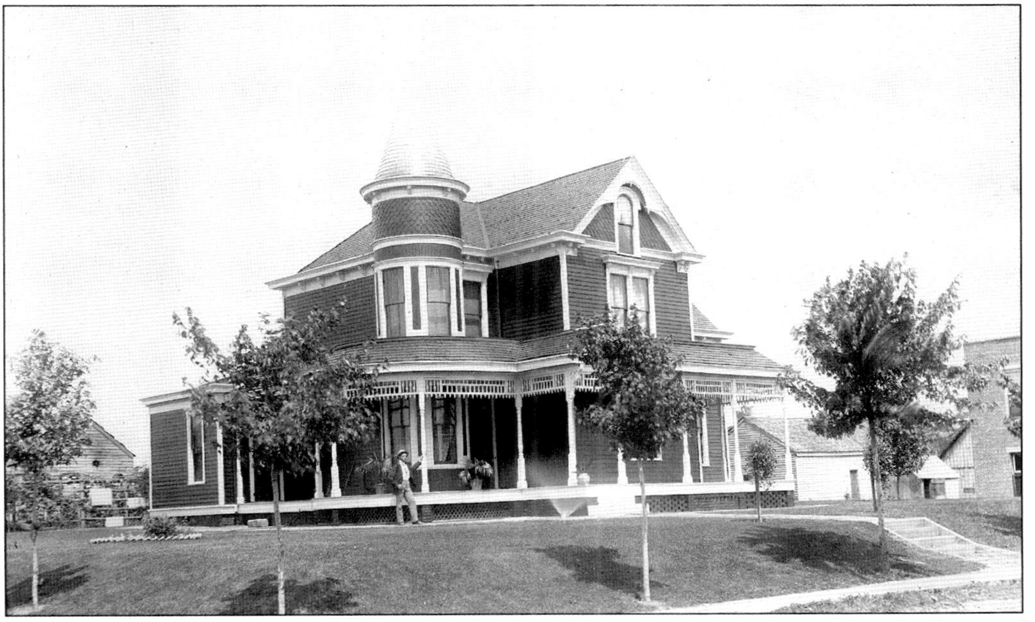

KREMPP RESIDENCE, 1005 NORTH MAIN STREET, JASPER, C. 1895. Pictured is the home of Charles and Louise Krempp. Note the early use of a lawn sprinkler. The Krodel family lived in the home for many years, during which the tower was removed and the porch lowered. (Photograph courtesy of John Fierst.)

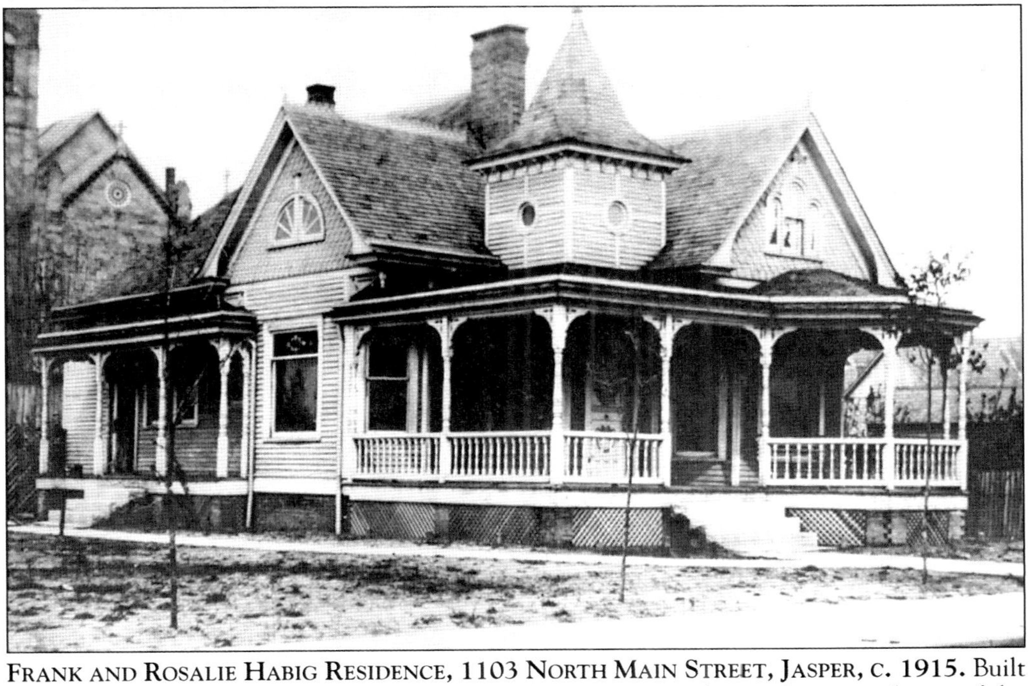

FRANK AND ROSALIE HABIG RESIDENCE, 1103 NORTH MAIN STREET, JASPER, C. 1915. Built in 1904 at the northwest corner of Eleventh and Main Streets, the residence was home of the Habig family, who owned and operated the brewery across the street. (Photograph courtesy of Barbara Habig.)

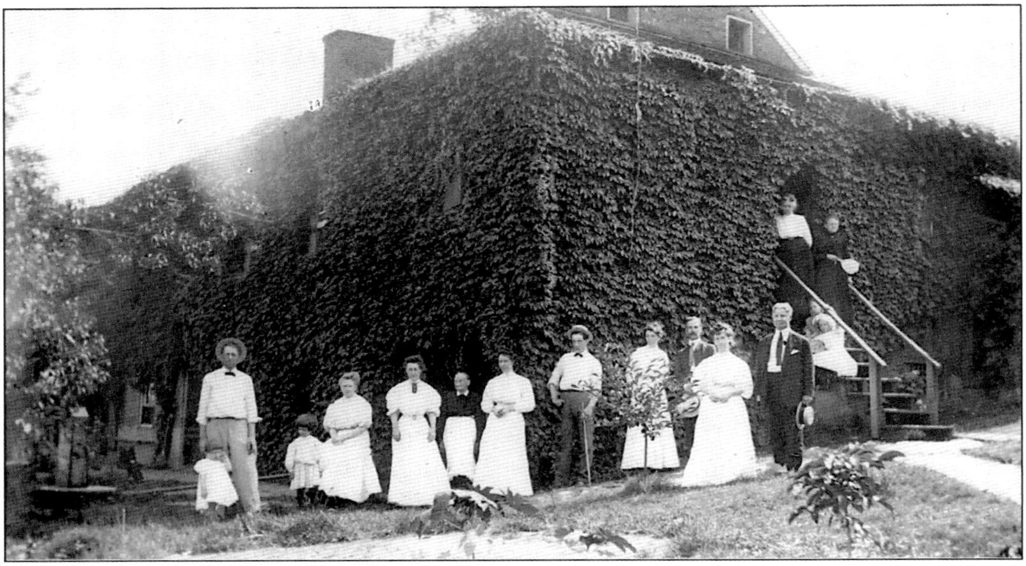

GEIGER RESIDENCE, SIXTH AND GEIGER STREETS, HUNTINGBURG. Colonel Jacob Geiger, an avid hunter, heard about the great hunting in the part of southern Indiana that would become Dubois County. Geiger purchased 1,920 acres of land in 1837 and moved here from Kentucky. The Geiger family had an illustrious heritage. Colonel Geiger was the son of Frederick Geiger who had served in the Revolutionary War. A slave owner when he lived in Kentucky, Geiger freed his slaves after moving here and became a member of the Freedom Settlement which was located just south of Huntingburg. Because of his love of hunting, Geiger incorporated the word in the name of the new town. The original Geiger home in Huntingburg, built in 1852, still stands at the corner of Sixth and Geiger Streets. (Photograph courtesy of the Huntingburg Public Library.)

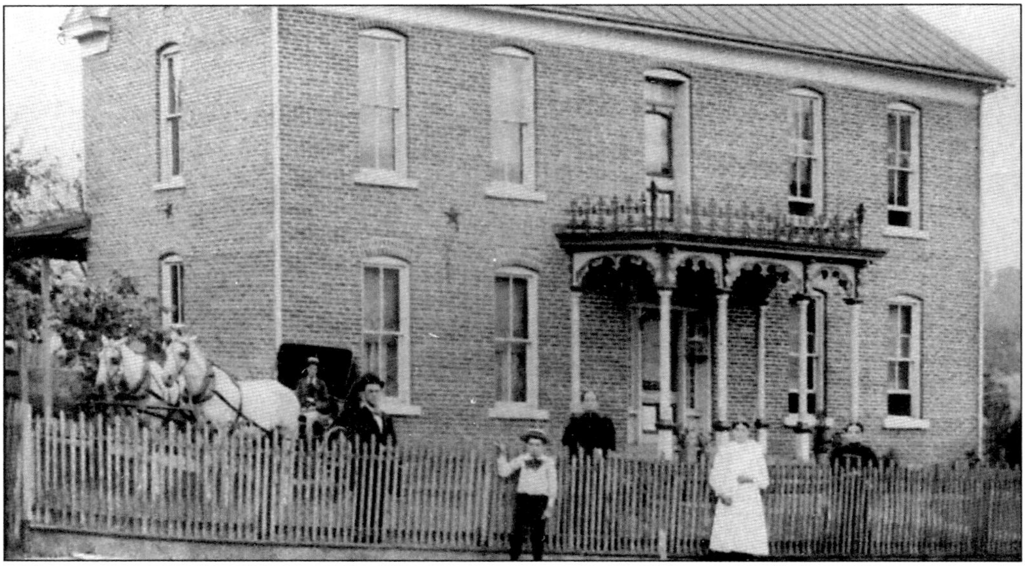

LANDGREBE RESIDENCE, 207 FIRST STREET, HUNTINGBURG, 1895. The home was built in 1874. This photograph was taken 21 years later, when the Landgrebes were still residents. Pictured in front of the house are Henry Landgrebe and Louisa Landgrebe. Henry also owned a building at 402 Fourth Street, constructed in 1887. (Photograph courtesy of the Huntingburg Public Library.)

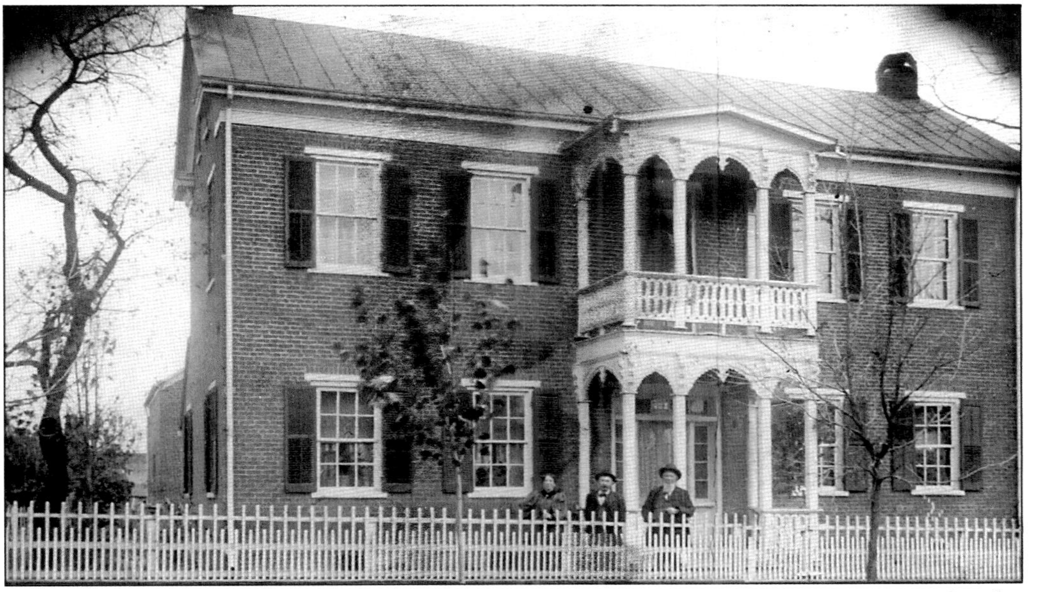

LEONARD BRETZ RESIDENCE, FIFTH AND GEIGER STREETS, HUNTINGBURG. In the photograph are Millie and Henry Bretz, with their father, Leonard. (Photograph courtesy of the Huntingburg Public Library.)

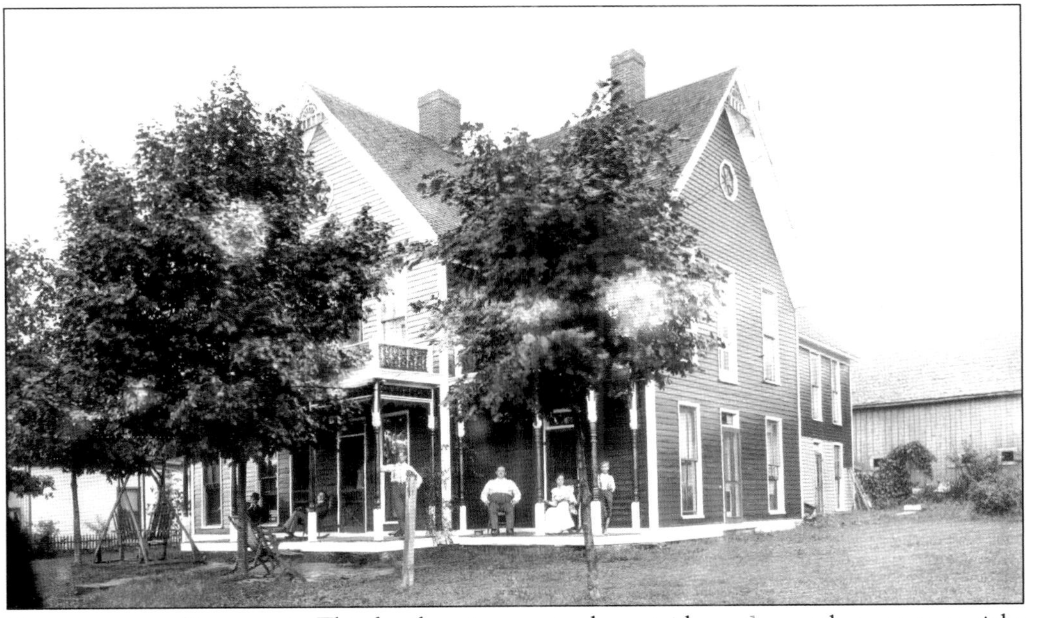

HUNTINGBURG RESIDENCE. This family enjoys a nice day outside on the porch, a common sight when this photograph was taken in the late 1800s. (Photograph courtesy of the Huntingburg Public Library.)

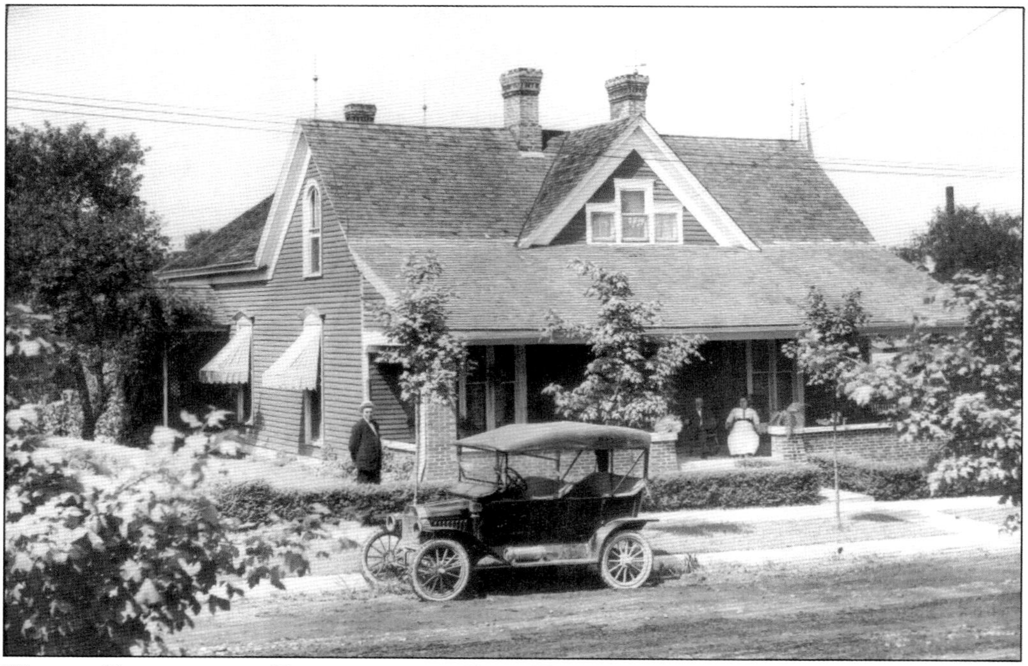

WALTER REUTEPOHLER RESIDENCE, 108 EAST THIRD STREET, HUNTINGBURG. This lovely home sat on the north side of Third Street. The steeple of Salem Church can be seen in the distance. Unfortunately, the site is now a parking lot. (Photograph courtesy of the Huntingburg Public Library.)

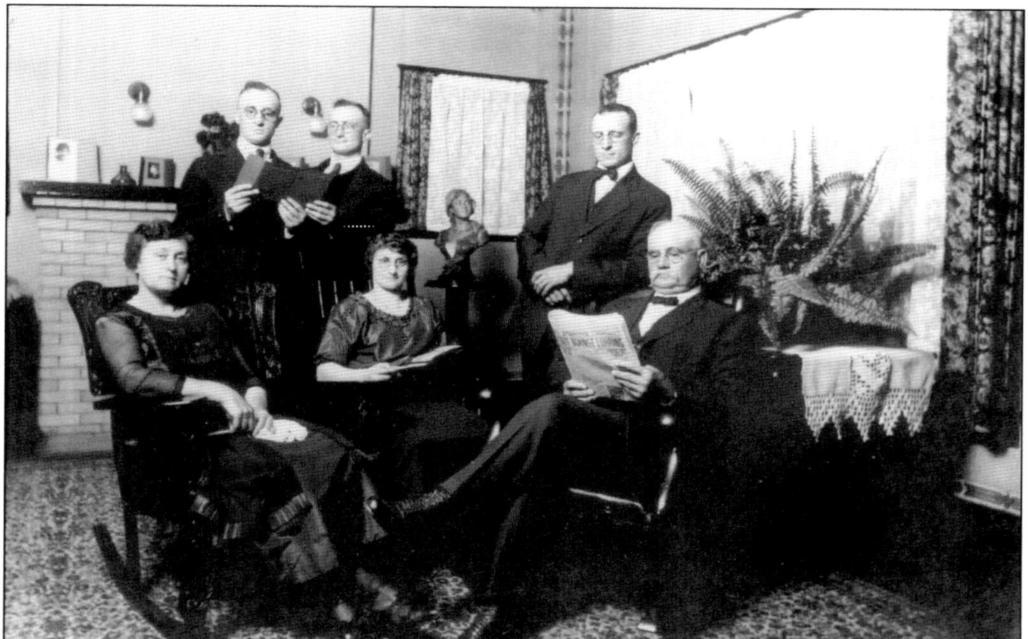

LINK FAMILY. Note Roy and Ray Link, the dapper insurance salesmen pictured on page 54, in the back. (Photograph courtesy of the Huntingburg Public Library.)

Nine

FERDINAND

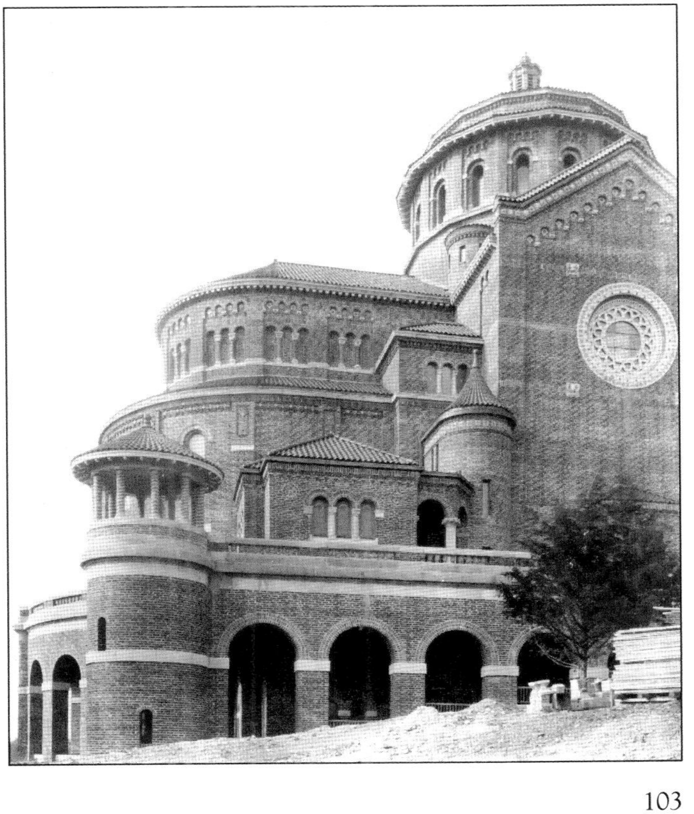

MONASTERY IMMACULATE CONCEPTION CHURCH EXTERIOR, 1916. The Byzantine Romanesque-style building is among the nation's most beautiful edifices. Located in Ferdinand in Dubois County, the Monastery, also known as the Castle on the Hill, was founded in 1867 by the Sisters of St. Benedict, an order whose roots go back to the sixth century when St. Benedict established his rules. (Photograph courtesy of the Monastery Immaculate Conception.)

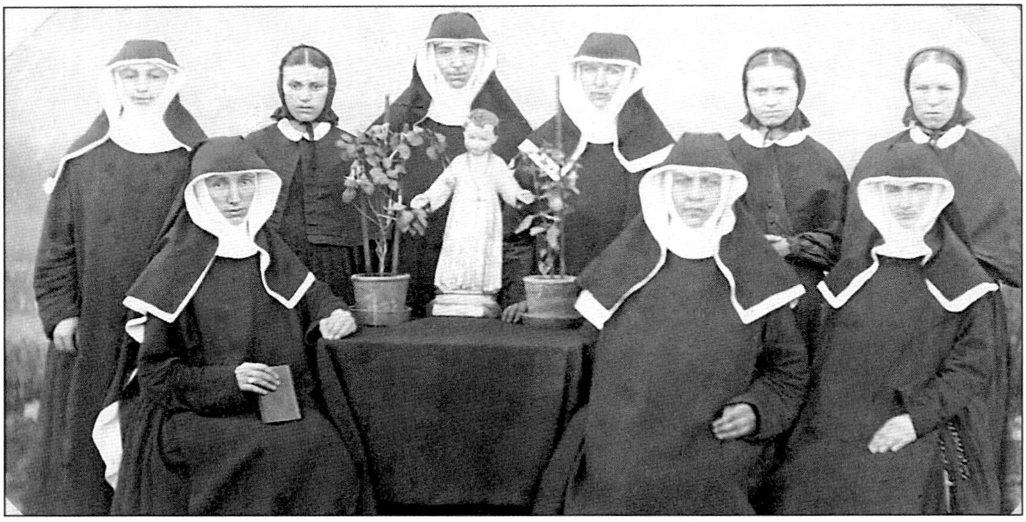

Community of the Monastery, 1870. Seated on the right of the statue is Sister M. Xaveria and standing directly behind is Mother M. Benedicta. The other sisters, from left to right, are Ferdinand Neu, Scholastica Stockman (later Rev. Mother) and Cecila Mehling. The postulants are (Caroline) Sr. Agnes Rumig, (Mary) Sr. Agatha Werb (later Rev. Mother), (Magdelena) Sr. Anastasia Stockman. According to *The Castle on the Hill* (Sr. M. Frederica Dudine, O.S.B., Ph.D., Bruce Publishing 1967), "During the first few years of their residence in Indiana, the Sisters of St. Benedict at Ferdinand had only ground enough for a small garden and a yard around the cottage. Mother Benedicta realized that if they wished to work and prosper in pioneering, and indeed even to stay alive and physically well, they must have a farm, some draft animals, cattle, hogs, many more chickens then they had and they must work the farm to gain a livelihood." (Photograph courtesy of the Monastery Immaculate Conception.)

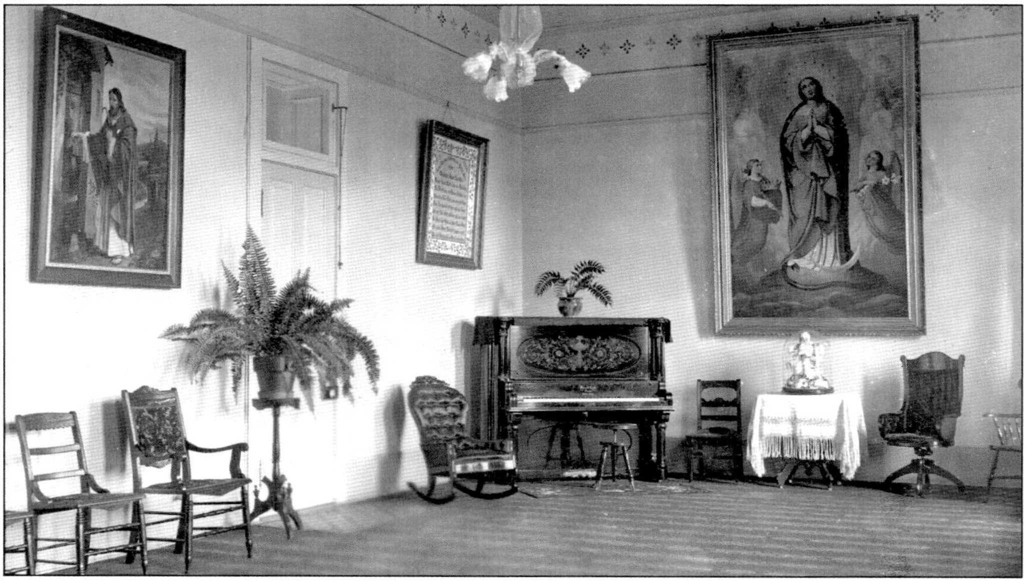

Reception Hall, Monastery Immaculate Conception. The beauty of the exterior of the monastery is matched by its interior. (Photograph courtesy of the Monastery Immaculate Conception.)

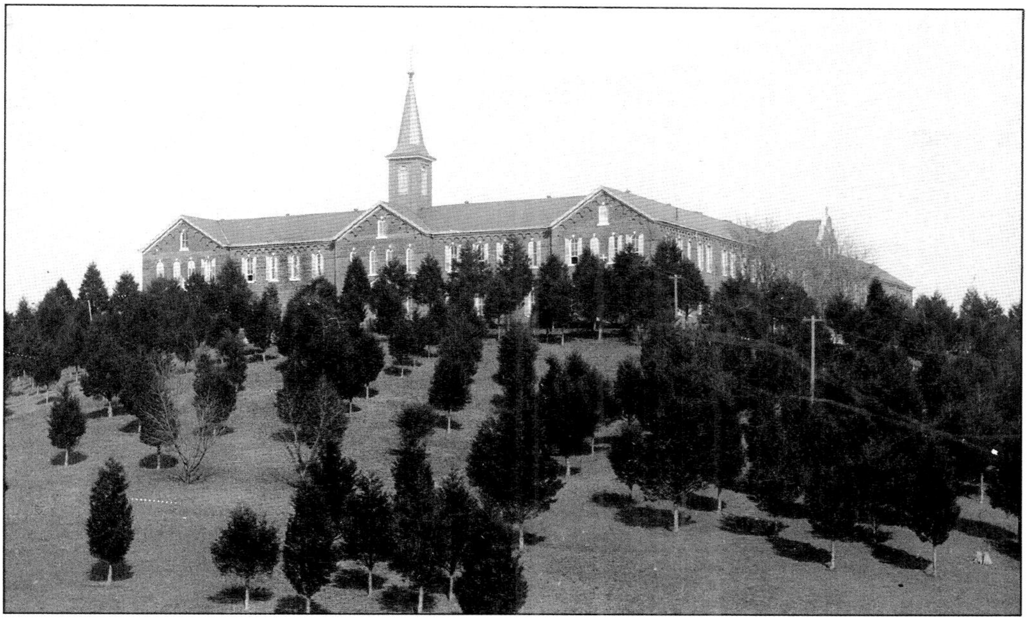

THE OLD CHURCH, 1867. Home to one of the largest communities of Benedictine Sisters in the United States, the Monastery Immaculate Conception was founded in 1867. It was in that year that four German Benedictine Sisters from the Benedictine St. Walburga's Abbey in Eichstaett, Bavaria, arrived in Ferdinand to teach and do missionary work with the German immigrants who founded Ferdinand. (Photograph courtesy of the Monastery Immaculate Conception.)

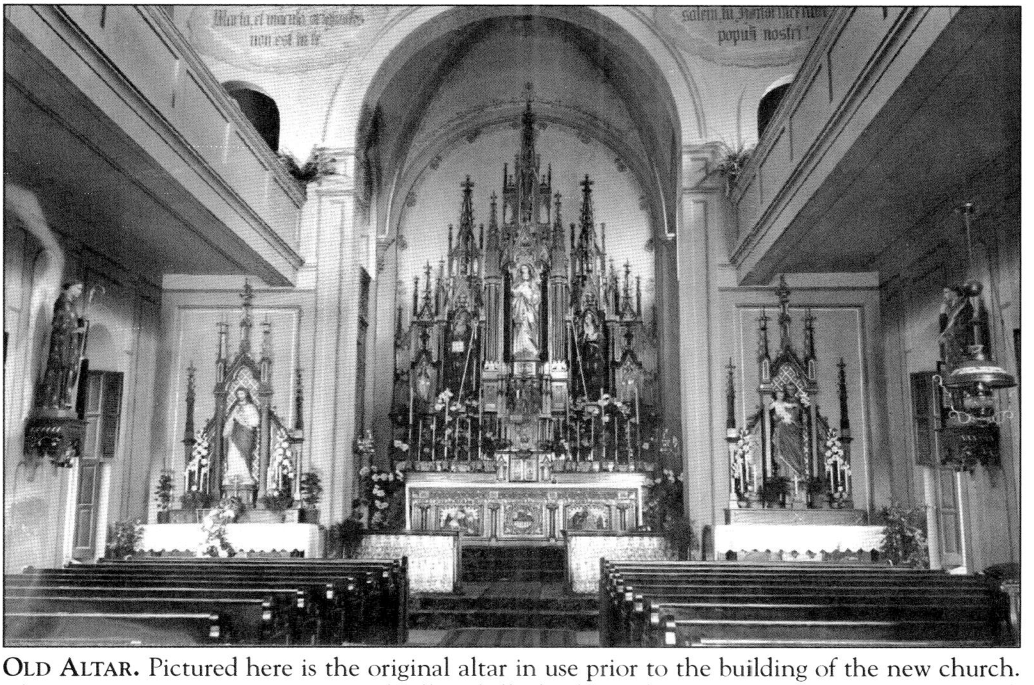

OLD ALTAR. Pictured here is the original altar in use prior to the building of the new church. The Monastery sits on 190 acres of rolling hillside above the picturesque town of Ferdinand. (Photograph courtesy of the Monastery Immaculate Conception.)

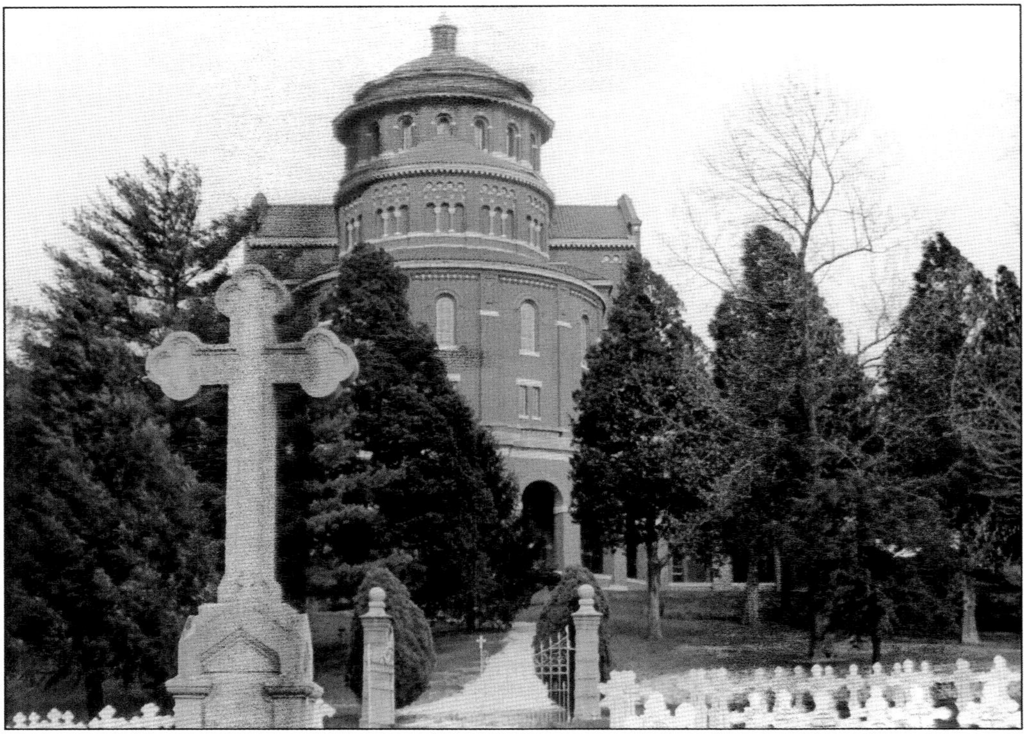

THE MONASTERY FROM THE CEMETERY. The dome of the monastery chapel rises 87 feet from the floor and is 13.5 feet in diameter. Angels are depicted in the 16 stained-glass windows around the dome. This angel motif is evident throughout the chapel; 94 angels have been counted. The architect seems to have taken a cue from the Rule of St. Benedict, in which Benedict says, "We gather to worship and praise God in unison with the angels." (Information courtesy of www.thedome.org. Photograph courtesy of the Monastery Immaculate Conception.)

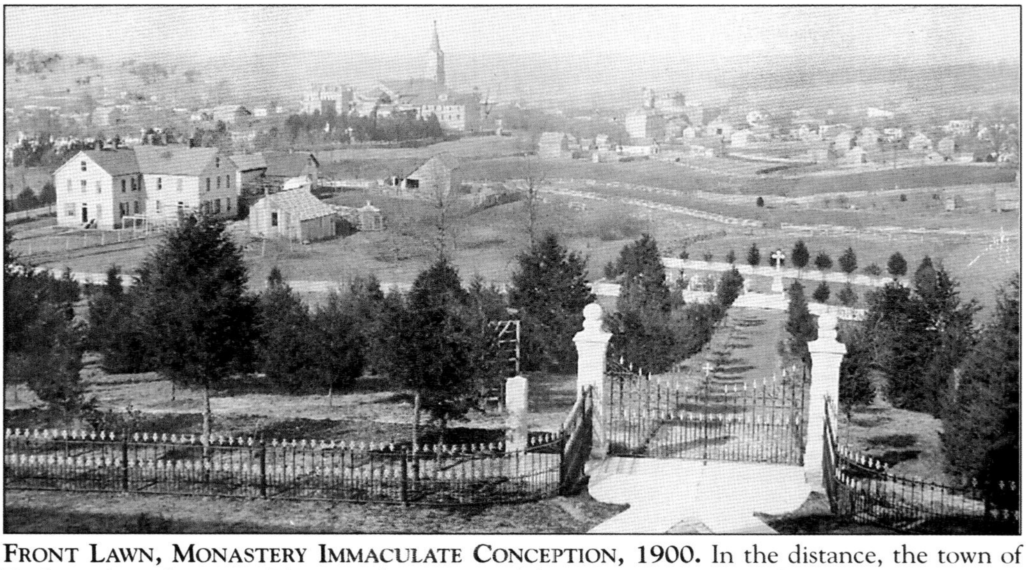

FRONT LAWN, MONASTERY IMMACULATE CONCEPTION, 1900. In the distance, the town of Ferdinand can be seen. (Photograph courtesy of the Monastery Immaculate Conception.)

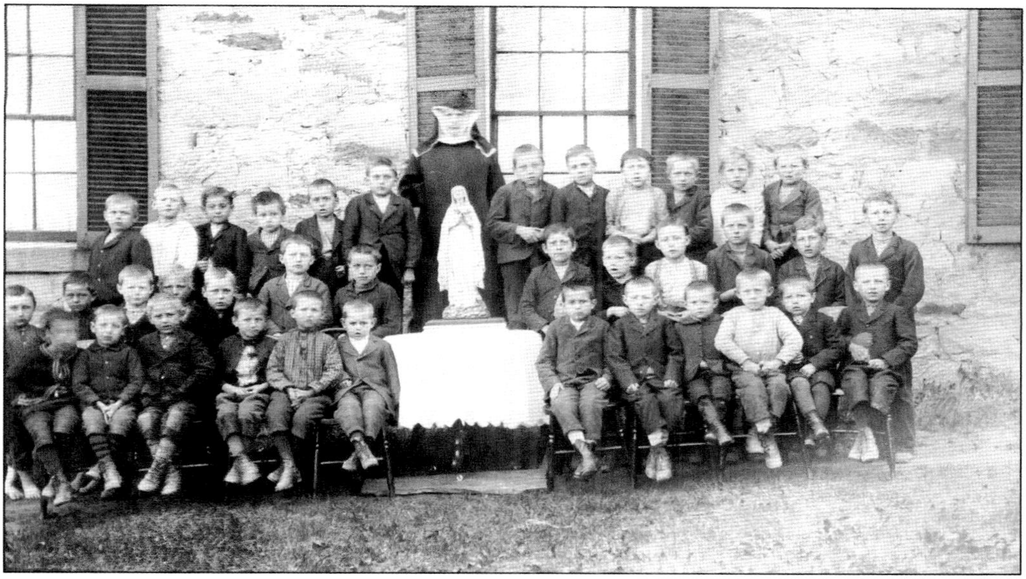

FERDINAND GRADE SCHOOL CLASS, C. 1870S. Education was a very important component of both the Monastery and the town of Ferdinand. (Photograph courtesy of the Monastery Immaculate Conception.)

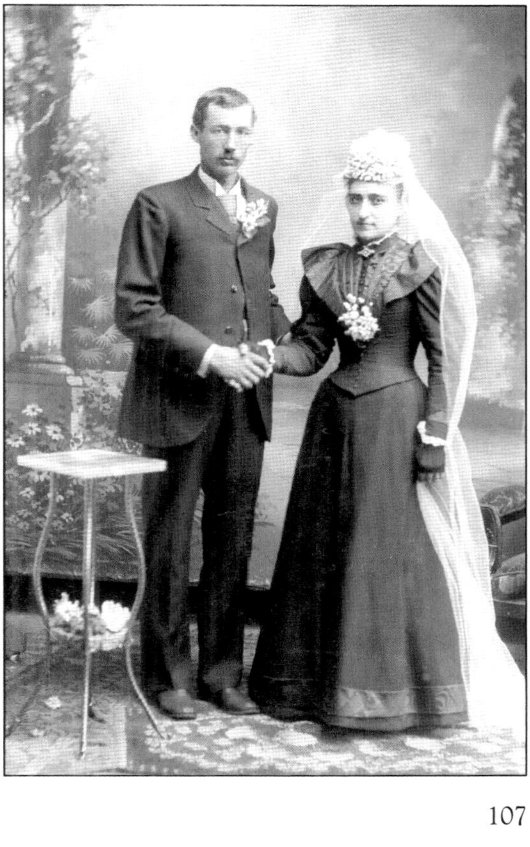

MR. AND MRS. BERNARD KRAMPE. Bernard was known as the Guardian Angel of the convent properties as he managed the farm from 1883, when he was hired by Mother Agatha Werb, to 1925 (one year before his death). He married Frances Jochem of Mariah Hill in 1892. Frances had two sisters in the Ferdinand Community—Srs. Cunigunda and Boniface. The Krampes had eight children, two of whom died in infancy. Their son, Albert, took over the management of the convent farms, a position he held from 1925 to 1975, when he became semi-retired, according to Monastery archivist Sr. Mary Dominic. Albert married Theresa Loechte on May 25, 1926, and they had seven children. His son Bernard Krampe became an Indiana state senator. Between father and son, the Krampes gave more than 92 years of service to the Monastery. They kept daily logs of all the activities on the farm, which are stored in the Monastery's extensive archives. (Photograph courtesy of the Monastery Immaculate Conception.)

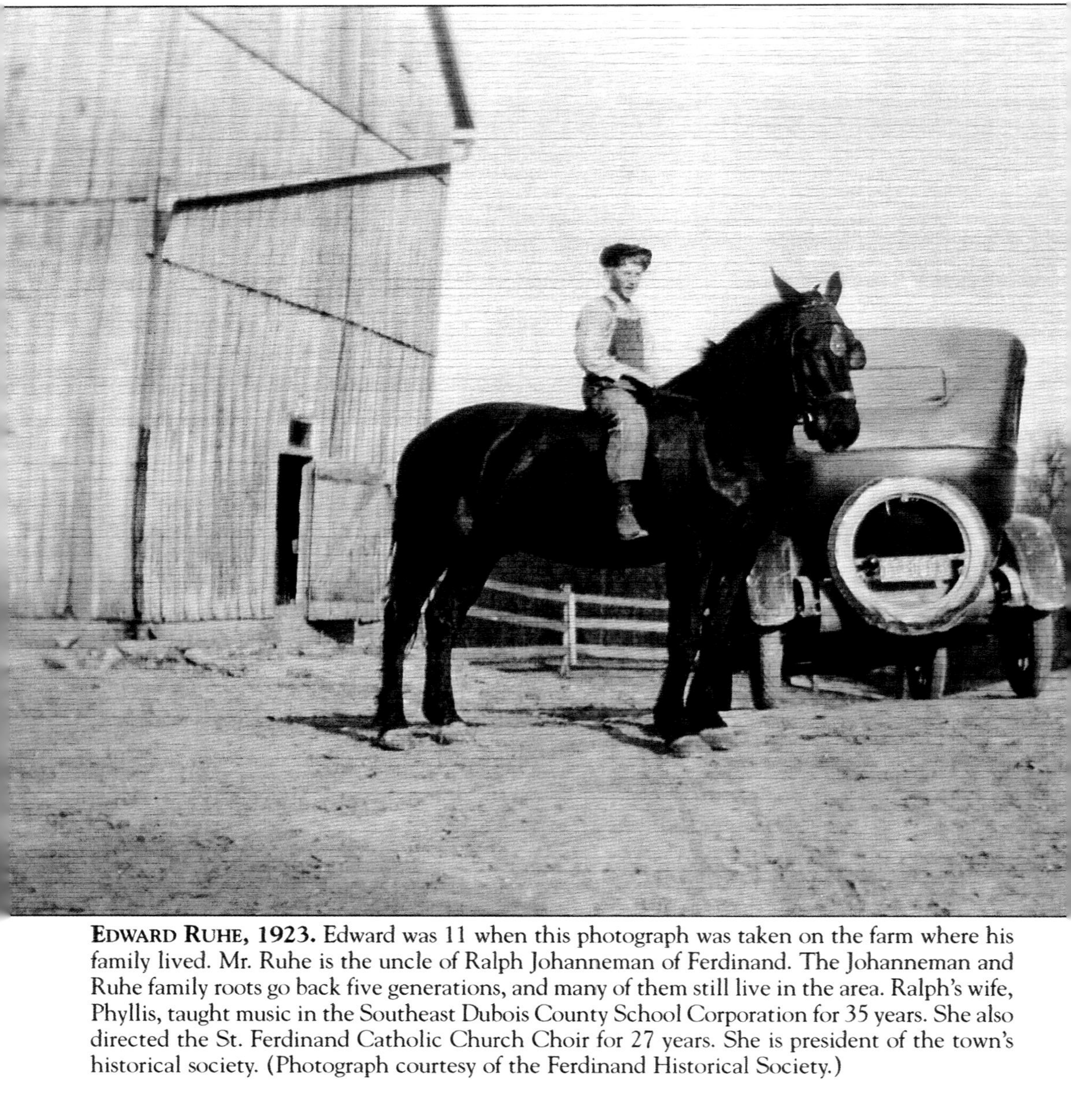

EDWARD RUHE, 1923. Edward was 11 when this photograph was taken on the farm where his family lived. Mr. Ruhe is the uncle of Ralph Johanneman of Ferdinand. The Johanneman and Ruhe family roots go back five generations, and many of them still live in the area. Ralph's wife, Phyllis, taught music in the Southeast Dubois County School Corporation for 35 years. She also directed the St. Ferdinand Catholic Church Choir for 27 years. She is president of the town's historical society. (Photograph courtesy of the Ferdinand Historical Society.)

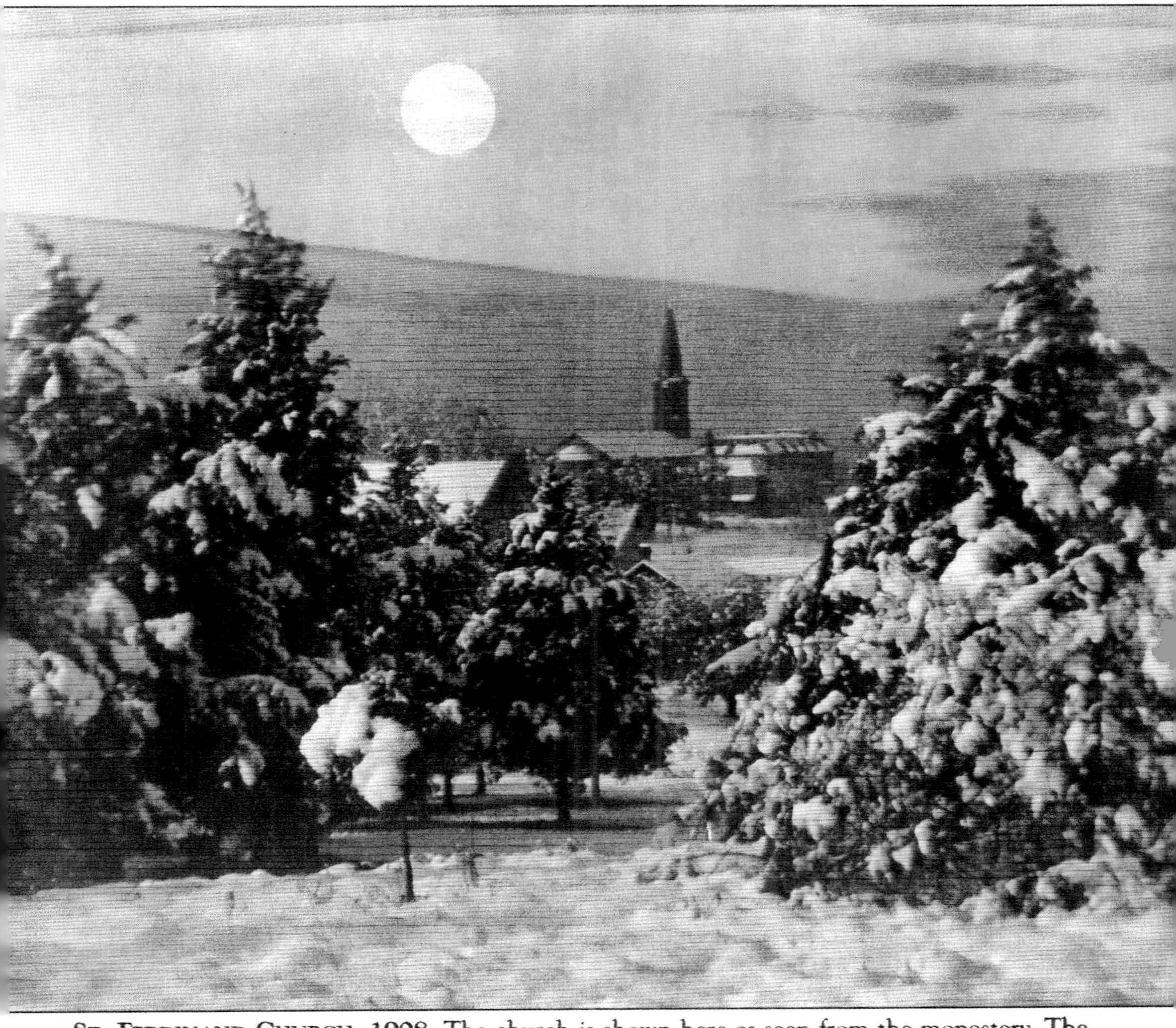

St. Ferdinand Church, 1908. The church is shown here as seen from the monastery. The town of Ferdinand was named in honor of Emperor Ferdinand of Austria, who was described in *The Castle on the Hill* as a devoted patron of German immigrants to America. The town was laid out in 1840 based on instructions given by Father Joseph Kundek. (Photograph courtesy of the Monastery Immaculate Conception.)

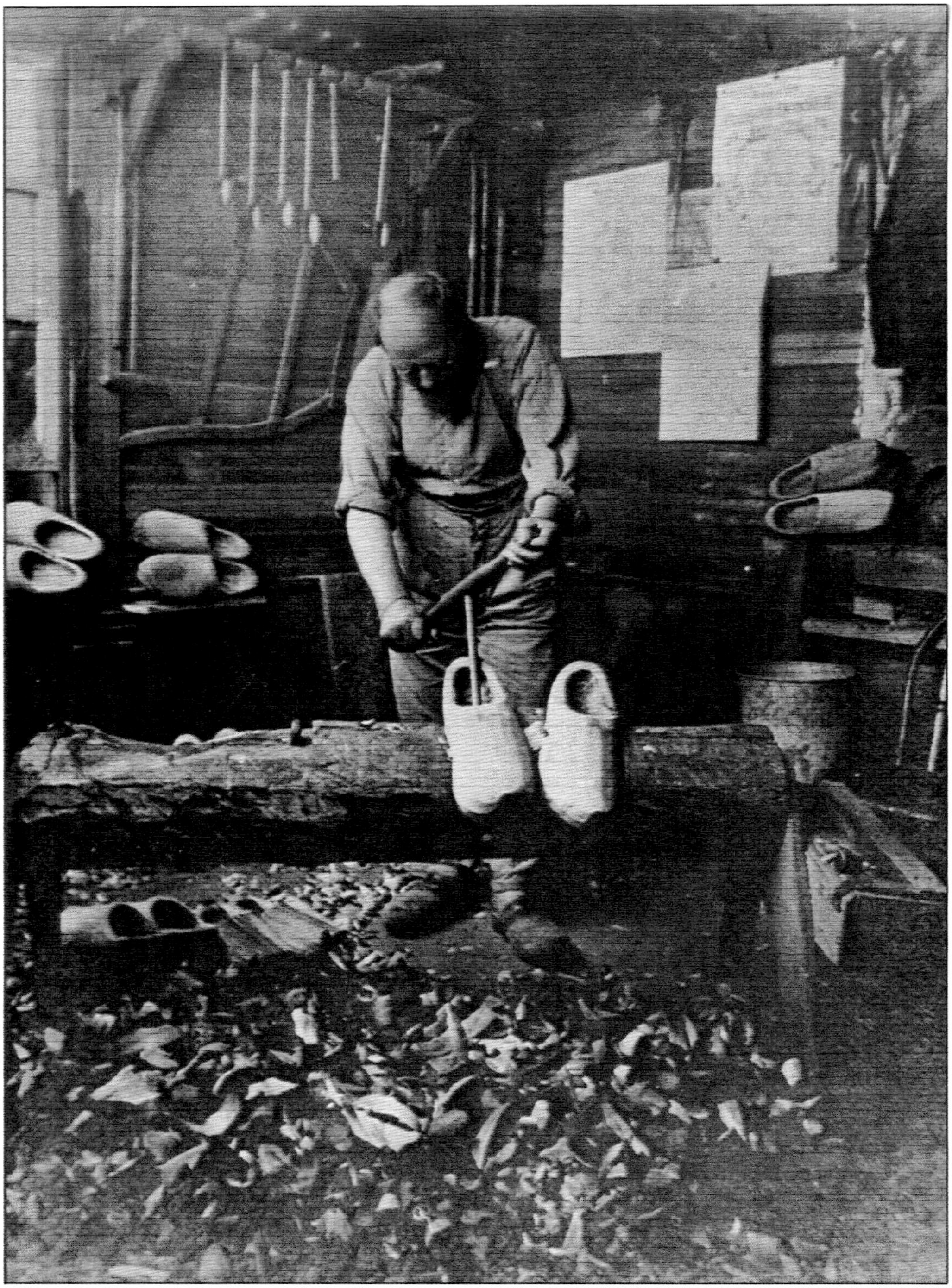

Wooden Shoe Cobbler. This early 1900s photograph shows Clemens Lueken Jr. carving wooden shoes out of birch and poplar wood. According to Phyllis Johanneman, president of the Ferdinand Historical Society, this activity earned Ferdinand the name "Wooden Shoe Township." (Photograph courtesy of the Ferdinand Historical Society.)

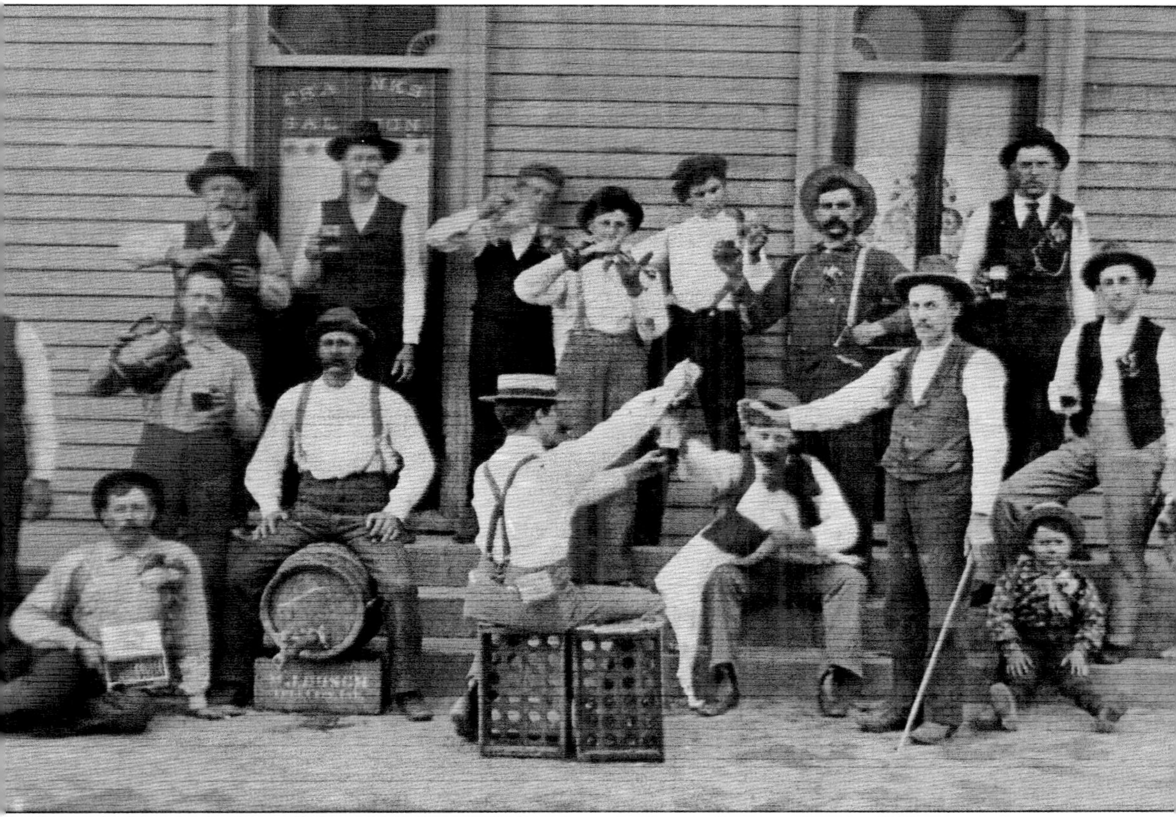

FRANK'S SALOON. This picture was taken in front of Frank's Saloon in Ferdinand. Pictured, from left to right, are: (seated) Frank Roos, Jake Haug, Hubert Quante, Joe Jochim (from Jasper), and Victor Roos (age five); (standing on left) Andy Hollander, Fritz Bromm (with pitcher), and Roehle Jasper (with dog "Honey"); (back) Joe Leppert, Frank Gehlausen, Ike Senninger, Ron Senninger, Albert Leppert, John Mehling, and Theodore Eckstein; and Andy Hollander holds Troy. (Photograph courtesy of the Ferdinand Historical Society.)

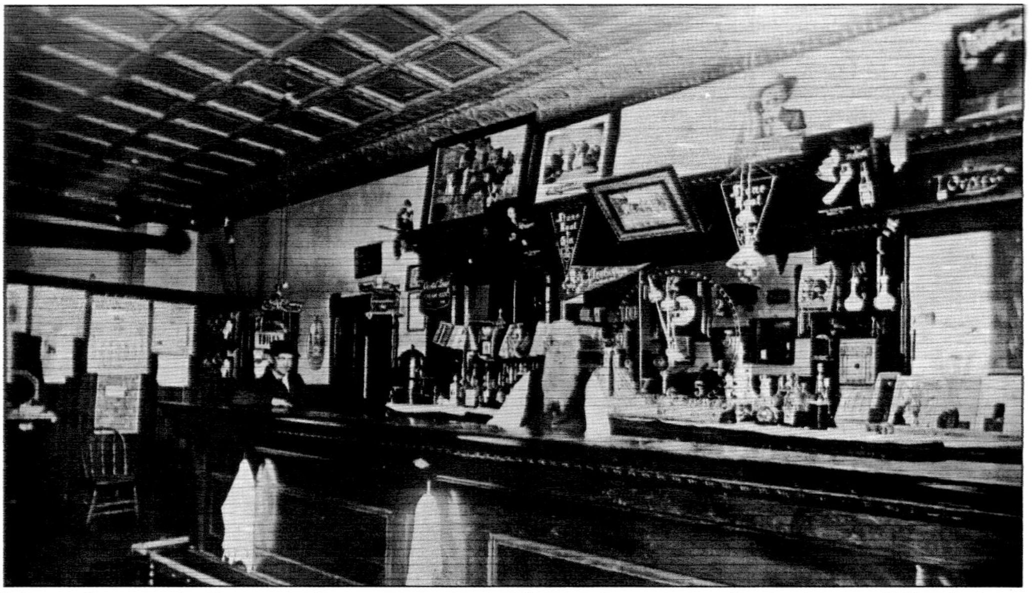

MATT OLINGER'S SALOON, INTERIOR, 1914. This is the present day location of Fleig's Cage in downtown Ferdinand. Pictured here are Carl Olinger and Matt Olinger Sr. (Photograph courtesy of the Ferdinand Historical Society.)

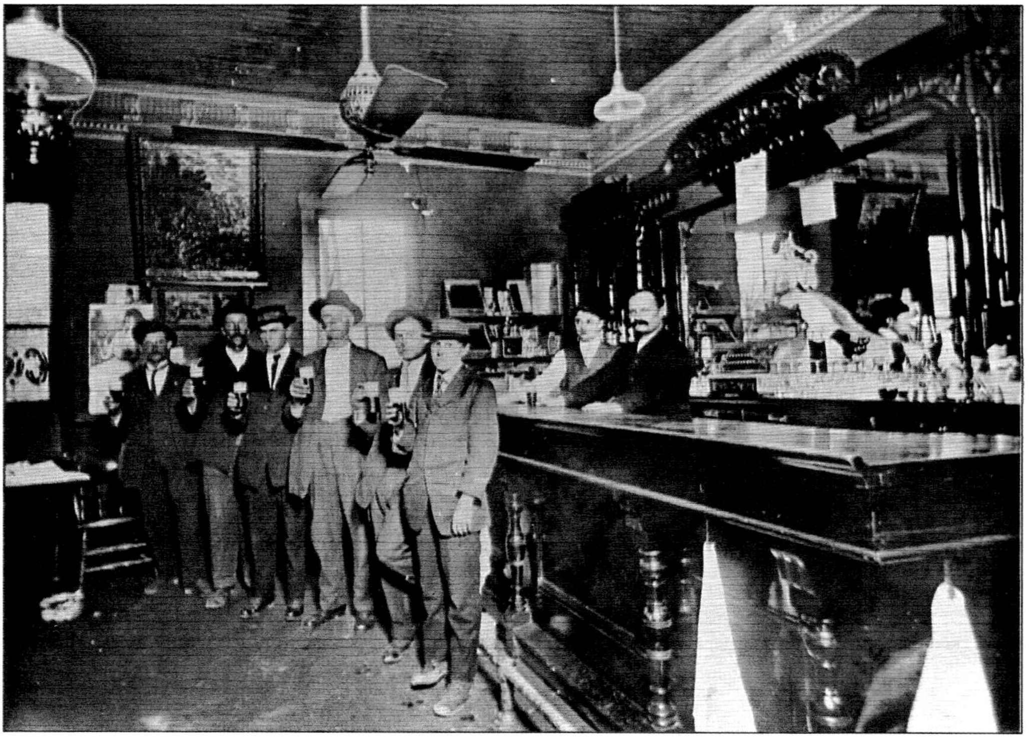

FLEIG'S SALOON, C. 1915. A photograph of Fleig's Saloon in Ferdinand shows, from left to right, Pete Durcholtz, Xavier Steiner, Fidelis Berg, Fred Albert, Rob Berg, Albert Fleig, and Valentine Fleig. (Photograph courtesy of the Ferdinand Historical Society.)

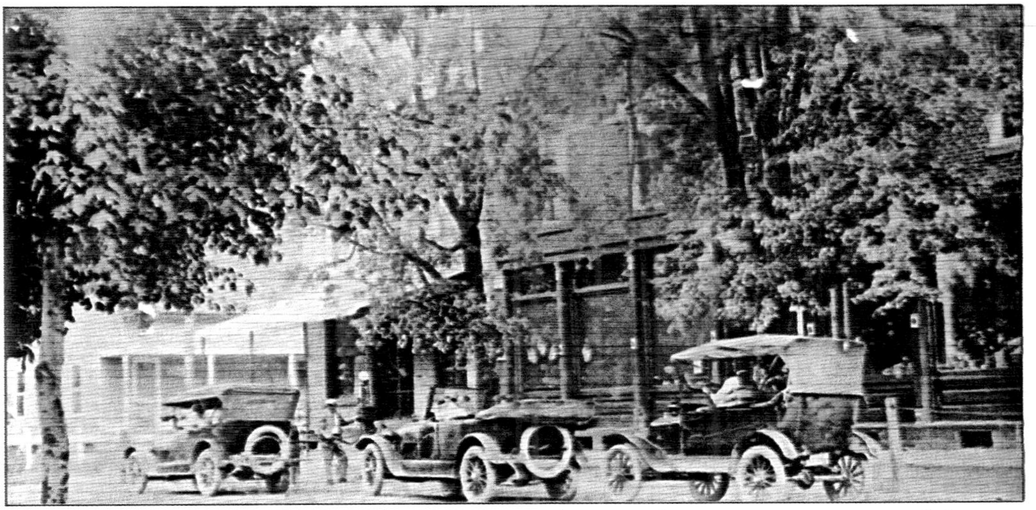

MOTHER OF INVENTION. Ferdinand was the center for several major inventions around the turn of the 20th century. This photograph, taken in 1913, shows autos getting gas from the newly invented, self-computing dispensing machine originated by the Petson Company. (Photograph courtesy of the Ferdinand Historical Society.)

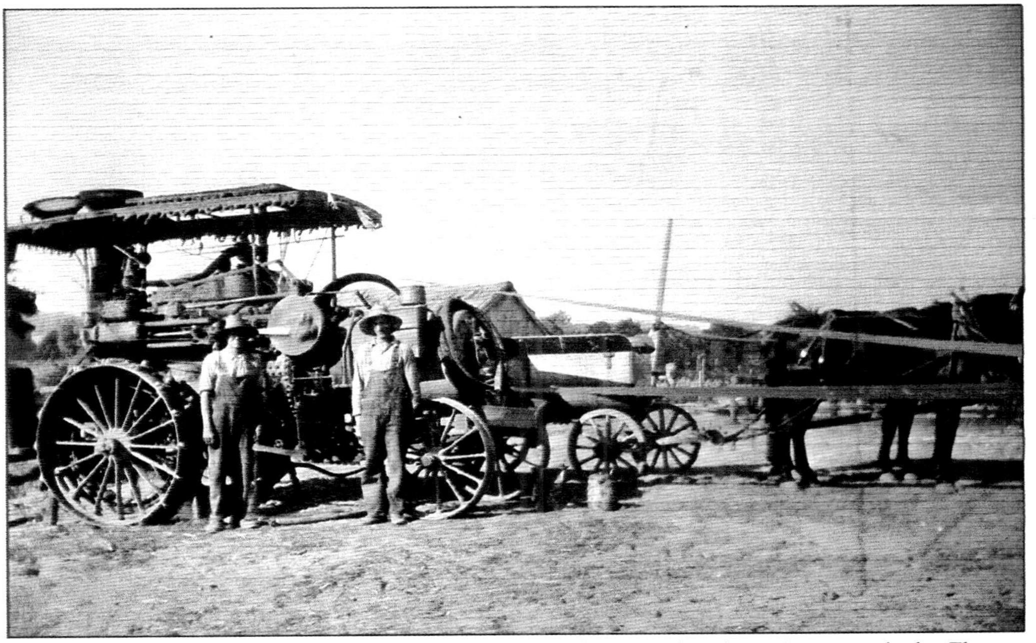

THRESHING OPERATION, 1922. Pictured here are Eddie Wessel and Leo Jasper with the Florenz Kitten Steam Engine, invented in Ferdinand. The town of Ferdinand was platted in 1840 by Father Joseph Kundek, who helped shape the community as one founded on both the principles of the Catholic religion and the strong work ethic of immigrating Germans. (Information courtesy of Phyllis Johanneman, president of the Dubois County Historical Society and active volunteer at the Dubois County Museum. Photograph courtesy of the Ferdinand Historical Society.)

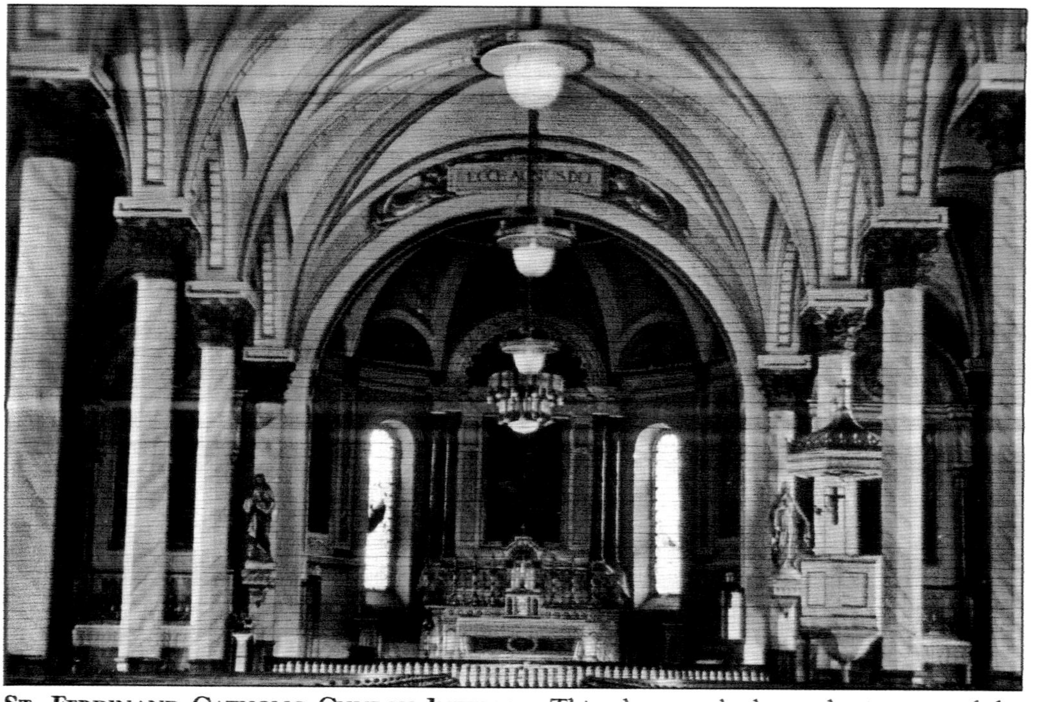

ST. FERDINAND CATHOLIC CHURCH INTERIOR. This photograph shows the interior of the St. Ferdinand Catholic Church before it was modernized. (Photograph courtesy of the Ferdinand Historical Society.)

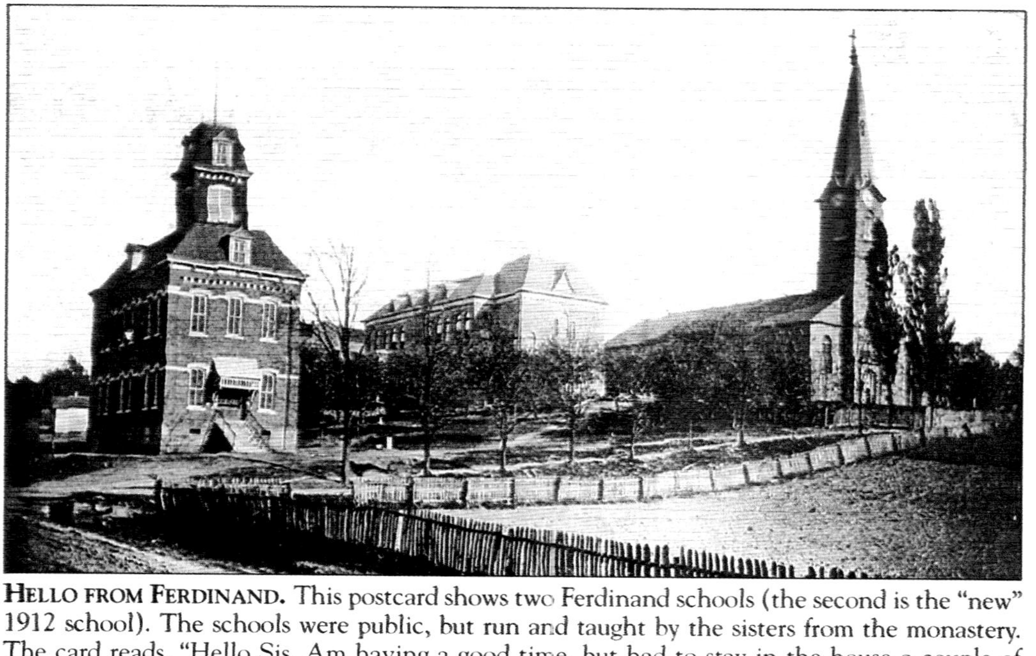

HELLO FROM FERDINAND. This postcard shows two Ferdinand schools (the second is the "new" 1912 school). The schools were public, but run and taught by the sisters from the monastery. The card reads, "Hello Sis, Am having a good time, but had to stay in the house a couple of days as we had some very heavy snows Saturday and Sunday. G." (Photograph courtesy of the Ferdinand Historical Society.)

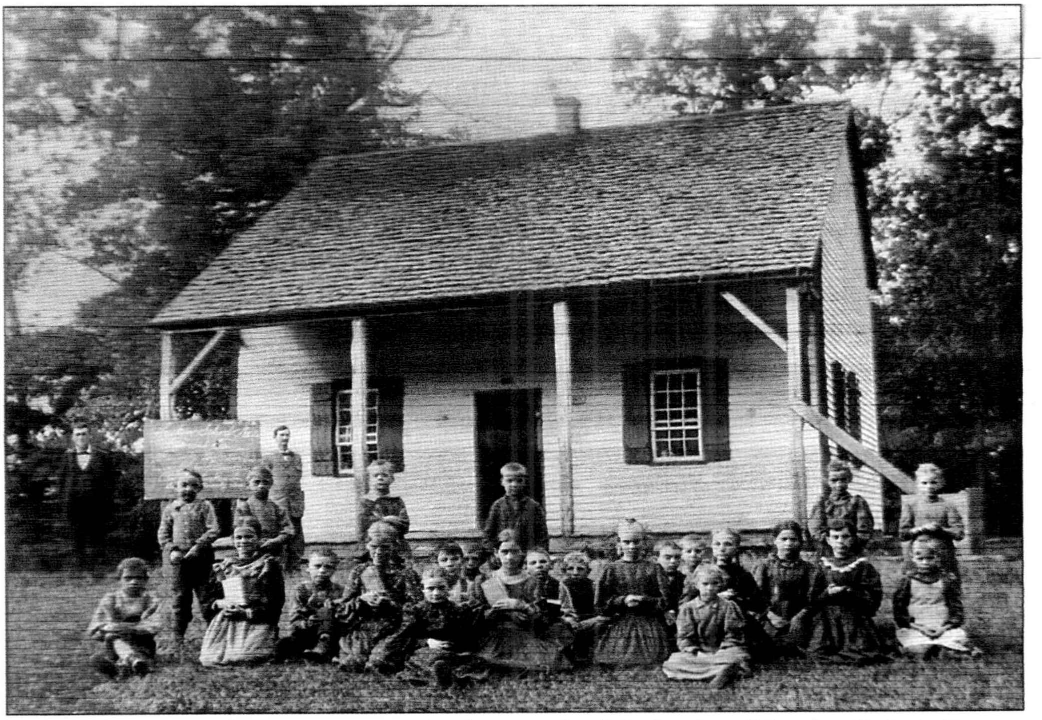

LUEKEN SCHOOL . Shown is a very early photograph of the Lueken School in Dubois County. Clemens Lueken was the teacher. (Photograph courtesy of the Ferdinand Historical Society.)

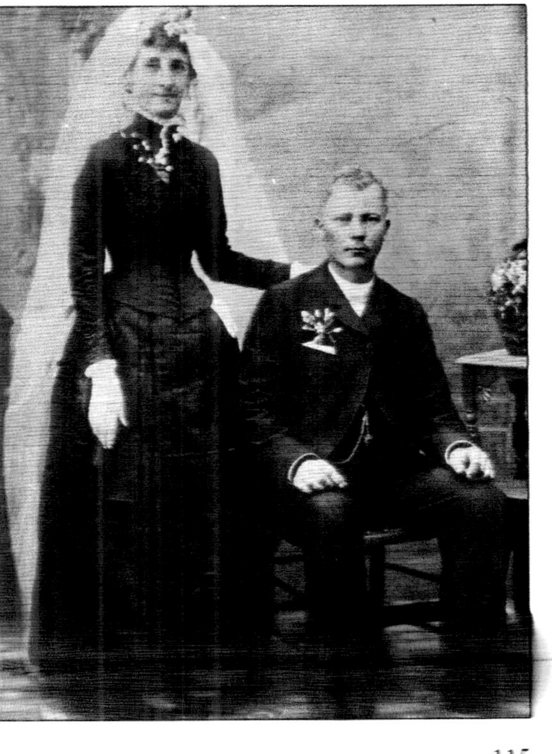

WEDDING PHOTOGRAPH, 1888. According to the Ferdinand Historical Society, Herman and Maria Diek, pictured here at their wedding in Cincinnati, Ohio, moved to the Ferdinand area and settled at the site of the present Ferdinand Forest Lake. In February 1934, they were the first couple to donate their large farm to the Ferdinand State Forest development; in return for their donation, they received a pension from the state government for the rest of their lives. Both are buried in the Ferdinand Cemetery. After their deaths, a marble-topped antique bedroom suite, along with many ornaments including glass domes, statues, expensive keepsakes, and wooden barrels of china which had never been unpacked, were found. It was believed that many of these items were never used. The find was even more intriguing as many believed that Mr. and Mrs. Diek, who lived a life of austerity, were very poor. (Photograph courtesy of the Ferdinand Historical Society.)

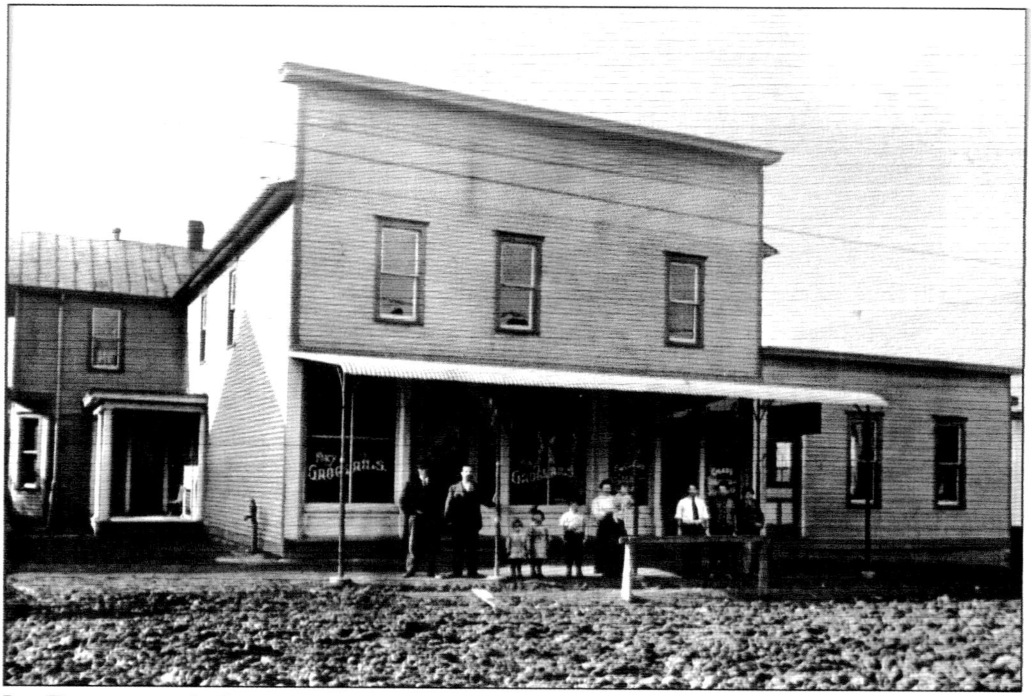

Joe Daunhauer's Confectionary and Pool Hall, 1920. This building stands on the site of what is now the Oasis Restaurant on Main Street in Ferdinand. Pictured here, from left to right, are unidentified, Joe Daunhauer, Earl Daunhauer, Myrtle Daunhauer, Walter Daunhauer, Mrs. Joe Daunhauer (holding Baby Cora), and other unidentified pool sharks—or candy lovers. (Photograph courtesy of the Ferdinand Historical Society.)

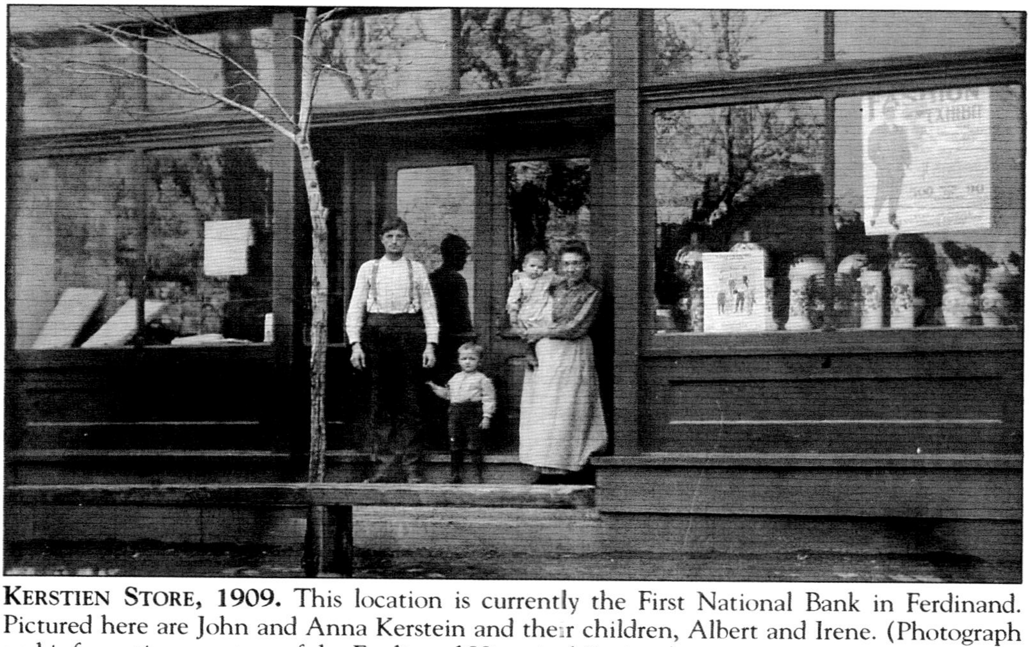

Kerstien Store, 1909. This location is currently the First National Bank in Ferdinand. Pictured here are John and Anna Kerstein and their children, Albert and Irene. (Photograph and information courtesy of the Ferdinand Historical Society.)

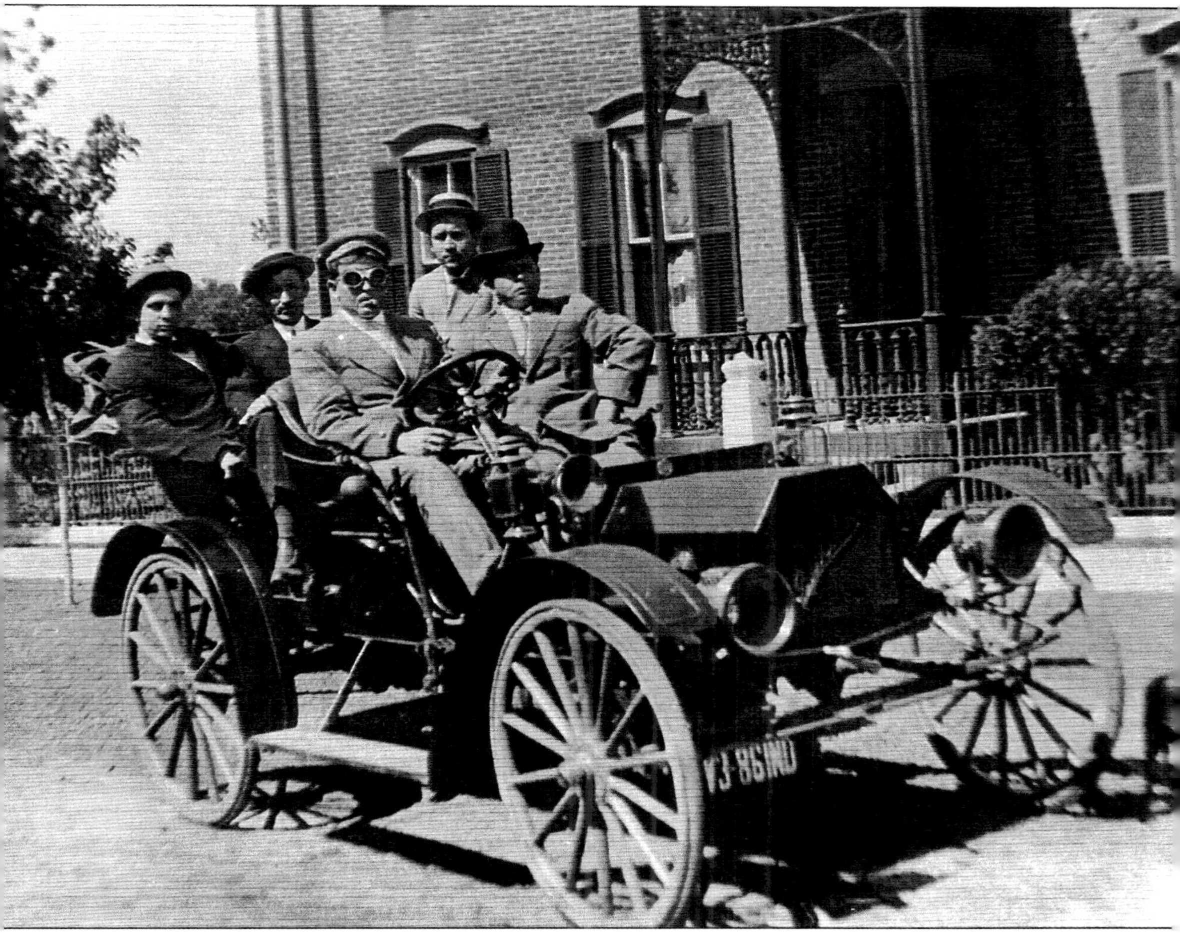

EUREKA. The Eureka automobile received by Peter Mueller was the first one in Ferdinand. This photograph was taken in front of the Mueller home at the corner of Ninth and Missouri Streets. Seated in the back of the auto, from left to right, are Herb Mueller, Charles Metzger, and John Ross. Son Joe is the driver, while Peter Muller is the front seat passenger. (Photograph courtesy of the Ferdinand Historical Society.)

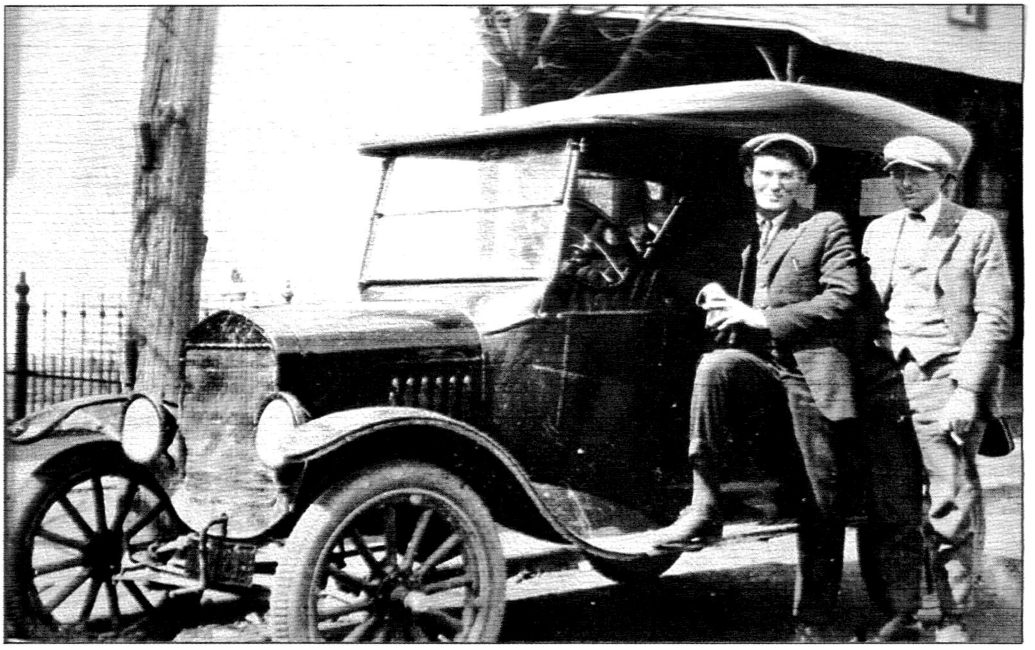

NEW WHEELS, 1923. Looking dashing and ready for fun with a new mode of transportation are Harry Ruhe and Slick Altman in front of today's Oasis Restaurant in Ferdinand. (Photograph courtesy of the Ferdinand Historical Society.)

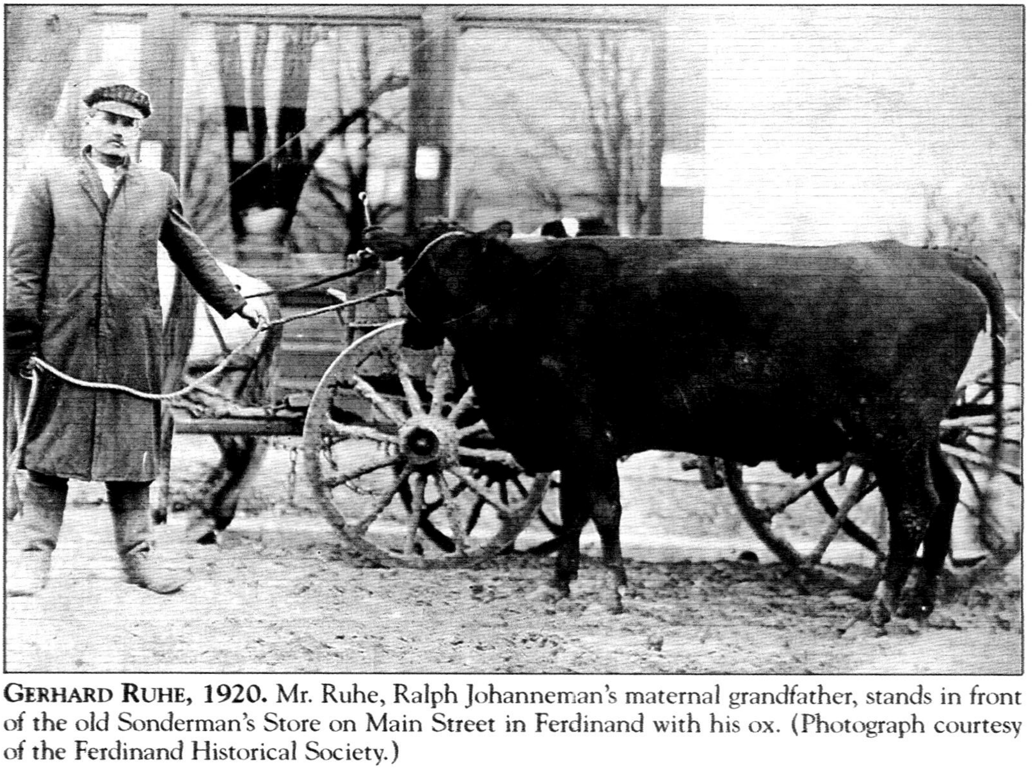

GERHARD RUHE, 1920. Mr. Ruhe, Ralph Johanneman's maternal grandfather, stands in front of the old Sonderman's Store on Main Street in Ferdinand with his ox. (Photograph courtesy of the Ferdinand Historical Society.)

Ten

IRELAND

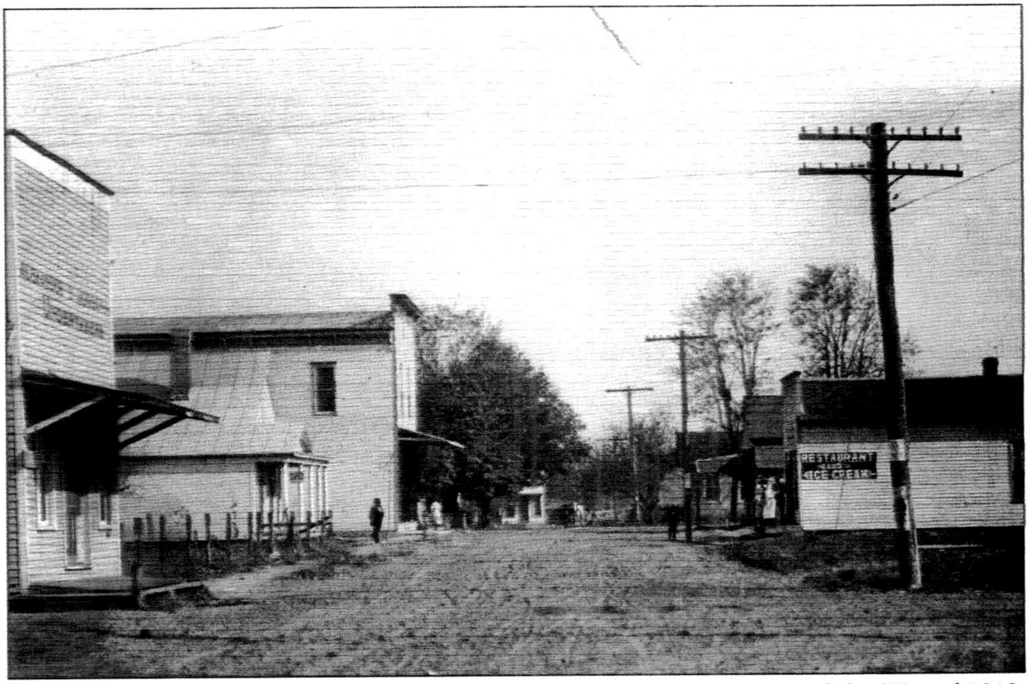

DOWNTOWN IRELAND, EARLY 1900S. In 1816, John Stewart, a veteran of the War of 1812, secured a deed from President James Monroe for the land that is now Ireland. John's son, James, named the town "American City," but the name was dropped when it was learned that there was already a town by that name. The community then became known as the Irish Settlement, or Ireland, named for the ancestral home of the Stewarts and many of their neighbors. In the photograph are the businesses that made up downtown Ireland in the early 1900s. On the left are the Alexander and Morgan funeral home, the office of Dr. Glezen, the Odd Fellow Hall, and, in the distance beneath the tree, a millinery shop. On the right is a restaurant and ice cream stand. (Photograph courtesy of Elsie [Morgan] Traylor.)

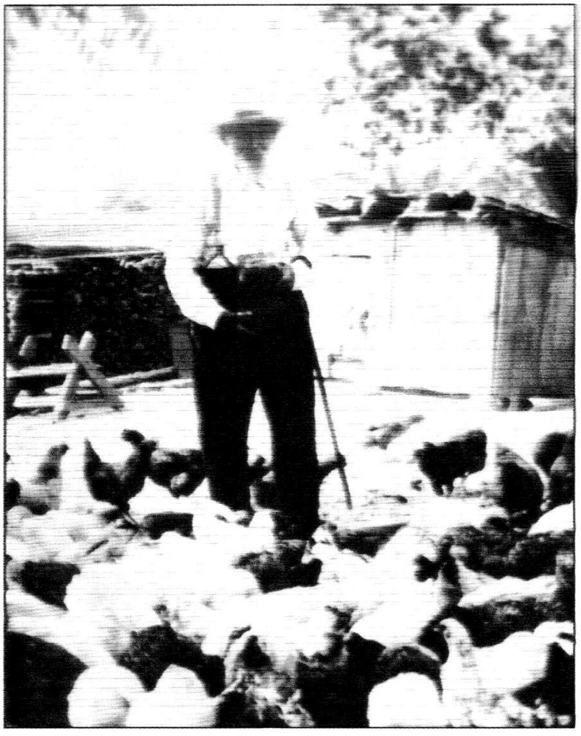

WILLIAM THOMAS HARDIN, C. 1940. William Thomas Hardin was a long-time resident of Ireland. (Photograph courtesy of Delbert Himsel Jr.)

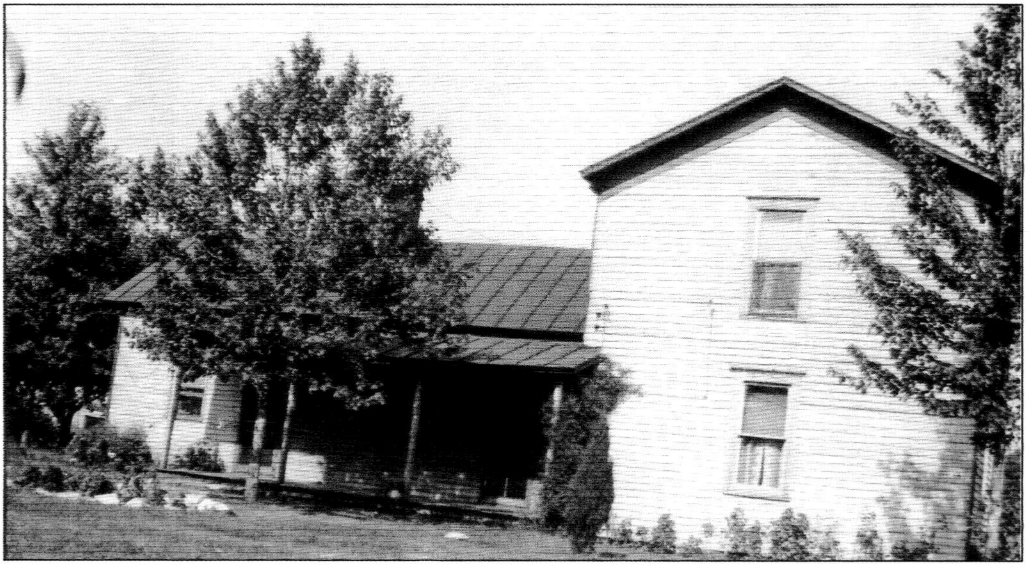

THE HARDIN HOTEL. This building is the oldest house in Ireland, the Irish settlement, just west of Jasper. The hotel was owned by William Hardin. Later, according to Delbert Himsel Jr., William's son Isaac ran it. William Thomas Hardin was the 11th child of the hotel owner, but never ran the hotel. The Hardin family (related to Delbert on his mother's side) used the names William and Isaac many times. According to Delbert's records, in 1877, the Hardin Hotel served meals for 12 cents and offered rooms (boards) for 60 cents. A Dr. Parr's bill for January 30, 1877, for 13 meals and 7 boards was $5.76. (Photograph courtesy of Roy Hardin.)

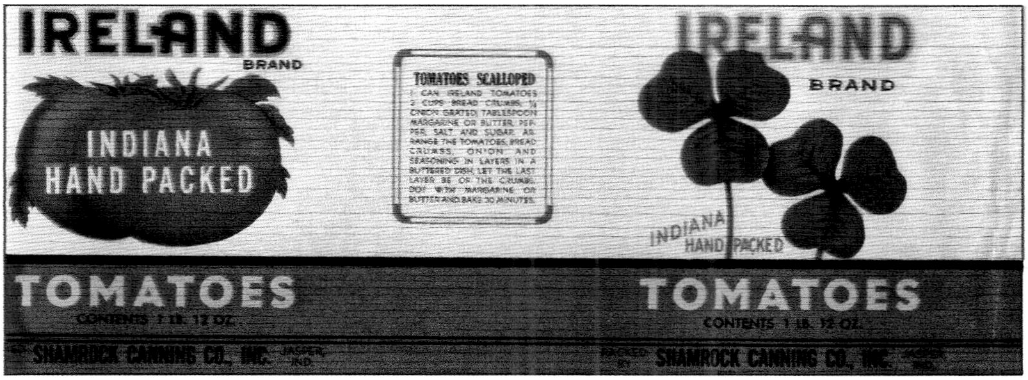

IRELAND BRAND TOMATOES LABEL. The Ireland brand was produced by the Shamrock Canning Company. The label touts that the tomatoes are "Indiana Hand Packed." (Photograph courtesy of Clara Mae [Gress] Braunecker.)

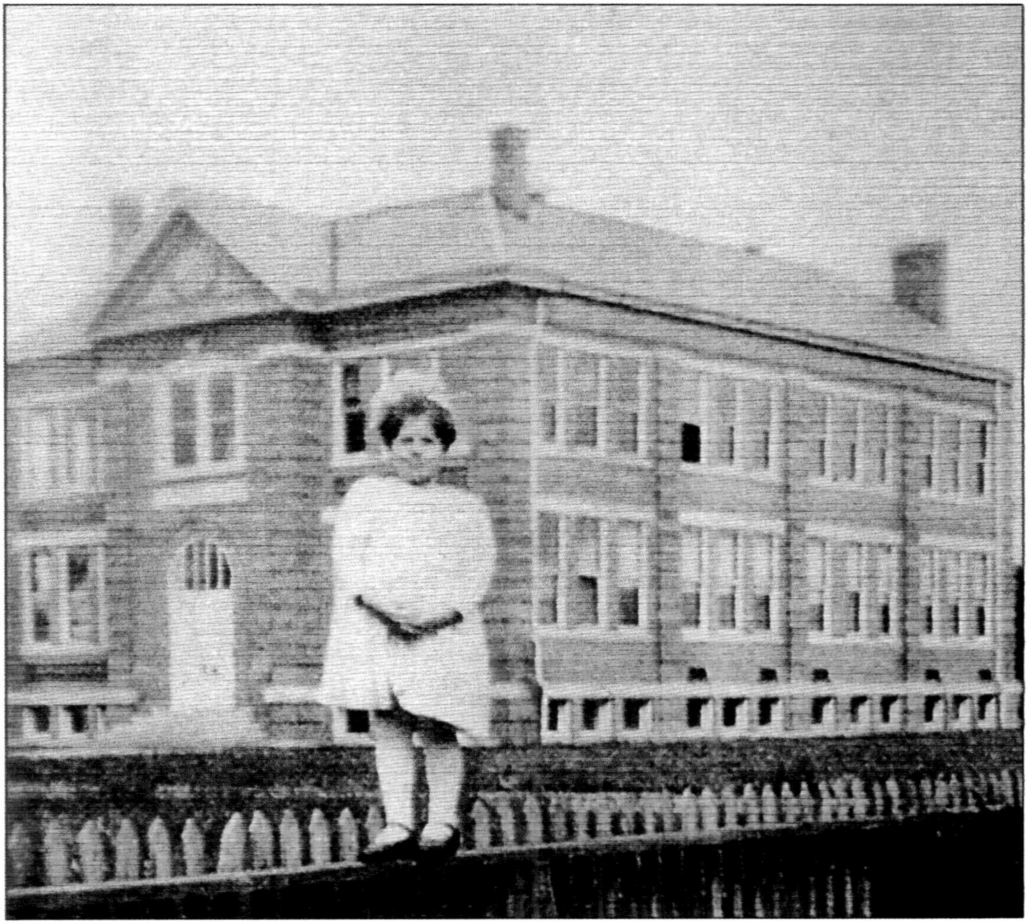

ALICE DILLIN, 1920. This photograph of the Ireland High School looks northwest. The high school was built in 1915 at a cost of $15,000. (Photograph courtesy of Delbert Himsel Jr.)

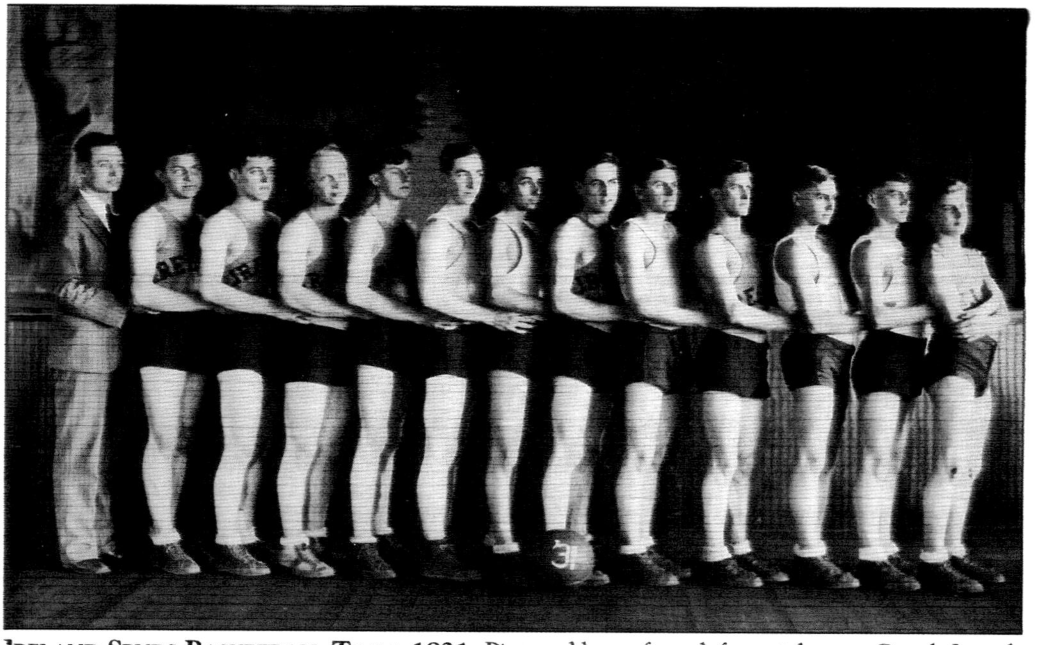

IRELAND SPUDS BASKETBALL TEAM, 1931. Pictured here, from left to right, are Coach Joseph Glezen, Raymond Buechler, William Stewart, Don Yates, Linus Rudolph, Lloyd Houchins, Ray Stenftenagle, Fred Houcins, Felix Schnaus, Basil Morgan, George Heim, Charles Stewart,and Amos Leinenbach. The photograph notes that "home games were played in the upstairs of the 1915 Ireland High School." (Photograph courtesy of Delbert Himsel Jr.)

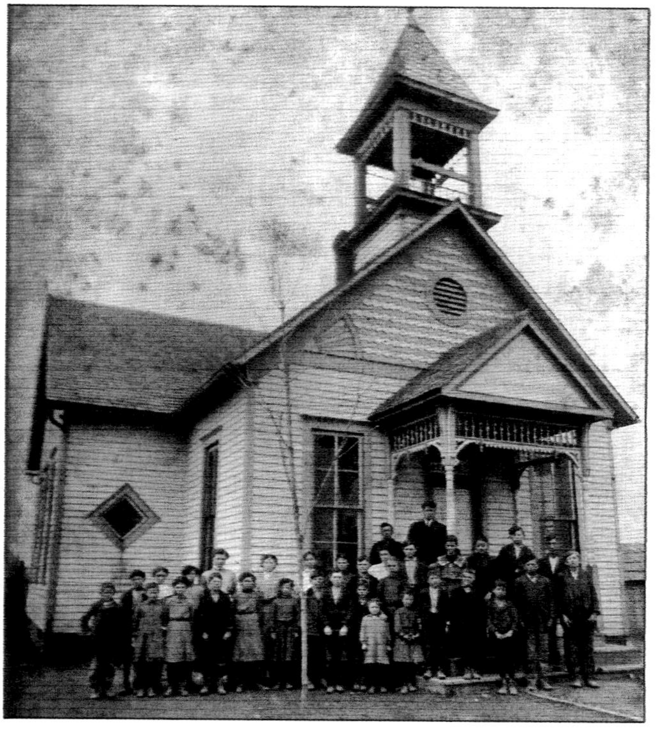

GREENE SCHOOL, APRIL 6, 1906. This school, built by school trustee G. M. Greene, replaced the original building that was torn down in 1903. The school was located in an area known as "Hog Heaven," a portion of southwest Madison Township that lay between the Postlethwaite and Flat Creek bridges. The school was closed in 1939. (Photograph courtesy of Delbert Himsel Jr.)

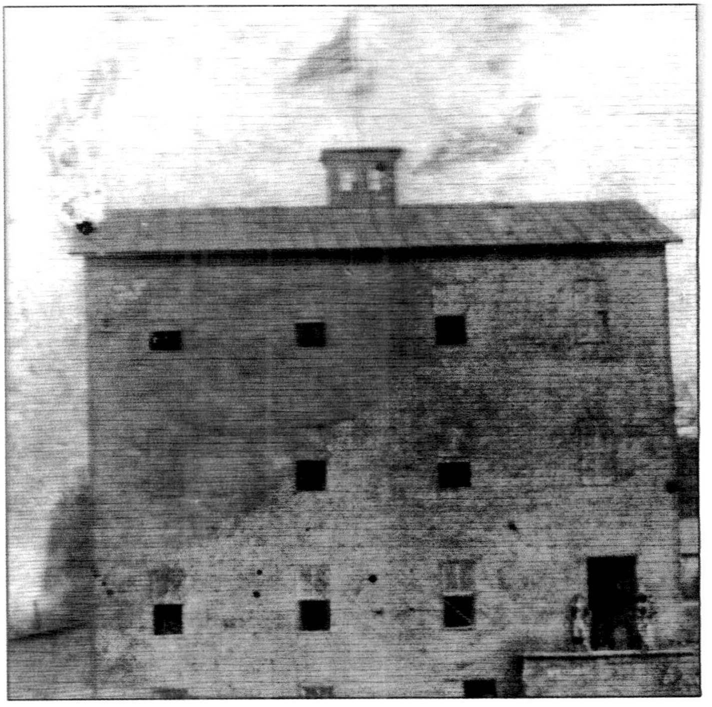

COOPER FLOUR MILL, WALNUT STREET, 1885. The mill had two additional owners after Mr. Cooper—Mr. Norman and then Mr. Glezen. It burnt once and was rebuilt, but abandoned after it caught fire a second time. Notice the flag on top of the building. (Photograph courtesy of Tom Kellams.)

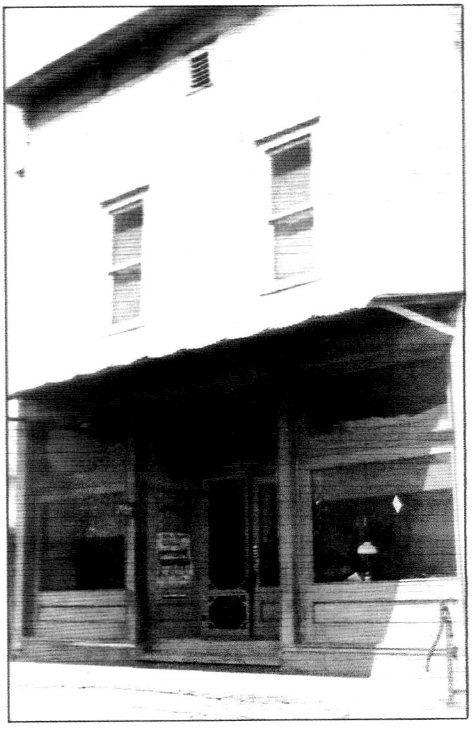

CHARLEY BISSEY GENERAL STORE. Bisseys' Store was on the bottom floor of the Odd Fellows Hall on Main Street in Ireland. The Odd Fellows met upstairs. (Photograph courtesy of Delbert Himsel Jr.)

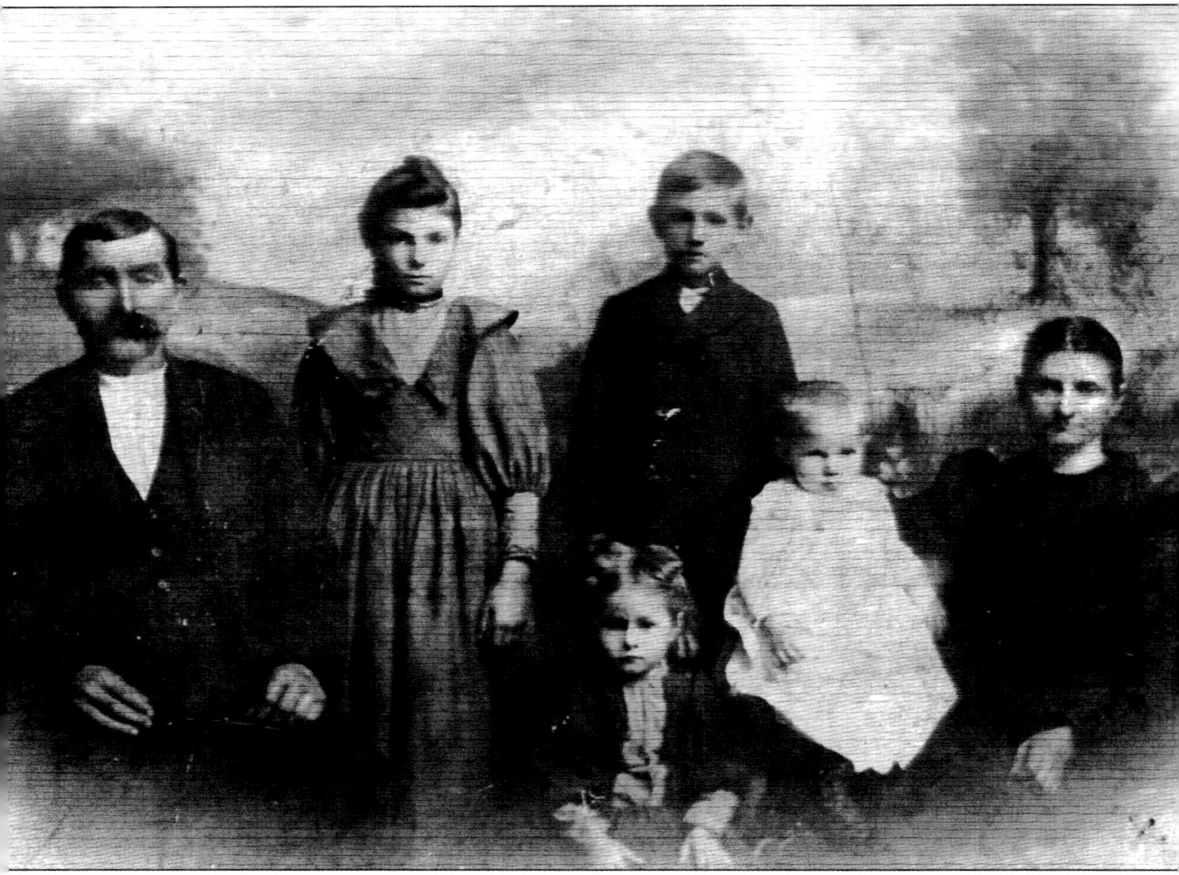

ALBERT HIMSEL FAMILY. Shown in this photograph is the family of Albert and Margaretha Himsel, who were the victims of a horrible drowning accident in 1899. The following account of the accident was taken from records of St. John's Lutheran Church, Boone Township, and was provided by Delbert Himsel Jr. The record states, "All these family members died on 8-16-1899, by drowning in the White River at Albert Himsel's farm, when they were attempting to cross the river. This sad accident happened as follows: Albert Himsel and his entire family were in Daviess County at his farm where they threshed oats on that day. His wife, Margaretha, did the cooking of the meals. In the evening they all started back home in Albert's wagon. When they intended to drive the wagon on the ferry, the post which tied the boat to the ferry broke, and the ferry went into the water where they all drowned. Only Albert and his son, Andreas, were able to save themselves. Albert also went under the water, however, he came out alive. His son, Andreas, jumped from the wagon onto the land and saved himself that way. The father, Albert, called to the others that they should jump from the wagon. They grabbed the small sleeping children. But in the meantime, the wagon and the occupants went into the water, where they drowned. Drowned, also, was another girl, an orphan child, Mary Alice Dillin, who was a babysitter for Mrs. Albert Himsel. The bodies of Hellmut and Katharina were found immeadiately. Margaretha, Albert's wife, on the next day at 10 o'clock in the morning, and Emilla was found around 5 o'clock in the afternoon on Thursday evening. Adam Johann on Friday at 1 o'clock in the afternoon." (Photograph courtesy of Delbert Himsel Jr.)

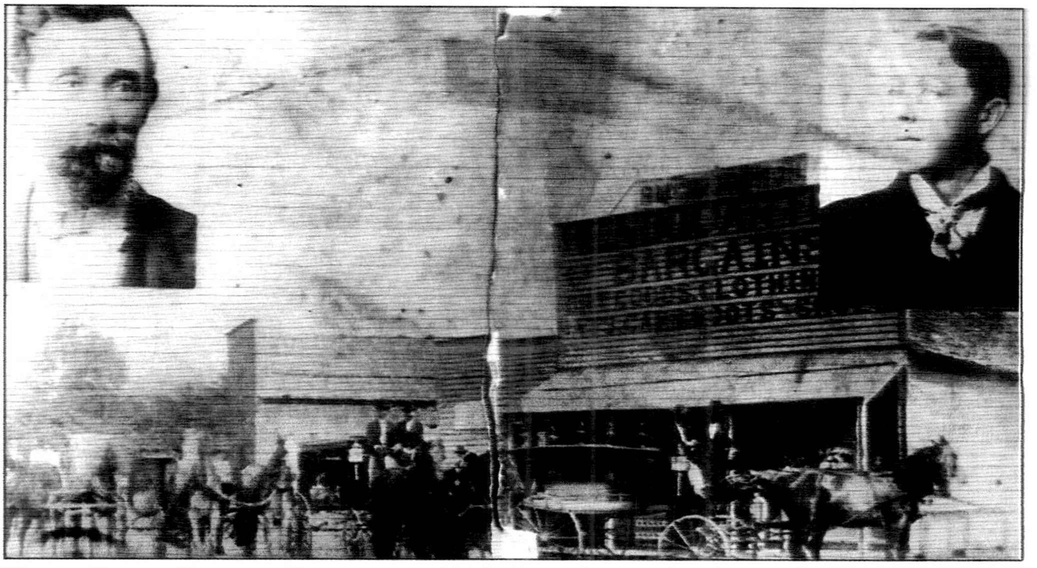

HIMSEL FAMILY FUNERAL PROCESSION, 1899. According to church records, "They [the Himsel family members] were all buried in the cemetery of this congregation. The orphan child's body was found shortly after the last body of the Himsel family was recovered and her body was taken to Pike County by her relation for burial. More than 2,000 persons came to the funeral and burial at the cemetery of St. John's congregation. Pastor F. W. Lange from Kellerville assisted Pastor Ronte at the burial and in the church with a sermon in English about Psalm 69: 1–3. Pastor Ronte preached in German abut Jeremiah 29:11. The funeral procession from the church to the cemetery consisted of four hearses and was more than a mile long. This shows how much the accident affected the whole community." (Photograph courtesy of Delbert Himsel Jr.)

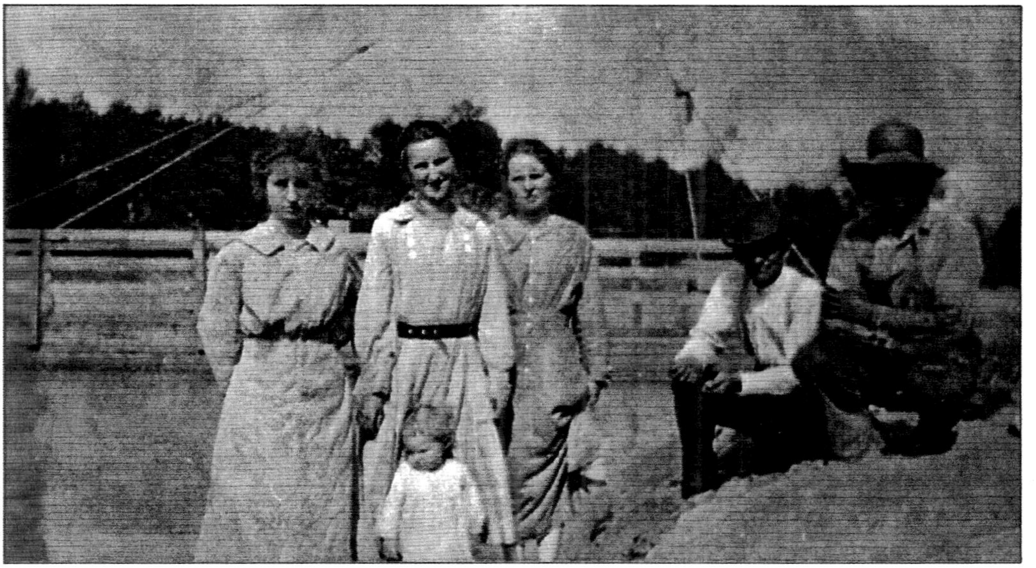

FLAT ROCK FERRY, AUGUST 31, 1919. This photograph was taken at the site of the Flat Rock ferry, which was located at the east fork of the White River in Boone Township. Pictured are Hilda Himsel, Helen Deppen, a Deppen child, Lottie Deppen, Samuel Himsel, and the ferryman, Bud Abbott. (Photograph courtesy of Delbert Himsel Jr.)

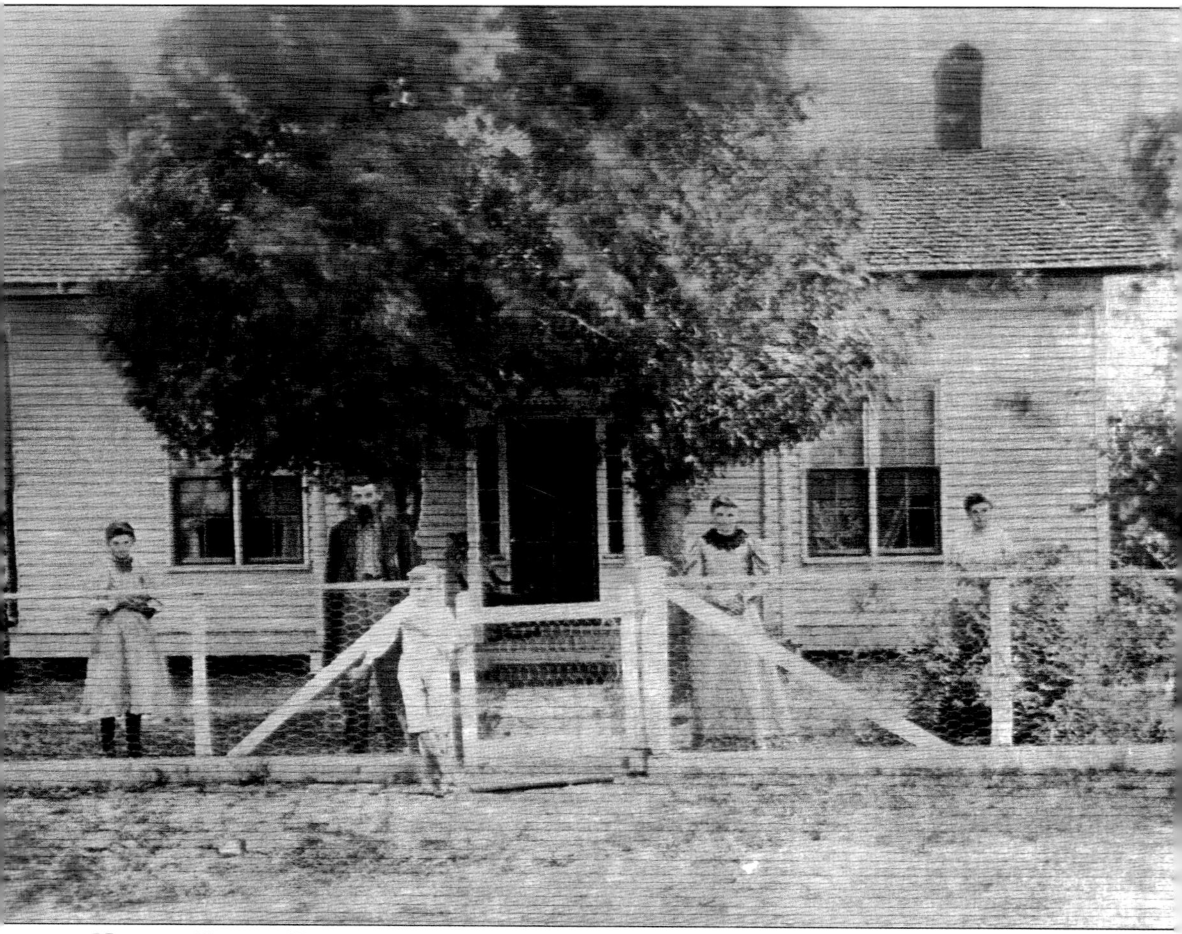

HARDIN FAMILY PHOTOGRAPH, 1892. Pictured here, from left to right, are Rilla, W. T., Orentus, Mary Florence, and Effie Hardin. (Photograph courtesy of Ethel [Hopkins] Hardin.)